A CELEBRATION OF

Petersfield

A Town and its People

Imagery ©2014 DigitalGlobe, Getmapping plc, Infoterra Ltd & Bluesky, Map data ©2014 Google

A CELEBRATION OF

Petersfield

A Town and its People

The Petersfield Society

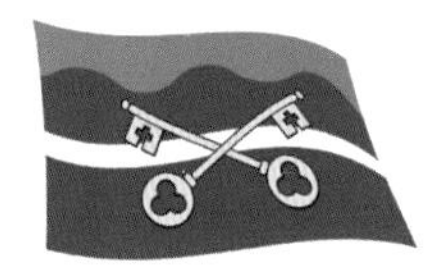

The Petersfield Town Flag, designed by Tony New

A Celebration of Petersfield

ISBN 978-0-9931901-0-0

First published February 2015
by The Peterfield Society, Winton House, 18 High Street, Petersfield, Hampshire GU32 3JL

CONTENTS

6 Town Map

9 Introduction

10 Foreword

12 The Petersfield Society

13 Architecture and Ambience

21 Business and Industry

33 Charities

47 Churches

57 Clubs and Societies

71 Community

81 Family Firms

101 Festivals

105 Folly Market

113 Health and Welfare

123 Independent Traders

143 Petersfield's Lanes

155 Markets

159 Music

167 Natural Environment

178 Out of Town

183 Town Council and Festival Hall

187 Pubs

197 Restaurants and Cafés

209 Schools

217 Sport and Leisure

229 Theatre

235 Young People

243 Sponsors

244 Acknowledgements

246 Directory A to Z

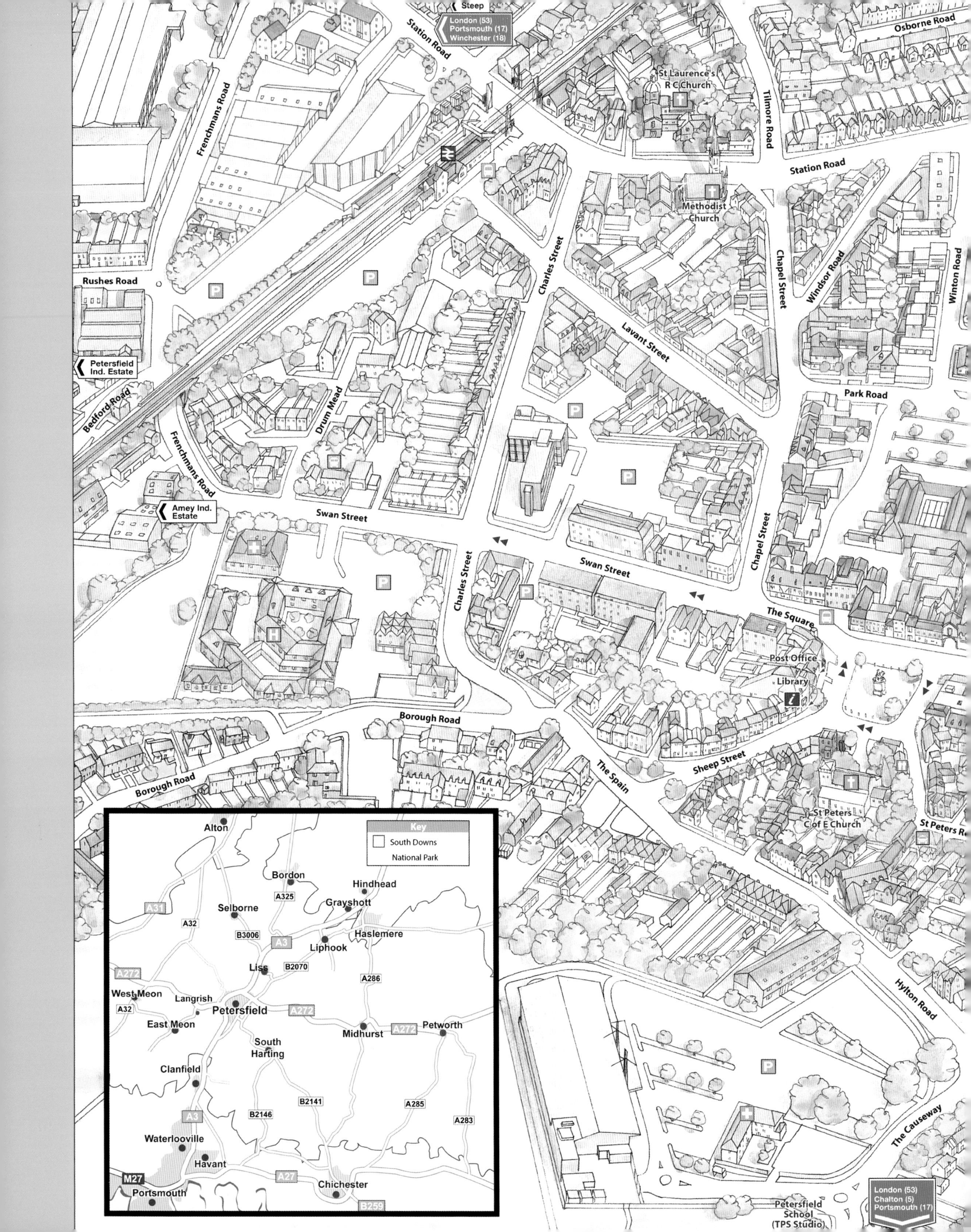

Steep
London (53)
Portsmouth (17)
Winchester (18)
Station Road
Frenchmans Road
St Laurence's
R C Church
Tilmore Road
Osborne Road
Station Road
Methodist
Church
Chapel Street
Windsor Road
Winton Road
Charles Street
Lavant Street
Rushes Road
Petersfield
Ind. Estate
Bedford Road
Drum Mead
Frenchmans Road
Park Road
Amey Ind.
Estate
Swan Street
Swan Street
Chapel Street
Charles Street
The Square
Post Office
Library
Borough Road
Borough Road
The Spain
Sheep Street
St Peters
C of E Church
St Peters R
Hylton Road
The Causeway
London (53)
Chalton (5)
Portsmouth (17)
Petersfield
School
(TPS Studio)
Key
South Downs
National Park
Alton
Bordon
Hindhead
A325
Grayshott
A31
Selborne
A32
B3006
A3
Liphook
Haslemere
A272
Liss
B2070
A286
West Meon
Langrish
Petersfield
A272
A32
East Meon
Midhurst
A272
Petworth
South
Harting
Clanfield
B2141
A285
B2146
A283
A3
Waterlooville
Havant
M27
A27
Chichester
Portsmouth
B259

Sheet
London (53)
Portsmouth (17)
Guildford (25)
Cemetery
Community Centre
North Road
Station Road
Registry Office
United Reformed Church
College Street
Grenehurst Way
Love Lane
Lydum Close
King George Avenue
Tor Way
Love Lane Playing Fields
Football Club
Upper Heyshott
Barham Road
Lower Heyshott
College Street
Physic Garden
Tor Way
Moggs Mead
Penns Place
Taro Centre
Open Air Swimming Pool
Folly Lane
Folly Market
Festival Hall
Folly Lane
Town Hall
Herne Road
High Street
Pages Court
Heath Road
Dragon Street
The Avenue
Weston Road
Heath Road
Heath Road
Cricket Club
Dragon Street
Avenue Pavillion
Tennis Courts
Sussex Road
Sussex Gardens
Heath Road West
Heath Pond
South Harting (6)
Chichester (12)
Boathouse

WILLIAM III
Rhona Russell
Library

INTRODUCTION

Damian Hinds, MP for East Hampshire

It was the founding of the market by the 2nd Earl of Gloucester back in the 12th century that created the spark of commerce that has built Petersfield into the success story which it certainly is today. We have some hugely successful businesses that provide products, services and jobs to the local area and further afield. They span a range of industries, from energy to manufacturing to technology.

We also have a wonderful hospital, great schools, a vibrant voluntary sector, and clubs and societies catering to every interest, from arts to amateur dramatics. It goes without saying that the calendar in Petersfield is constantly full of events, from the Spring Festival to the Christmas Market.

When you look around, it is no surprise that through the ages new families have chosen to settle here, in one of the most beautiful parts of the United Kingdom. We are nestled amongst outstanding scenery, with the South Downs National Park, Queen Elizabeth Country Park and Butser Hill to our south and the Hampshire Downs to our west.

This makes Petersfield attractive not only to those who live here, but to the visitors who are welcomed. Watching history unfold at Butser Ancient Farm, experiencing the Physic Garden, cycling the Shipwright's Way – there is a wealth of things to be discovered.

But more than anything it is the people who live here who make Petersfield. It is the children who fill the schools, the traders who make the market buzz, the business people who keep the local economy turning and the families who choose to make their lives here. The town will evolve in future, as it has done in the past, but I have no doubt that the spirit of Petersfield will remain the same forever.

FOREWORD

The Petersfield Society is delighted to publish this book to celebrate the life of Petersfield in 2015. We have been involved in the town and its surrounding district for seventy years and have always sought to ensure that the best of our town, villages and countryside is protected and enhanced for future generations.

Civic and amenity societies such as ours can be found throughout the UK and are active within their communities - undertaking environmental projects, promoting conservation areas, campaigning for the better protection of local assets and recognising local achievements in planning and architecture. This book is slightly different and takes us in a new direction by illustrating how all the different groups in the town are active in their community. It is a unique approach to celebrating the town for residents and visitors alike and its contents lavishly illustrate the variety, depth and vast range of Petersfield's cultural, sporting and social activities.

We believe that it is both a compendium and a celebration of all those aspects of a town which make it an attractive place in which to live and work. We are proud to undertake this new publishing venture - reflecting and supporting our work in safeguarding and enhancing the town's qualities. In doing this we both mirror our community and trumpet its successes!

This book and its contents might encourage you to join a group, participate in a new activity, visit a business or seek out one of the places illustrated. Petersfield is a wonderful place, much appreciated for its special character and quality of life by its local residents, businesses and visitors. We very much hope that you agree and enjoy reading this celebration of our town and its community.

Christopher Napier, President

Tony Struthers, Chairman

Heath Lake by Flora Twort - oil on wood

The Petersfield Society

Margaret Paren (Chair of the South Downs National Park Authority) with Christopher Napier (President of The Petersfield Society) and members of the Society planting the English oak on the Sheet Link roundabout.

At the end of the Second World War, the Hants and Sussex News (the predecessor to The Petersfield Post) had declared that the future prosperity of Petersfield stood or fell on the careful preservation of its atmosphere of an old English country town and that the group best placed to maintain such vigilance over the town's development was The Petersfield Society.

It was Edward Barnsley, the master furniture craftsman whose workshop in Froxfield still exists today, who instigated the 'Group for the Preservation and Improvement of Petersfield' in July 1945. He foresaw the potential dangers in the rapid post-war development of the town which, "if these [changes] are not carefully organised and controlled, there will be a grave danger that irretrievable damage will be done." Local luminaries such as Flora Twort and Dr Harry Roberts were among the first to support this new group and its energetic founder secretary, Miss Mary Ward, made frequent visits to Whitehall to fight various preservation causes.

Seventy years later, The Petersfield Society is still pursuing these aims with its interest in local planning, design, the environment and, above all, the character of the town. Its work complements that of the local councils by canvassing public opinion and commenting on the proposed development plans of individual developers and public statutory bodies. The Society's expertise in the historical, architectural and planning issues associated with such developments allow it to influence the decision-making process. The strength and commitment of its membership adds weight to these deliberations and its regular meetings offer a democratic opportunity for the public to express their opinions on the most pressing matters of the day.

The Society has campaigned for the protection and conservation of Petersfield since its inception and, in 1980, instigated its annual President's Owl award for the best contribution to improving the environment of the town, whether an architectural heritage site, a sympathetic building design, or a scheme for the improvement of a local amenity.

In past years, the Society published plans for the future of the town and for the enhancement of the Square, effected the removal of overhead power lines in The Spain, planted trees on the Heath Pond island and daffodils in Tor Way, and supported the use of the old Magistrates' Court as the Town Museum. More recently, it initiated the Blue Plaque Trail within the town, strongly campaigned for the inclusion of Petersfield in the South Downs National Park, published the Town Design Statement, and directly assisted the teams upgrading the local Conservation Area and writing the Neighbourhood Plan.

The Petersfield Society's President's Owl Award

This award takes the form of a wooden owl, sculpted by George Taylor of the Barnsley Workshop in 1980, and is presented annually to an individual or a group who have improved, refurbished or restored the environment within the Petersfield area.

In 2009, the Owl was presented to Margaret Paren, Chair of the SDNPA (right), for her support in endorsing the Society's bid to have Petersfield and the Western Weald included in the South Downs National Park.

Architecture and Ambience

Architectural Heritage

The signs leading into Petersfield proclaim 'Historic Market Town'. So what do we expect from this and are we conscious of our own history?

52 Miles From LONDON
Petersfield
17 To PORTSMOUTH

The Market Square is a fine starting place for an assessment of Petersfield: St Peter's Church marks the spot where, in the 12th century, a chapel of ease was built to allow the local, rather isolated, rural community to participate in worship on a Sunday. The oldest stones in Petersfield can still be seen in St Peter's magnificent chancel arch.

For almost 900 years, people have been able to go to market in the Market Square, officially established by Charter under William, Earl of Gloucester in 1184.

Top: *Cattle market in the 1930s*
Above: *The Square circa 1910*
Left: *Market Square by Flora Twort*

Did you know?

William III statue

People often ask: "Why is William here in Petersfield?" The answer links local history, British monarchs and European religions.

The strictly Protestant Jolliffe family, who provided our MPs over five generations and dominated Petersfield life for 150 years, were strongly opposed to a Catholic succession to King James II. Sir William Jolliffe, Petersfield's MP, was one of a group who had persuaded the Dutch monarch, William of Orange (King Billy) to contest the crown and the succession at the Battle of the Boyne in 1690. William's victory was celebrated by the erection of statues in various British towns in the 1730s: Bristol, Hull, Glasgow and London all have equestrian statues of William dressed as a Roman emperor, so Petersfield is unique in being the only small town to own one.

Bequeathed by Sir William, our statue was cast in lead – and originally gilded – in 1753 and symbolises the Jolliffes' patriotism and Protestantism, which still attracts a handful of Orangemen at an annual ceremony of dedication. The statue is now a scheduled ancient monument.

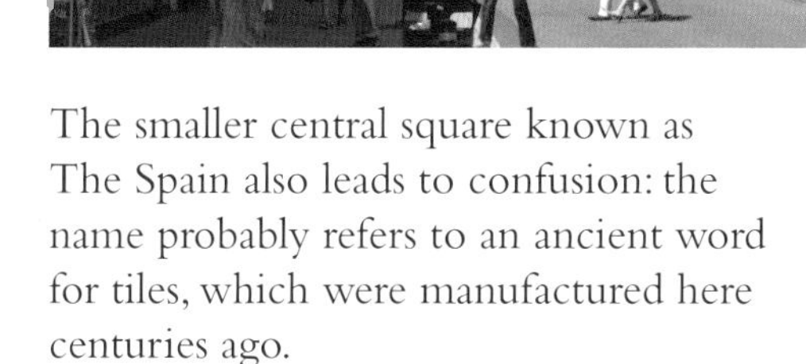

The smaller central square known as The Spain also leads to confusion: the name probably refers to an ancient word for tiles, which were manufactured here centuries ago.

Petersfield's mediaeval pattern of roads is still visible, radiating from the Square and along the ancient High Street. One of the original burgage plots (now the site of the Physic Garden) reminds us of the commercial basis and wealth of the town: a shop within a dwelling facing the road and a long garden behind for cultivating produce or housing a workshop.

Top left: *High Street today, looking west* Above: *High Street c.1910, looking east* Left: *Late 16th century house in The Spain* Right: *Petersfield Police Station of 1858* Below left: *Poor House given by Jolliffe family and memorial plaque*

Above: *The oldest private house in Petersfield in College Street, dated 1350* Below: *The Spain*

The High Street has now lost most of its ancient inns which catered for hundreds of passing visitors and traders in the early coaching days of the 17th and 18th centuries, but Dragon Street still retains some hostelries which date back to that period.

To the east lies the jewel in the crown of Petersfield: the Heath, carefully preserved from over-development and a place of relative solitude for walkers, anglers and wild-life enthusiasts. The Heath Pond has also only seen restricted exploitation, while the surrounding heathland is about to reveal its oldest settlements below the Bronze Age barrows, currently being scientifically investigated and, hopefully, historically explained.

Top & inset: *Aerial and moonlit view of the Heath and Pond* Far left: *Herne House on Herne Farm (once called Horn Farm)* Left: *Edwardian houses in Weston Road* Right: *15th century Wealden houses in Sheep Street* Below left: *St Peter's Court in the church close*

More recently, it was the arrival of the railway in 1859 which brought new housing and commerce to the town and the railway line soon defined the extent of the town to the north-west. There existed practically no buildings beyond the railway until the 1930s, when Petersfield experienced its first major development in the form of the Bell Hill estate. This development has been matched over the past 30 years by the Herne Farm estate to the east.

Sadly, the town has had its fair share of historic losses over the past century: a Tudor mansion and some 17th century merchants' houses in the Square, coaching inns of the 18th century, Victorian civic buildings and private dwellings of various periods have all fallen victim to random destruction by developers. Fortunately, however, we can still marvel at the beauty of half-timbered houses in Sheep Street and College Street, some elegant Georgian frontages in the High Street and our beloved Heath and Pond are conscious reminders of our history as well as modern attractions for our families and visitors to the town.

Far left: *John Goodyer's house in The Spain with explanatory plaque* Left: *The early Victorian Bell Inn in St. Peter's Road (now a restaurant)*

Petersfield Museum enjoyed an exciting year in 2014. At a large, innovative event in the Square commemorating the First World War children and young people told the story of the local population and their experiences during the Great War through the medium of dance.

The summer also saw the start of a four-year archaeology project to reveal the history of the Bronze Age barrows cemetery on Petersfield Heath. Professional archaeologists are carrying out the research in collaboration with local volunteers, while the museum is sharing the results with the wider community through exhibitions, walking tours and school activities.

Another exciting project has been the plan to buy Petersfield Police Station and link it with the Old Courthouse in order to make a larger and improved museum. The new museum aims to be fully wheelchair accessible, with a new display and activity spaces and a sound environment for all collections. Plans included the establishment of an Edward Thomas Study Centre, and education activities focusing on the history of crime that features the two buildings, including the original Victorian police cells.

In 1999 the Petersfield Area Historical Society opened the museum in the Old Courthouse next to the Police Station. Thanks to the generous bequest of the late Freddie Standfield, the Society was able to employ the first professional curator Kathryn Pieren (left) six years later. Since then, the museum has employed an education and outreach officer, expanded its collection to include historic dress and fine art, as well as acquiring a second venue, Flora Twort's former home and studio in Church Path.

Petersfield Museum has social history, fine art and dress collections. The earliest garments and accessories date from the late 18th century and the collection is particularly strong on women's dress from the 19th century. The social history collection encompasses thousands of photographs and archival records relating to Petersfield and the surrounding areas, plus artefacts ranging from Mesolithic flints to domestic goods from the 20th century. The museum also owns the largest collection of watercolours, drawings and prints by the late local artist Flora Twort (1893-1985) who produced a vivid visual memory of old Petersfield (below) and many accomplished portraits.

Petersfield Museum is no dusty musty place. Its ever growing programme of events includes holiday activities for children, regular adult learning talks and guided town walks. The museum also engages with local schools through workshops and loans boxes that respond to the demands of the National Curriculum. There are reminiscence sessions with community groups, and local artists have a chance to showcase their work in temporary exhibitions.

Currently the museum has three staff members, two of whom work part-time, and over 40 volunteers who provide valuable support by meeting and greeting visitors, caring for the collections, aiding in the installation of displays or carrying out research.

Did you know?

Petersfield's historic walls

Geologically speaking, Petersfield is located in an area rich in a variety of rock formations, from the flint found in the local chalk and limestone Downs, through the malmstone in the upper greensand of Sussex, to the ironstone from south of Midhurst. The underlying clay deposits have also produced the raw material for bricks and tiles.

The Causeway Brick and Tileworks were founded in the 1840s, providing most of Petersfield's requirements for private housing and commercial buildings. The original brick-drying shed transferred to the Weald and Downland Museum in Singleton in 1979.

In the 1920s Larcombe's Brickyards (hence the road name) had a kilnyard opposite the old Jolly Sailor (now Kennet Road). Bricks were used by Larcombe for Causeway houses on the east side from no. 150 to Causeway Farm Entrance.

The 1930s houses in Cranford Road by Larcombe's used 1,000 bricks per day per man (pay was10 shillings), with loam and clay from land behind the works. Also, they were used for facing bricks, fancy tiles (for fireplaces etc) and pipes (for land drainage). Larcombe's closed in the Second World War (the glow from the kilns lit the sky), and its original brick-drying shed for brickworks is now at the Weald and Downland Museum. Mr Nightingale's brickyard (hence the road name) and 'clampyard' was on land now owned by Reeves.

More ornamental and decorative work, such as the facing tiles for fireplaces and the insertion of ironstone chips (galleting) into layers of mortar, are to be seen all over the town, usually indicating the wealth of the buildings' owners.

Tileworks: In The Spain (Norse: Spann = wood chip tile), some of the houses had clay tiles or wood shingles. There were Mathematical tiles in Sheep Street and College Street, to avoid the brick tax of 1784.

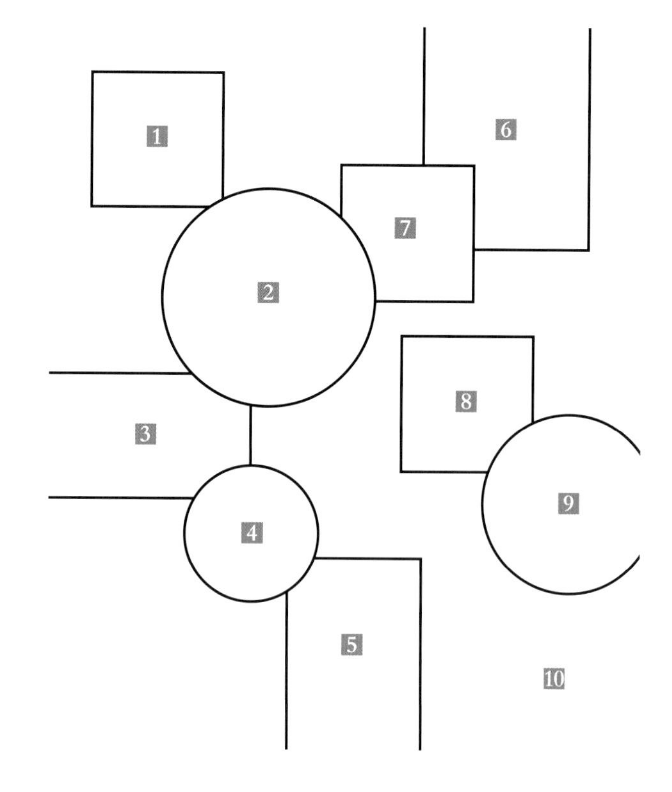

Key

1 *Wattle and daub wall to be seen inside Willow (6a High Street)*

2 *Brick with malmstone and ironstone galleting (decorative ironstone chips)*

3 *Malmstone with galleting (Sussex Road)*

4 *Limestone wall with 'S' brace (Bowen Lane)*

5 *Brick and flint wall (Police Station)*

6 *Knapped flints, (Methodist Church)*

7 *Brick with traditional half-round capping (Sussex Road)*

8 *"Mathematical" tiles - created to avoid the brick tax of 1784 (Sheep Street)*

9 *17th century (lower) wall of John Worlidge's house (Dragon Street)*

10 *[Backdrop picture] Ironstone with galleting in herringbone pattern (St. Peter's Road)*

Factfile

Ironstone – from poor soil, seams found south of Midhurst (Storrington).

Malmstone – a hard, grey-white sandstone, specifically from the upper greensand of Surrey and Sussex.

Flint – a hard form of quartz, chiefly found in chalk and limestone (flint tools from the Stone Age have been found on the Heath).

Hidden Corners

All around the town there are many nooks, crannies and interesting places.

1 *This oval drawing room with domed ceiling and elegant French doors opening onto the garden was a Victorian addition to the shop at the rear of 6, The High Street.*

2 *An appropriate recent addition to The Old Dairy beside the Station Road level crossing, this beast reminds us of the original function of the building – the offices of South Eastern Farmers Ltd, a wholesale dairy and milk processing depot.*

3 *The only Edwardian postbox in Petersfield – in Station Road close to Windsor Road.*

4 *Tombstones in St Peter's Churchyard re-erected around the path in 1950.*

5 *The original foundation stones of the Home from Home services' canteen situated near here and run by Kathleen Money-Chappelle during the Second World War.*

6 *Tablet in the wall in front of St. Peter's commemorating the Queen's Golden Jubilee in 2002.*

7 *The Georgian gravestone of John Small and his wife and three daughters. He was a renowned Hambledon cricketer, whose family owned a shoemaker's shop in the Square for 100 years.*

8 *Tudor Window above Ask Restaurant in the High Street.*

9 *A Victorian well pump – situated in the back yard of the Police Station in St Peter's Road.*

10 *The original door to Antrobus House, a 17th century almshouse, opposite in College Street, which was demolished when a fire struck the adjacent Luker's brewery in 1933.*

11 *A fire-mark of the Royal Insurance Company, guaranteeing protection by the local Fire Brigade for this Sheep Street property.*

12 *Metasequoia glyptostroboides (Dawn Redwood) trees on path to rear of Physic Garden. Grown from seed by John Bowen, donor of the Garden.*

Business and Industry

6a Vision

A property design and construction firm in The Spain, 6a Vision focuses its main operations in and around Petersfield. The firm builds between 3 and 8 units per year and is headed up by James Allen and Peter Noe, who were both brought up in Petersfield. They have recently won the Petersfield Society Owl Award for local projects.

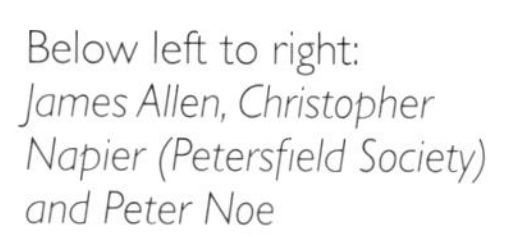

Below left to right: *James Allen, Christopher Napier (Petersfield Society) and Peter Noe*

The head office is next door to a recent project at 32 The Spain. One of the key challenges was the characterless, hard-square LBC brick that was widely used then. "We spent many days researching and testing various products until we found a product that could really soften the building and round the hard edge," said Peter Noe. "Other buildings on The Spain have soft bricks and then centuries' worth of paint build-up. We finally managed to create this look and are very happy with the results."

Although time-consuming and costly, they consider this attention to detail is worthwhile. "This is an industry where every detail counts, and the huge time we invest at 6a makes a difference," Peter added. "Design, build quality, materials, layouts, finishes, light, space, storage, kitchen and bathroom design are all painstakingly considered. The building must fit the surroundings and the setting, and we put in the time to ensure that every one of these details works."

Their professional team includes an experienced team of local craftsmen and architect Paul Masser, who designs every home 6a Vision produces. He has a wealth of experience and an uncompromising approach to creating the best layouts.

James Allen summed up: "Building is one thing; building with the care and attention that would be afforded to your own home every time is the key. It takes huge time and dedication, but it makes a difference, and this is how 6a Vision works. We build homes, not products."

Agincourt Contractors Ltd

With 48 staff, including 4 directors, Agincourt Contractors maintains a close working relationship with local Petersfield architects and its mostly private clients. Residential new build and refurbishment form the bulk of its commissions.

Recently completed works in the commercial sector include John Peter hairdressers in Chapel Street and Meon Travel in the High Street. Agincourt was also instrumental in building the new visitor centre at Butser Ancient Farm.

Below: *Meon Valley Travel shop frontage showing before (inset) and after refurbishment*

The company was established in 1990 and operates from its base in Petersfield, serving an area stretching west to east from Winchester to Midhurst and north to the London suburbs.

Before (inset) and after: *A malm and brick house built by Agincourt in 2013/14 stands on the site of a 1960s Colt house. With traditional cedar cladding and roof tiling to complement the farm buildings next door, its air source heat pump, and the photovoltaic solar panels providing electricity, are absolutely contemporary*

Antrobus Accountants

Mike Kirby has owned and managed Antrobus Accountants since 2006, but it has existed since the early 1990s and was established by Allan Tarver and Anne Deakin, who both still live locally. Antrobus tries hard to manage a delicate balance between a modest-sized country practice and the ability to handle the most challenging and complex financial issues. In this regard Mike was trained at one of the Big Four chartered accountancy practices and has substantial international experience as a finance director. Sarah Macnaughton, Director of Audit, Accounts and Tax, has been with Antrobus all her working life. She was born and educated in Petersfield and seems to know or be related to a significant minority of its population.

Antrobus works with very small one-person owner-managed businesses and those people who just need a little help with their tax returns as well as larger more complex businesses, often with international aspects. Where they have insufficient experience of a specific area, they will know where to go to get expert advice and assistance.

Antrobus House in College Street not only houses Antrobus Chartered Accountants, but is also home to Antrobus House Business Centre, which offers secretarial services, mail accommodation and phone answering services to other businesses and has several serviced offices. These are let out to businesses that find this sort of accommodation very cost-effective as they don't have to worry about the cost and time of running an office themselves. There is also a meeting room, suitable for training courses or small seminars of up to about 15 people, which can be hired by the hour or day.

L to R: *Rob Stephens, Sarah Macnaughton, Samantha Buckingham, Mike Kirby, Toni Cady, Nicky Gander*

Cluson Engineering Limited

Cluson Engineering Ltd was first formed in 1970 as a small family business and became incorporated in 1975. The founding directors began by offering engineering services locally and after a considerable amount of commitment, aided later by a loyal and dedicated team, now take pride in servicing an international community with Clulite products.

Clulite takes its name from the original orange square torch, designed and manufactured by Cluson over 40 years ago. These high-powered rechargeable torches are the main core of their product range and they remain market leaders in the field, keeping up with new technology as it is developed from their own factory in Petersfield. Recognised strongly within the farming fraternity, some of these lamps remain in use today and, remarkably, can still be serviced. This fact marks high for British manufacturing and has earned Cluson much respect within the industry.

In addition to their original business Cluson run a highly successful country-wear store just off Bedford Road. Here there is an astonishing and indispensable variety of country clothes including boots, hats, socks, waterproofs as well as farming and gardening tools and household items.

J B Corrie and Company Ltd

J B Corrie and Company has been in existence for over 100 years, first as a partnership in the 1890s and then incorporated in 1925. The founder, John Bradford Corrie, started the company in London in partnership with Fred Weil as agent for a number of machine tool companies.

John Bradford Corrie went on to obtain a patent for dropper fencing, a fence design developed originally in Argentina, which he had manufactured by William Bain of Scotland, and became the sales agency for these fencing products.

It was in 1931 that Corrie's were able to purchase a manufacturing plant to make the fencing products themselves. Originally in Middlesbrough, the manufacturing plant enabled Corrie's to develop the business rapidly during the 1930s with contracts obtained throughout the British Commonwealth countries.

There were setbacks during the war when their offices in London were destroyed, but it was the takeover of the Flextella Fencing and Engineering Company that brought Corrie's to Petersfield in 1946. The subsequent transfer of the Middlesbrough manufacturing to Petersfield cemented Corrie's as a major manufacturing centre for fencing in the area.

Richard Corrie joined the Company in 1950, marking the third generation of the family to enter the business. The company was growing strongly with markets for fencing products being established around the world as well as in the UK. Product lines were expanded through innovative design as well as the purchase of other fencing companies.

The current Chairman, John Corrie (left), is the fourth generation of the Corrie family in the business. The day to day running of the company is now led by a strong management team with broad experience to take the company into the future.

It is significant that employee loyalty has been a major factor in the success of J B Corrie. More than a quarter of the Petersfield employees have been with the company for over 25 years and the average length of service is close to 14 years.

Kebbell Development Ltd

Petersfield's largest-ever housing development – 78 acres at Herne Farm (originally Horn Farm) - was begun in 1972. Kebbell Development Ltd eventually received planning permission for the whole area to be developed over several decades, containing over 800 houses for roughly 2,300 new residents, thereby boosting the population of Petersfield by about 20%.

After their initial joint visit to Kebbell's previous development at Carpenders Park in Hertfordshire, the developer, the architects and the councillors agreed on the style of houses and the overall concept of the estate.

The major aim of the architects, Meacher, Moyes and Partners, was for a variety of styles of houses and layout at each stage of the building programme, and for mixed designs and rooflines to reproduce a village street atmosphere. The names of the first roads were Butser Walk and Moggs Mead (meaning "marshy pools" and named after the boggy field which stood there before development). Alongside the housing units, Kebbells envisaged a riverside walk (Tilmore Brook) and recreational facilities.

Care was taken over the construction of decent brick walls, landscaping, footpaths and the creation of occasional cul-de-sacs for safety and privacy.

Inevitably, architectural styles and public tastes developed over the course of construction of the estate and individual buyers demanded different criteria; this in turn led to clear differences between the houses of the early 1970s (at the Pulens Lane end of Moggs Mead) and the 1980s and 1990s (towards Tor Way), where greater density has also been a consideration.

One aspect of life on the estate which made it unique in Petersfield was its resident-operated management company, which is responsible for the running of the estate's social and leisure activities. The sale, in 2010, of the last property on the estate marked the end of 30 years of development.

One of the outstanding features of Kebbell's developments both in the

North and South of England are the inclusion of sports and leisure facilities solely for the use of residents. In Petersfield, this concept embraces a heated swimming pool, two squash courts and a multi-purpose hall. Dances, film shows, children's play groups, jumble sales, coffee mornings and many other activities for all ages have been regularly held in the hall since it was built and this has helped create a compact community that continues to thrive.

Andrea Fawell, Kebbell's Sales and Marketing Manager, says: "We have always been keen to support the local Petersfield community and over the years made a number of contributions to charities and schools in the area. We have sponsored the annual *Life in Petersfield* awards for six years now, we are previous sponsors of Petersfield in Bloom, and we have made donations to Petersfield Town Juniors Football Club and local youth club, the Kings Arms."

KEBBELL Homes

Location Landscapes

Location Landscapes specialise in soft landscaping and garden maintenance in private gardens in and around Petersfield and the Home Counties. They work with clients, and garden designers, to create gardens that bring the greatest pleasure to their owners. Planting and specimen tree planting are two of Location Landscapes' specialities.

Callum West, Stepan Sliva, Sam Day, Jonathan Harrington, Charles Blumlein & Matt Johnson.

Managing Director Charles Blumlein, whose passion and expertise is in plants, studied horticulture at Sparsholt and Merrist Wood Colleges, and served his apprenticeship at Winchester College.

Charles launched the business in September 2013 with a team of experienced gardeners, and Tracey Harding who deals with the administration of the company. "Our team is carefully chosen;" says Charles, "they are the public face of the business and they must be skilled, knowledgeable and courteous. Whether we are looking after a small garden, or one of several acres, we value the relationship we have with our clients."

He was delighted that in their first year of trading Location Landscapes had the opportunity to plant the No Man's Land Garden for designer Charlotte Rowe at Chelsea Flower Show 2014. The garden was created to commemorate the First World War for ABF The Soldiers' Charity, and won a Gold Medal. "It was a great privilege to be part of it," says Charles.

The company are hoping to work on show gardens at Chelsea in 2015 and also at the Hampton Court Flower Show. Charles said, "Our passion is creating domestic gardens and planting a show garden gives us the opportunity to show off our skills on the world stage."

Petersfield media

Petersfield has a diverse and successful media. And traditional values are maintained in the modern, multi-platform environment.

Newspaper publishing has a long tradition in the town, with the Hants and Sussex News established in 1883. After changes in ownership, premises and title over the years, the current *Petersfield Post*, based at 33 High Street, offers a wide range of community news, entertainments and sports coverage.

The Herald was established in Petersfield in 1976 to serve the local community with local news and provide a record, both in words and pictures, of the major events and celebrations in the town and surrounding villages.

Meanwhile, *The Messenger* newspaper has been involved in Petersfield life for more than three decades, covering events across the town, from jumble sales and school sports days to the spring festival and the arrival of the Olympic Flame in 2012.

All aspects of community life feature in *Life in Petersfield* magazine, which shines the spotlight on the outstanding achievements of people, businesses and charities across the local area at the annual Petersfield Business and Community Awards.

Tindle Newspapers own the *Post*, the *Herald* and Life Magazines. Now in the Newspaper Society's list of the 10 biggest UK publishers, the Group is still run by Sir Ray Tindle, who began it with £300 demob money given to soldiers at the end of the Second World War.

The other publication familiar in the town is the *Directory*, which was launched by Denise Lloyd in Petersfield in 2005. The Directory Group says it delivers to 89,500 homes and businesses every month in different areas in Hampshire and Sussex.

Did you know?

Sir Ray Tindle CBE DL

Sir Ray Tindle was born in 1926 and educated at Torquay Grammar School and the Strand Grammar School in London. During the Second World War he was a Captain in the Devonshire Regiment and served in the Far East. His love of print began then, as he sailed to join his regiment and made his first newspaper on board.

After the war he wanted to be a journalist: "I wrote to every Fleet Street editor but I never made it." Instead, he used most of his £300 army pay to buy the *Tooting Gazette* with a circulation of 700.

Through launches and acquisitions the group now has more than 220 titles, with an audited weekly circulation of more than 1.4 million and turnover above £50 million. Sir Ray attributes his success to a dedicated staff led in recent years by Brian Doel and Wendy Craig and 30 general managers running the newspapers locally. According to Press Gazette writer Jon Slattery, a clue to his success "may be that the Tindle family coat of arms, which is carried by all his newspapers, has the motto 'Noli Cedere', which translates as Never Surrender".

As well as owning hundreds of newspapers Sir Ray also has several veteran cars, his other passion. He was knighted in 1994 for his services to the newspaper industry.

RAK Ceramics UK Ltd

Founded in 2002 the company came into being as a collaborative effort after RAK Ceramics, based in the United Arab Emirates, approached Rob Jull Agencies to start their UK subsidiary. Originally based in Easebourne, West Sussex, RAK moved into the Paris House premises on Frenchmans Road, Petersfield, in 2007 to be closer to the A3.

RAK Ceramics, named after Ras Al Khaimah where the main factory is based, is a $1 billion conglomerate that exports to over 150 countries around the world. RAK has opened factories in Bangladesh and China and produces over 12,000 sanitary ware pieces and 360,000 sq m of tiles per day.

Left: *Robert Jull, Managing Director*
Above: *Ben Jull, Veronica Jull, Heather Farnden, Jeannette Newman, Alice Hunt, Michelle McDiarmid and Scott Adams*

From modest offices in West Sussex, the company has grown rapidly to occupy premises in excess of 7,000 sq ft office space, nearly 34,000 sq ft warehouse space and with a showroom of over 6,000 sq ft. The company employs around 50 people and delivers RAK products nationwide.

MD Robert Jull says, "As with all RAK products, we impress our customers with cutting-edge style and fabulous quality, then shock them with how affordable they are."

RAK
ceramics

RAK in the community

John Anscombe of RAK UK gives his free time to help the children of the Chernobyl Children Lifeline, a charity set up to help the children affected by the 1986 nuclear explosion in Chernobyl. Although Chernobyl is in the Ukraine, most of the nuclear fallout was taken up by south east winds to its neighbouring country Belarus.

The charity's main purpose is to bring children over to the UK for a month's 'health break', when they are away from their own polluted homeland and build up their strength and immune systems to cope better with disease.

Whitman Laboratories

Whitman Laboratories, one of Estée Lauder's largest global manufacturing sites, plays an important part in the economic life of Petersfield. Located in the town since 1982, with an earlier presence in the Hampshire area dating back to 1962, the plant employs some 1,000 people, producing 53 of the Estée Lauder Company's top 100 global products, in part or in whole.

Supporting Breast Cancer research

Mike Gladman, General Manager

The vast majority of staff are local, although more than 32 countries are represented in the diverse workforce. Many employees still happily recall the visit of Estée Lauder to Petersfield in 1984.

"A large number of local lives and families are intertwined with our business," says the company. "We have been lucky to have enjoyed so much success and growth with such a skilled, loyal, and hard-working workforce. It is a tribute to the values of the local community here, and also to the high levels of education and training standards set by our local authorities."

Whitman Laboratories employs people with a wide range of expertise – accountants, microbiologists, mechanical and chemical engineers, logistics and distribution specialists, factory and production staff, quality technicians and team managers. "We have some of the most experienced and brightest talent in any manufacturing site in the South of England and we are proud of our association with Petersfield."

The company has solid, long-lasting relationships with many local suppliers. Their Corporate and Social Responsibility initiatives have seen some high-potential employees involved with community projects in Petersfield, and in the refurbishment of facilities designed to help disadvantaged children in the local area. Also, Whitman Laboratories has sponsored the Petersfield Youth Theatre for several years, and contributes to many other local charities and community causes.

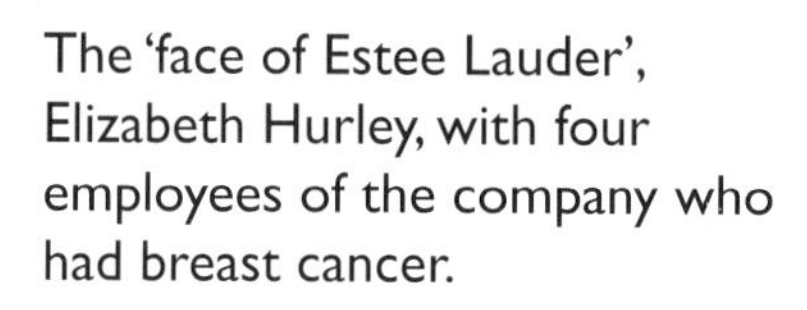

The 'face of Estee Lauder', Elizabeth Hurley, with four employees of the company who had breast cancer.

The Plant is rumoured to have been named after Walt Whitman, the famous American poet. In his poem 'My 71st Year', Whitman celebrates his life and, in a memorable phrase, pledges to remain '*Here, with vital voice*'. "Whitman Laboratories hope that the vital voice provided by the Petersfield Society, as it enters its 71st year, continues to be heard for very many years to come."

WHITMAN LABORATORIES

Did you know?

Michel Focard de Fontefiguieres
Michel is a well known professional photographer, which he describes as "the best job in the world". With a French father and English mother, he started his working life making crepes at his own restaurant in Paris.
Now he combines the best of French flair and English pragmatism as a photographer who can name Joanna Lumley, Philip Green and Mary Portas among his clients. His photo shoots include Virgin Galaxy, historical re-enactments at Chawton House and exotic locations in Vienna and the Middle East – as well at this book for the Petersfield Society.

Did you know?

Sam Farrow, Founder of Farrow Creative has more than 20 years' experience in the graphic design industry. After getting a degree in Design and Communication, she earned a Masters in Graphic Communication at Kingston University, where she was also a member of the teaching faculty.

She says she has spent most of her career "at the coalface", working as a professional graphic designer in several agencies before being appointed Senior Designer at Meridian Television. From there, she went to Surrey County Council, where she headed up a major re-branding project that produced savings of almost £2 million across the authority.
In 2003 she returned to the private sector as a creative director.

Then in 2006 she launched her own graphic design and marketing agency, Farrow Creative. The Petersfield-based business has gone from strength to strength, with clients including the South Downs National Park, Radian Group, and Karren Brady, a star of The Apprentice.

Sam has assembled a specialist team who, she says, "share my passion for design and dedication to producing top-quality creative work in print and online". She is also proud of her "wicked sense of humour".

Petersfield Industry

Petersfield is already home to a wide range of international companies and high tech start-ups in Bedford Road and the adjacent Ridgeway Office Parks and Rotherbrook Court. The District Council is keen to attract both established industries and new businesses and, in the Petersfield Neighbourhood Plan, the industrial area is set to double in size over the next 15 years.

As well as the familiar names of **Whitman Laboratories** and **Clusons**, there are several trade counters, joineries, motor workshops, builders' and plumbers' merchants as well as a tool hire company and kitchen manufacturer.

Others include the **CPI** card group - an international high tech company at the forefront of smartcard technology with Petersfield as the European card production centre for Europe.

Neural Technologies provide risk management and business intelligence software to the financial and telecommunication sectors. It is an international company with facilities around the world and with its European headquarters in Petersfield. In 2015 the company celebrates 25 years in this industry.

The **Ridgeway Office Park** is a modern office estate adjacent to the A3 and accessed by way of Bedford Road.

Rotherbrook Court is the location for small offices and start-up units for new businesses and entrepreneurs.

The **Vestey Food Group** is an international company represented in over 70 countries around the world They are well known for supplying, processing and distributing chilled, ambient and frozen products, everything from meat and fish to fruit and vegetables.

Charities

Artscape

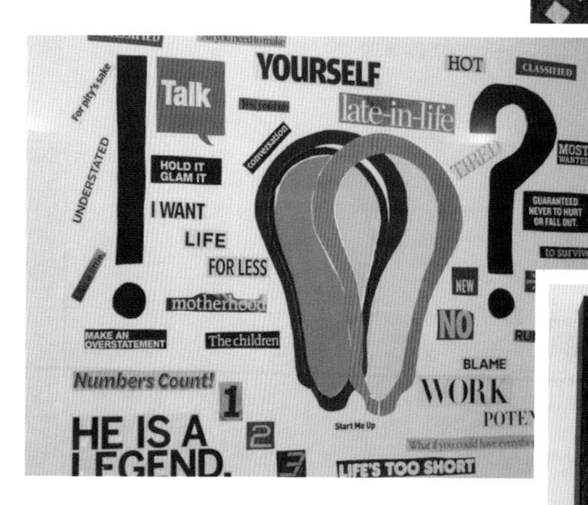

Artscape is an arts-based charity for adults in recovery from long and enduring mental ill health, and combating addictions and related disabilities. The charity's aims are to help alleviate personal stress, and increase self-confidence and social inclusion in a safe, welcoming environment which is full of acceptance, banter, creativity and fun. Over the years many participants have returned to work, education and employment.

Below: *Artscape Director Mandie Saw, Petersfield Town Mayor Sue Harwood and Cllr Julie Butler, at an exhibition celebrating a year at Winton House*

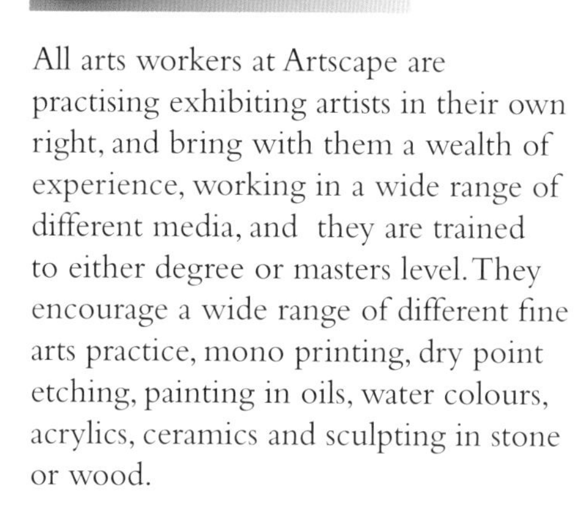

Experiencing any form of mental ill health is extremely isolating and Artscape people are not art therapists. They work in a unique way using art as a catalyst for enabling healing to begin to take place and to help people feel valued.

Above: *Mural created for the Open Air Swimming Pool*

All arts workers at Artscape are practising exhibiting artists in their own right, and bring with them a wealth of experience, working in a wide range of different media, and they are trained to either degree or masters level. They encourage a wide range of different fine arts practice, mono printing, dry point etching, painting in oils, water colours, acrylics, ceramics and sculpting in stone or wood.

Regular exhibitions are held in Petersfield and in such places as The Pallant House Gallery in Chichester. Various public projects have been achieved, such as the mural outside the Petersfield Open Air Pool.

Participants can be referred to via their local Community Mental Health Teams, their doctor or can enquire for themselves through Artscape's website.

The Royal British Legion

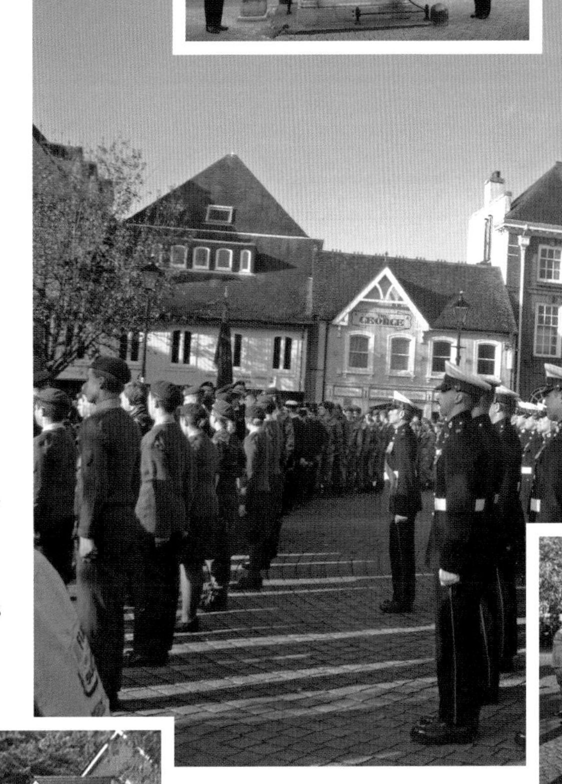

The Petersfield branch of the Royal British Legion has more than 50 members, with a mission to provide welfare, comradeship, representation and membership for the Armed Forces community. As welfare plays a major part of the Legion's work, the annual poppy appeal occupies much of its time.

For Remembrance Sunday, there is a parade and service held in the Square and at the War Memorial. Troops from REME and the Royal Marines join many other organisations to pay homage to the fallen in both World Wars and subsequent conflicts. The people of Petersfield always respond magnificently, and in 2014 in excess of £28,000 was raised.

"The people of Petersfield always respond magnificently"

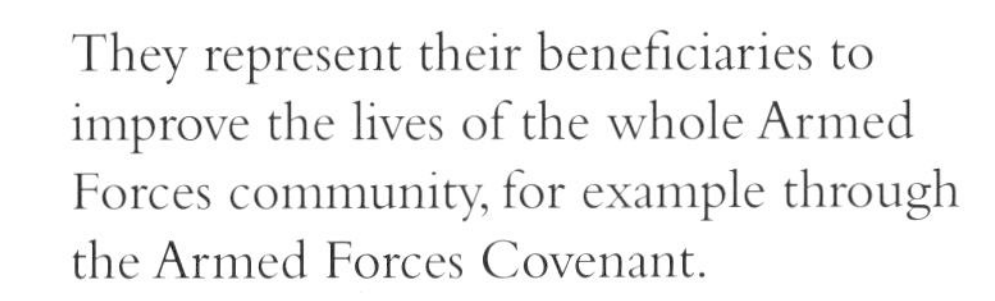

They represent their beneficiaries to improve the lives of the whole Armed Forces community, for example through the Armed Forces Covenant.

Comradeship comes through shared experiences in the Armed Forces. The branch organises annual trips to First and Second World War sites, such as Ypres and Arnhem, which gives them the opportunity to pay their respects to those from the Petersfield area who made the supreme sacrifice.

Members parade with representatives of Petersfield Town Council to raise the Armed Forces flag on Armed Forces Day. The involvement of the Town Council in the parade and their maintenance of the War Memorial is appreciated.

The Petersfield branch was founded in July 1921 and members cater for the needs of other members by visiting them, taking them out and generally tending to their requirements.

Receiving a cheque from Waitrose Community Giving

FitzRoy

Petersfield is proud to be home to the head office of FitzRoy, the national charity supporting adults with learning disabilities.

As little as 50 years ago people with learning disabilities were institutionalised, hidden from everyday life, and had few opportunities to enjoy life. Shocked by the lack of understanding, respect and support shown to her son with Down's syndrome, Elizabeth FitzRoy was determined to change things. She had a pioneering spirit and passionate belief that people with learning disabilities should have the support they need to fulfil their potential.

"On a typical day at any FitzRoy service our staff are providing the support and encouragement needed for extraordinary things to happen."

Elizabeth FitzRoy championed the idea that people with learning disabilities should hope for the best care possible in a safe and loving home. This led to a new kind of social care, one we take for granted today, but one that was once unimaginable.

Her vision became reality in 1962 when she set up her first family-sized home to provide a comfortable, safe environment in which the residents could flourish – this was Donec Mews in Grayshott which is still supporting local people.

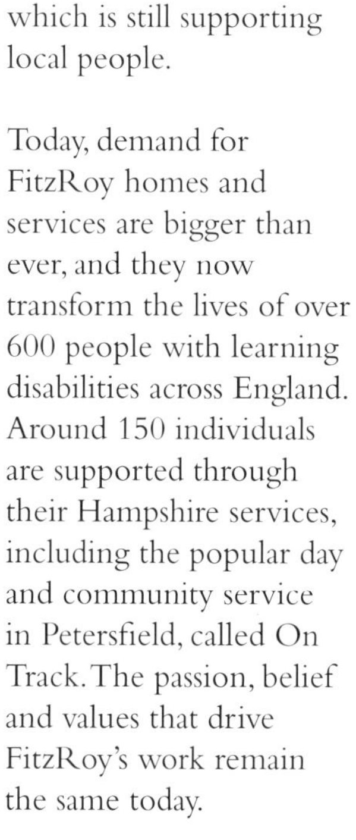

Today, demand for FitzRoy homes and services are bigger than ever, and they now transform the lives of over 600 people with learning disabilities across England. Around 150 individuals are supported through their Hampshire services, including the popular day and community service in Petersfield, called On Track. The passion, belief and values that drive FitzRoy's work remain the same today.

Anna Galliford, Chief Executive, FitzRoy, says: "On a typical day at any FitzRoy service our staff are providing the support and encouragement needed for extraordinary things to happen. Whether it is teaching someone to tie their own shoelaces at 18, taking the time to give someone the confidence to speak after years of silence, encouraging skills and confidence so they can freely develop friendships and relationships, FitzRoy staff are there, encouraging and bringing hope to families."

FitzRoy
transforming lives

Friends of Petersfield Hospital

Friends' committee member, Monica Taylor (left) and June Brooks, President (right)

The aim of the Friends of Petersfield Hospital Charity is to provide equipment and support that is beyond the scope of the NHS, both for the benefit of patients in the hospital and to the wider healthcare community within the Petersfield area. Formed in 1954 and a registered charity, it raises funds by membership subscription (currently £5 minimum per year), fundraising events, donations and legacies.

In the 20 or so years since the Hospital was rebuilt over £160,000 has been raised and spent on a range of benefits. These include curtains, blinds and bedcovers for wards, specially designed chairs to suit patients' needs, electric hoists, electrically adjustable beds, a birthing bed, and a treadmill. Other contributions are maintenance costs and many smaller items for use by doctors, nurses and patients.

"In the 20 or so years since the Hospital was rebuilt over £160,000 has been raised..."

A valued service to patients is the self-funding Hospital Trolley shop manned by a rota of members of the Friends of the Hospital. Three times weekly the trolley shop enables patients in the wards to purchase small but appreciated items.

In the year of the Queen's Golden Jubilee the Charity, having made an initial financial contribution to the garden outside Cedar Ward, undertook a project to design and build two areas of garden on either side of the main hospital corridor. A landscape gardener, specialising in the designing of healing gardens for the use of patients, visitors and hospital staff, was employed. These gardens are wheelchair friendly and are planted to give year-round interest.

A rota of committee members and Friends ensure the general upkeep of these much loved areas, and in the last year over £5,000 has been spent on some further replanting and the refurbishment of parts of the garden outside Cedar Ward together with new garden furniture and shady umbrellas. The work and commitment of the Charity continues and it is hoped that new members will join to keep this worthwhile group functioning.

Jackie Phillips, Acting Chairman (left) and Elizabeth Granger (right) help staff with the Trolley Shop

Home-Start Butser

Home-Start Butser supports 80 families and 200 children, on average, each year and continues to make a difference to many lives. This branch of the local family support charity is based in Petersfield and covers the southern area of East Hampshire District.

The charity's approach is simple and effective - helping parents to help themselves. Families need help for a number of reasons including social and geographical isolation, financial difficulties, health issues and depression. Often the families have multiple needs and the stress of any of these factors can cause other problems to escalate.

Each local Home-Start is managed by a board of volunteer trustees and a small staff team. Volunteers from the local community who have parenting experience are recruited, trained and then matched with families who have at least one child under five. The volunteers visit the family regularly for a minimum of two hours a week offering practical and emotional help. They support parents to grow in confidence, strengthen their relationships with their children and widen their links with the local community.

"With Home-Start's help I got through a terrible time, and now my house is full of hope and laughter."

Home-Start Butser, one of 314 local Home-Starts in the UK, and with British Forces in Cyprus and Germany, was launched in 1998. This followed a local public meeting in November 1995, when it was agreed there was an unmet need for an organisation which could support families with young children going through a critical time in their lives. A steering group was set up to establish a local Home-Start scheme.

In 2007 two Home-Start Family Groups were established in Petersfield and Horndean. One parent says: "With Home-Start's help I got through a terrible time, and now my house is full of hope and laughter."

Lions Club of Petersfield

There are 25 members of the Lions Club in Petersfield & District. They share the aims of this international organisation, which was started by Chicago businessmen in 1917 and now has 1.4 million members worldwide.

One of the Lions' main aims is to help those with eyesight problems, especially in Africa and India. The Petersfield club, opened in 1972, has made donations to help relief from the earthquake in Haiti, the typhoon in the Phillipines as well as flood relief in Britain. Locally they have supported Home-Start Butser, Elizabeth FitzRoy, Town Juniors football club, Kings Arms youth club, Age Concern, Canine Partners, Hounds for Heroes, Marie Curie cancer charity, Macmillan, Save the Children, National Childbirth Trust, Holidays for Disabled People and many more.

The Petersfield club organises the collection of used spectacles from over 60 Lions clubs in the Southern Counties, collected in the previous year. This is known as SpecTrek and takes place on a spring Sunday when the Lions borrow several vans and collect

more than 100,000 pairs, totalling more than 2 million in the last 30 years. These are processed and graded in several stages, always through Lions clubs.

Funds are raised locally through street collections, stalls at country fairs, an autumn quiz, and by running the bar at the Music Festival in spring. Every penny donated to the Lions is spent on charity, because the administration costs are covered by the members. They enjoy a number of social activities and new members are always welcome.

The Lions Clubs took up their international challenge from the late Helen Keller and promoted the use of the white stick. The Lions started the first school for training guide dogs for the blind.

Lions Club of Petersfield

Petersfield Open Air Swimming Pool

An oasis in the heart of the town, the Petersfield Open Air Swimming Pool is the only outdoor heated pool in Hampshire. On a hot day it echoes to the sound of children enjoying the water and playing in the paddling pool. Meanwhile parents relax in the sunshine knowing that the children are both safe and happily occupied.

The pool is open throughout the summer and holds a number of events appealing to a wide variety of tastes. Sponsored swims, demonstrations of synchronised swimming, a 'pink' swim and even a midnight swim on midsummer's day. There is a lot of fun as well as the opportunity for serious swimming and keep fit.

The pool is very much part of the community and appeals to all ages, as witness the babes-in-arms and octogenarians who have been coming for many years. Run as a charity, it celebrated its golden anniversary in 2012 with some of the original supporters and swimmers in attendance. Over the years there have been many improvements and these continue to be made.

Much of the enjoyment comes from the friendly atmosphere that the pool has always had. Both staff and customers contribute to this, and the staff know many of the customers by name. For many of them, socialising with fellow swimmers is part of the appeal.

Swimming in the outdoors under the sky is a world removed from a chlorine-infested sports centre. It provides an exhilarating sense of pure enjoyment that is hard to match. The town is fortunate to have its very own pool. Enjoy it.

Probus

There are two Probus clubs in the town – the Petersfield & District Probus Club and the Petersfield South Downs Probus Club (PSDPC). They are part of a worldwide organisation of 4,500 clubs, offering a regular opportunity for retired business and professional people over the age of 55 to meet, make new friends and expand their interests. The clubs are non-sectarian and non-political.

The Petersfield Probus Club has 40 members and is for men only, although wives and partners take part in many of the club's activities, such as the monthly pub lunch and walk. Established in 1977, the club meets in the evening of the last Thursday of the month at the Half Moon pub in Sheet for a two-course dinner followed by a speaker drawn from the membership or from outside. Talks cover a wide range of topics, such as the Wey and Arun Canal, charitable dentistry work in Uganda, and the Hampshire Air Ambulance.

Outings have taken members to the Mary Rose, to Bletchley Park, to the City of London, and to the theatre. Visits to Salisbury Cathedral and other places of interest are planned. A highlight of the year is the club's Christmas lunch held at a local venue.

The club raises money for local and national charities, which often provide speakers. The Chairman for the year chooses a charity to support during his year in office. Currently they are supporting the Not Forgotten Association, which helps serving and ex-service personnel who have been injured and suffer disability, and works with Help for Heroes.

Lunchtime meetings for PSDC

Established in 1995 to accommodate an excess of members at the other local club and to satisfy the demand for lunchtime rather than evening meetings, the PSDPC meets monthly at the Half Moon.

The club has an average membership of about 50 and is open to both men and women.

Professional speakers entertain members on various topics, and there are well-supported visits to places of interest. Some members meet up at classical music concerts, theatres and Gilbert & Sullivan performances. One group even organised a three-day visit to Paris. The monthly walks are jolly occasions and can end up in pubs where the calories are put back on!

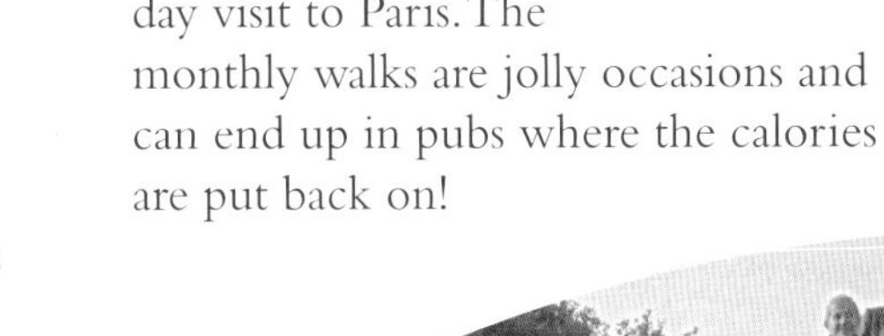

The Rosemary Foundation

Established in 1997, The Rosemary Foundation is a small local charity that provides much-needed palliative care and support to patients and their families in their own homes. The Rosemary Foundation is widely considered to be one of Petersfield's favourite charities, and anyone whose family has had contact with their nurses will know why.

The team of qualified nurses provides care and support where it is needed most, by patients suffering from cancer or other life limiting conditions who wish to spend their final days in the familiar and comfortable surroundings of their own home.

The foundation actively seeks to provide a cost-effective service with much of its administration and fundraising carried out by volunteers. Unfortunately charitable giving has been in decline in the recent economic downturn. There is a very real need for charitable giving as this is vital to the existence of The Rosemary Foundation, which receives no income from any statutory body.

Above: *(left to right) Lindy Coles, Barbara Pettegree (joint manager), Elspeth Dixon, Elaine Biles, Penny Powell and Jill Boucher* Below right: *(left to right) Julie Cotsell (Joint Manager), Penny Powell, Jeannette Burrows, Jill Boucher and Lindy Coles*

The Rosemary Foundation's team of trained, specialist nurses is available 24 hours a day and seven days a week without charge to the patient or carer. Should medical needs become more complex and dictate specialist outside expertise, The Rosemary Foundation can access, and work in partnership with, the Rowans Hospice, based in Purbrook, and the Macmillan team in Midhurst.

Coping with the loss of a loved-one is never easy, and, as well as providing a high level of care, the Rosemary Foundation offers counselling and bereavement support during these difficult and uncertain times. The Foundation's care does not end with the passing of the patient as the nurses remain to help the family come to terms with their loss.

The Rowans Hospice

The Rowans Hospice is a local charity which provides specialist hospice care and support to people affected by life-shortening illnesses in Portsmouth and South East Hampshire. They promote a philosophy of care that reaches far into the community through a dedicated team of clinical practitioners and trained volunteers.

They provide nursing care and practical support to people at home, thus avoiding unnecessary hospital admissions. They work in partnership with GPs, NHS community health care teams, social carers and other like-minded charities such as The Rosemary Foundation 'Hospice at Home' service.

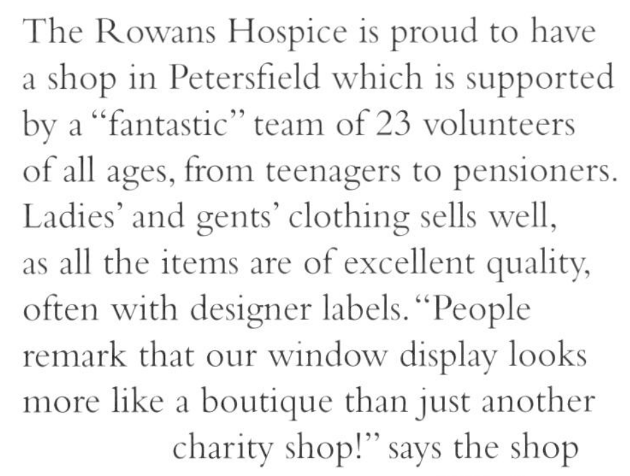

The Rowans Hospice is proud to have a shop in Petersfield which is supported by a "fantastic" team of 23 volunteers of all ages, from teenagers to pensioners. Ladies' and gents' clothing sells well, as all the items are of excellent quality, often with designer labels. "People remark that our window display looks more like a boutique than just another charity shop!" says the shop manager. "We have a large number of regular Petersfield customers as well as many who come from the wider district.

"The range of opportunities for our volunteers include community fundraising. We are very pleased to offer a sponsored cycle event which, for the most energetic cyclists, includes a route which takes in the beautiful countryside that surrounds Petersfield."

In October 2014, The Rowans Hospice celebrated 20 years of service to the growing number of people who need help and support regardless of age, diagnosis, financial means, culture or religion. This includes the development of the 'Living Well Centre', a community building that will support people to plan their future care needs, access therapies, information and support.

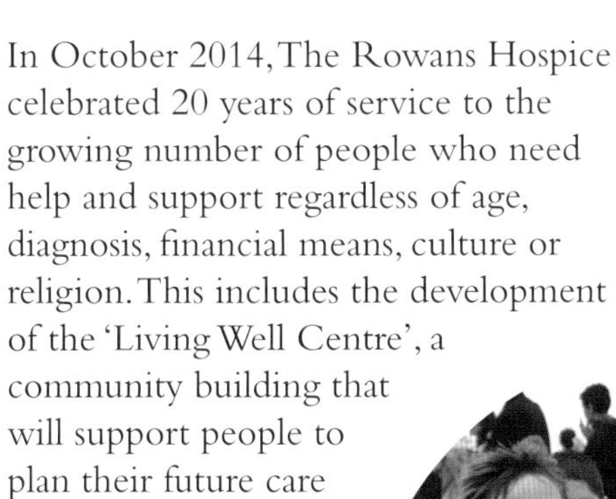

Save the Children

You might think that a group that raises money for a national charity – Save the Children – might be a friendly, energetic and hard-working gang and you would be right. But they also have a huge amount of fun while raising more money than any other branch in the UK – over £60,000 in 2014.

In 2013, when they celebrated their 50th anniversary, they were rewarded for their hard work by a visit from HRH Princess Anne (above) to their biggest event – the now famous three-day Big Sale in the spring. About 160 volunteers joined them for this year's Sale which raised over £20,000 and offered everything from a new wedding outfit to a pair of wellies, from a designer jacket to a vintage suit, and from a new suitcase to fancy jewellery or a pretty china tea-set.

Top: *The Catering team* Above: *Volunteers with items donated for an auction*

The diverse talents of the group lead to varied activities, which might inevitably include making cakes, playing bridge, selling good-as-new clothes, manning stalls at a Gift Fair, working with local schools to put on a Christmas concert, and taking part in cycling or running fund-raisers (even the London Marathon).

Save the Children

Did you know?

The branch chairman, Pauline Kneen, has visited Save the Children projects in Cambodia and is now a very well-informed ambassador for the charity. Her trip wasn't entirely glamorous and she met quite a challenge when invited to eat a tarantula – a new idea for an event perhaps?

Petersfield Voluntary Care Group

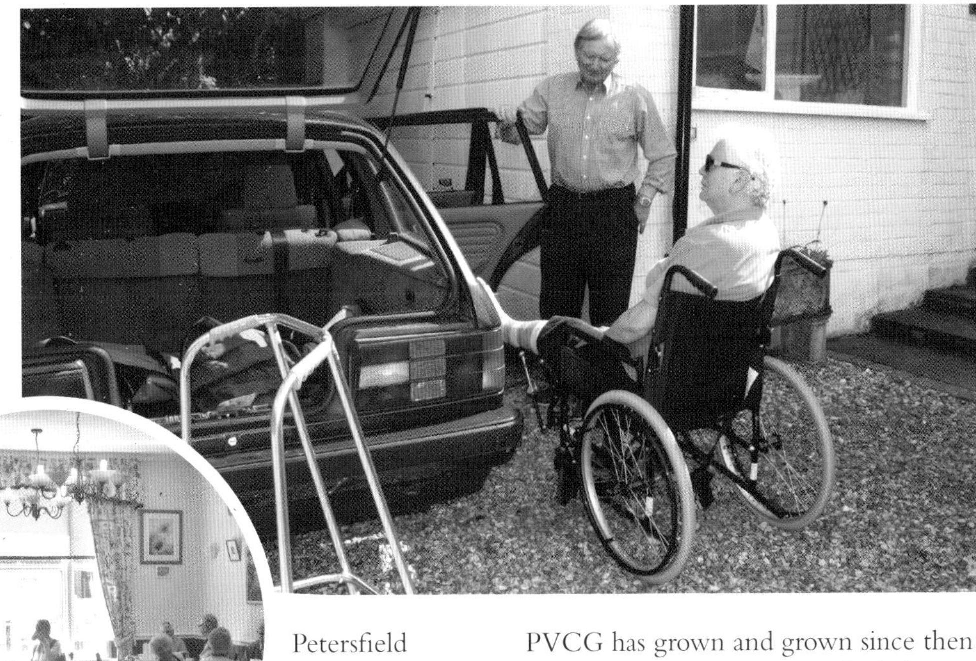

Petersfield Voluntary Care Group started as a result of a meeting in September 1974, when people from various local churches met in St Laurence Church to discuss the possibility of setting up a Voluntary Group to help local people who might need assistance in various ways. By the spring of 1975 the group was in action, driving people to hospital, dog walking and occasionally changing a light bulb.

PVCG has grown and grown since then and the number of requests for help seems to go up each year. Most of them are for shopping for the housebound, visiting relatives in care homes, visits to doctors and dentists' appointments, and taking people to hospitals – sometimes as far away as Southampton, Salisbury, Portsmouth and Guildford. PVCG ask for a donation for each trip: the clients are very generous.

The drivers give of their time but get a token petrol allowance; the coordinators get a phone allowance to cover their expenses. All the drivers have a clean driving licence and a CRB check, paid for by the Portsmouth Diocese at £50 a time.

Volunteers Nina Taylor, Maureen Willett and Christine Newman

Winton House Centre

Anyone walking along Petersfield's High Street notices the elegant Georgian building at number 18. Behind the façade are two surprises: an adapted Tudor coaching inn and a modern charity, the Winton House Centre, also the home of the Petersfield Voluntary Care Group. Here many of the needs of Petersfield's residents are met.

On the right of the front door is the Pop-In tea-room, open every day and on Saturday mornings for a restorative, reasonably priced pot of tea. On the left is the Office, an Information Centre, which acts as the registered address for many local organisations, including The Petersfield Society. Rooms can be hired, photocopying done cheaply, and a wealth of knowledge offered by friendly volunteers, including representatives of Age Concern.

Winton House has been used by the community for over 30 years in its present form, thus continuing a tradition spanning several centuries.

Dealing with customers, booking hospital transport, serving home-made cakes to regulars, and being part of peoples' lives draws a cross-section of people to volunteer to help in the office or behind the counter in the Pop-In. Why not drop in and see for yourself, any weekday between 10 and 4pm?

Did you know?

David Weeks has spent all his 73 years in the same house in Petersfield. As a boy, he developed an interest in the animals in his neighbour's (Fred Kimber's) menagerie in Tilmore Road and was introduced to the world of circuses and fairgrounds, eventually becoming a fairground 'spieler' himself. After a lifetime working on the railways, David enjoys helping with events in the town, his favourites being *Railway 150* in 2009 and the *Queen's Diamond Jubilee* celebrations in 2012.

Petersfield Area Churches Together: PACT

Above: *Remembrance service in the town square*
Below: *Good Friday March of Witness*

PACT is the association of Christian churches in the Petersfield area. Its objectives are "to seek every opportunity to worship and work together in united witness and service to the community and to work towards deeper commitment and fellowship between Christians". Petersfield was one of the first towns to record how churches were working together, as early as 1874.

Above: *PACT Messy Church event*
Inset: *Harvest Supper celebrations*
Below left: *Fundraising in Rams Walk*

In 1968, the Petersfield & District Council of Churches was formed, and the range of joint projects continued and expanded. In 1973, a group of members under this umbrella banded together and made donations to form a fund to help in the housing of people whom local government could not assist. From this grew the Petersfield Housing Association. Other examples of practical activities which continue to serve the community are the Society for Special Needs, the Voluntary Care Group, the Social Concerns Group and the Holiday Club, to name but a few.

Christmas 2013 saw 5,000 people attending churches within Petersfield, with 1,000 on any other Sunday service. PACT helps to demonstrate that churches are still a large part of Petersfield society and community life.

In addition to these practical activities, many of a more spiritual nature, involving all the churches, began in the 1960s and continue today, including Lent Bible Study groups, 'Carols in the Square' at Christmas time, with singing accompanied by the Salvation Army band, the Procession of Witness on Good Friday starting from the Methodist Church and finishing with a service in the Square, and the joint Pentecost Service.

St Peter's Parish Church

Reverend Will Hughes, the present vicar, believes St Peter's and the town of Petersfield are very good at looking after people. "Petersfield is a historic town but one which is not frozen in time," he says. "It is the sort of place where people stop and talk and are friendly – and that says a lot about the town itself, too."

One of the initiatives he introduced was to open a cafe – the 'Refresh Cafe' which now thrives inside the church on a Thursday morning. Will particularly enjoys the conversations he has in the town - from the charming gentleman on a motorbike "who wanted to tell me what was wrong with the country" or the passer-by in St Peter's Road who asked the way to the mosque (in fact, located in St Peter's Hall, but without the minarets!), to the half a dozen conversations he has every time he goes shopping in Petersfield.

Reverend Will Hughes, Vicar, (right) and Reverend Tom James, Assistant Curate

St Peter's, which gave the town its name, dates from the mid 12th century and its Norman pillars, arches, transepts and, above all, its magnificent chancel arch have attracted worshippers and visitors for nearly 900 years. The only Grade 1 listed building in Petersfield, it is also the oldest and was here when Petersfield was no more than a hamlet. The Domesday Book records that a small chapel dedicated to St Peter had been built on the site, then just a crossroads.

Over the centuries, most notably during the Victorian era, many alterations and additions to the building have taken place. In 1874, Sir Arthur Blomfield raised the nave roof and added a clerestory which brought extra light into the church. The most recent improvements came in 2000, when a new floor was installed, ancient pews were removed and the Lady Chapel, meeting room and servery were added at the west end. This enhanced the bright, open atmosphere of the whole building, transforming it into a space adaptable for concerts, plays, exhibitions and various community events.

Many fine memorials and tablets, including several dedicated to members of the Jolliffe family, are collected together in the Lady Chapel and meeting room. They chronicle the lives and deaths of parishioners through hundreds of years.

Petersfield Methodist Church

Apart from normal Sunday worship, the Church runs Youth groups once a month, a Women's Fellowship with speakers to which all are welcome, and two Bible study groups which meet in people's homes.

Special events often involve visiting or being visited by others in the East Solent and Downs circuit (anywhere between Haslemere and Gosport), when all the ministers in the circuit take part. As has always been the case historically, Methodist ministers generally move around the circuits after three or four years in one place. The current Minister is David Rice (below).

They are actively involved in the PACT events: about 60 children enjoy the Messy Church after school finishes at 3.30pm and they come along with their parents to do painting or craftwork – and even breadmaking sometimes – followed by a short service and tea. The Petersfield Christmas lunch takes place in the church hall for anyone who finds themselves alone on 25 December. It is much appreciated, of course, and attracts about 80 people who eat, drink, sing and are entertained for the afternoon by various individual performers or groups.

'Prayer breakfasts' are very popular: after the meeting for prayer at 8 am, bacon and sausages – and occasionally croissants! - are served to everyone! If you prefer coffee and a chat, then come along to the Saturday morning sessions.

Did you know?

The first Wesleyan Methodist Gospel Mission Caravan was dedicated in 1886 in Selby in Yorkshire. This impressed the Reverend Thomas Champness, who was at that this time editor of the 'Joyful News' newspaper. He immediately started an appeal for the first 'Joyful News Gospel Mission Car'. The aim was to pass on the Gospel in a rural setting, which would then be carried into the towns and cities. In 1896, the jurisdiction of the cars was passed to the 'Home Missions Committee' and the number of Gospel Mission Cars continued to increase. Their heyday was in the period 1890 to 1907, when there were up to 30 cars - then in 1904 they moved their base from Rochdale to Cliff College at Calver in Derbyshire. Each car had a number and a name. By examining this photograph carefully, it can be seen that above the door it says 'Gospel Car No 1 Faith'. The use of Gospel Cars gradually declined, and by 1921 there was only one left in service.

St Laurence Roman Catholic Church

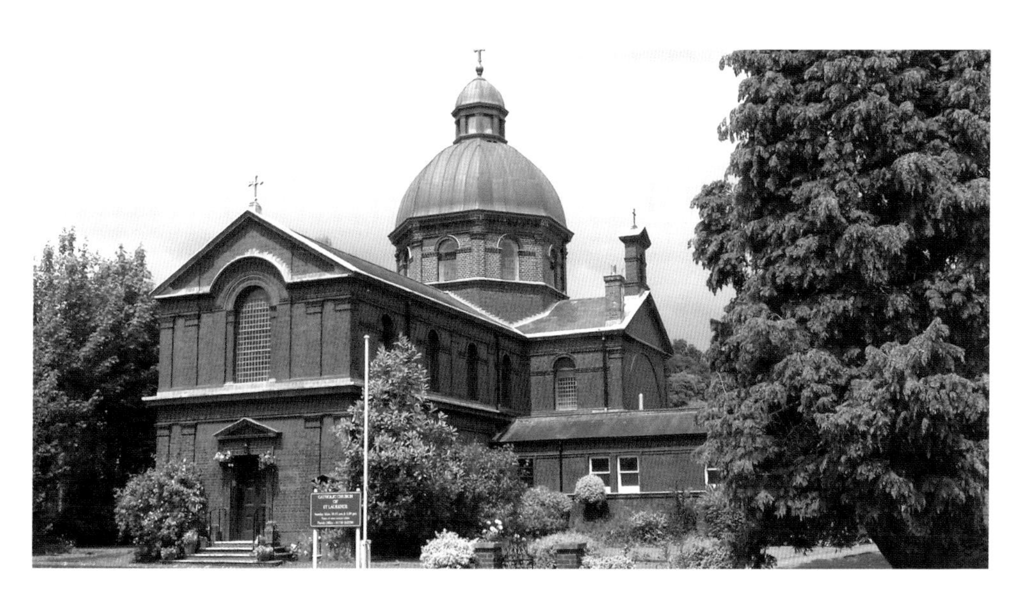

Father Peter Hollins is the fifth parish priest of St Laurence Roman Catholic Church in the last 70 years. Some 400 parishioners include those at St Agnes, Liss, and from as far afield as West Meon, South Harting and Finchdean. Attendees come from many countries – including Poland, Slovakia and the Philippines, and a regular Mass is held in Malayalam for Indian parishioners.

Former parishioners include Sir Alec Guinness who attended Evening Mass regularly with his wife, Merula. Once, a 10-year-old boy whispered excitedly to his father, "Obi Wan Kenobi is in front of us!" Another well-known parishioner was the late Katie Pitt MBE, former Petersfield Mayor and Councillor, who did an amazing amount of fund-raising for the former local Leonard Cheshire Home and also street-collections for major disaster appeals.

The foundations of this simply-furnished Victorian church were built in 1890 thanks to the generosity of

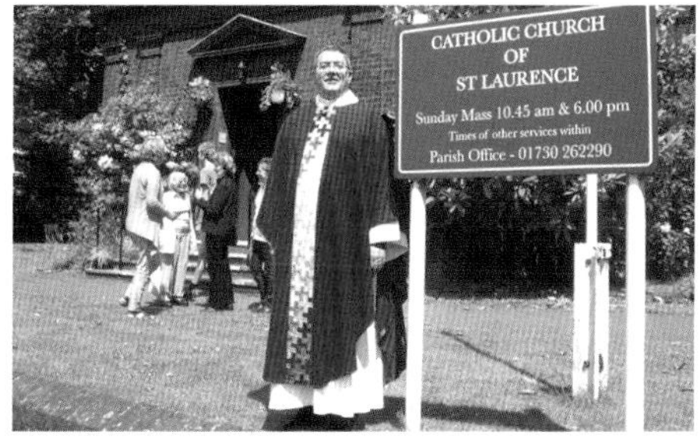

Top: *Father Peter Hollins* Middle: *Women's World Day of Prayer Service* Above: *Quiz Night in aid of Cabrini Children's Society* Inset: *Katie Pitt with her Benemerenti Medal*

Laurence Trent Cave. He died in 1891, and was buried just outside the walls but, following the extension of the left transept, his grave came within the church itself. The church's patron saint, St Lawrence, has his name spelt with a 'w' but in honour of Laurence Cave, St Laurence's is spelt with a 'u'.

A new copper dome completed in 2011 transformed the green oxidised dome to the brown one, which is a prominent landmark in the town. St Laurence also had a large electric organ installed and, with its excellent acoustics, the church is often used for concerts.

It is said that a church is the people, and many at St Laurence are living out their Christian faith daily with prayer and by involvement in community projects such as Home Start and the Soup Kitchen. St Laurence takes an active part in Petersfield Area Churches Together (PACT), in the annual Women's World Day of Prayer, and more recently has formed a Justice and Peace Group. Social events such as quiz nights and harvest suppers help to bring this widespread parish together.

St Mary Magdalen, Sheet

What could a pile of spare zips, a prize-winning garden and dozens of used biros possibly have in common? Well, they are just three of the ways Sheet Church lives up to its green agenda. The zips are for newly-qualified dressmakers in Africa; the church garden boasts its own water butt and compost heap; and the biros are 'upcycled' to save waste.

No one expects a church to care for the planet without caring for people as well – and St Mary's is no exception. The under-14s took a break from their pirate camp water-fight one summer weekend to make a short film on why the church needed a full-time youth worker. In the following weeks, church members responded with gusto, pledging £90,000 to cover a three-year contract and the new Youth Worker duly arrived just over a year later.

Above: *The new Youth Worker is front page news!* Left: *Actor Jenny Parkes in action* Below: *'Did he really change the time on Anne's watch?!' Friends Chair John Dunt and Anne Allchurch enjoy the Magic Show*

The Friends of Sheet Church (who raise funds for new sound systems, heating, organ or building repairs) organise great events, such as the Magic Supper in March. Amazing magician Simon Alexander plied his trade amongst the hors d'oeuvres, lasagne and chocolate puddings.

Seeing is believing, they say, so church activities include films and plays. The 2013 Nativity was unforgettable, from the disco-dancing angels to the puppet wise men and two heart-stopping solos from an eight-year-old Mary and a five-year-old sheep!

Other events included a sketch about tastes in worship when four Mary Magdalen actors had a field day, all cheerfully defying typecasting. John King, donned cravat and cap and took his voice down an octave to personify the traditional reactionary. Nikolai Gibbins, at the grand old age of nine, went even further, armed with 17th century texts and decrying all Victorian and modernist nonsense. The eminently respectable Dr Jenny Parkes became a radical who wanted everyone up and dancing. Computer buff Jon Ritchie became a silent meditator. Amongst all the laughs, there was the unmistakable message that however we worship, it's actually the thought – or rather the heart – that counts.

The Salvation Army

The Salvation Army in Petersfield is close to the centre of the town, located just off the Square. Its 'Open Door' offers an opportunity for people to visit the church daily and has proved a worthwhile venture, providing lonely and homeless people with a warm place to meet, chat, and have something to eat.

People can give to the food bank, which is managed by them on behalf of Petersfield Area Churches Together. Those who have fallen on hard times can collect a food parcel.

Along with representatives from other churches, the Salvation Army is embarking on a new initiative to go out and meet other homeless people, who are generally not on the radar, and initially provide them with something warm to eat once a week.

The Salvation Army also offers many other opportunities for the community's benefit from their small suite of buildings. As well as 'Open Door', they provide: a weekly lunch club for more than 40 people; space for more than 20 families to play and meet each other at the Parent & Tots Club; games and crafts for more than 20 children aged 5-12 at the Junior Club; a coffee morning, a mid-week 'Come and meet each other'; and, of course, an opportunity to worship each Sunday. All these activities are run by members of the church.

The Church Band participates in many annual town events during the year, including the Good Friday 'Act of Witness', the spring and summer festivals, and the Remembrance Sunday parade. During December, they visit many of the residential homes, schools, carol services, and other venues to sing Christmas Carols.

Life Church Petersfield

Life Church came together to celebrate 35 years in Petersfield by inviting previous members of the Church to a celebratory meal. Formerly Petersfield Christian Fellowship, the Church started in its present form when a group of Christians from Portsmouth, originally at the Polytechnic, merged with another house church group who moved from Canterbury in the late 1970s. Today they meet on Sundays at The Petersfield School, in the Main Hall.

You may have noticed the illuminated Crown in the window of the Life Church Office in Station Road, where Sandra Coombes (left), their secretary, welcomes visitors. Among her many activities she runs Knit & Knatter, where knitters, crafters and crochet makers meet once a month. This started small but has now expanded to a group meeting in the Herne Farm Leisure Centre, and works on projects for charity each month as well as individual projects.

Life Church is a keen member of PACT, and John Callaghan (left), one of the Leaders, is Chairman. Life Church is part of several PACT projects, like the Town Chaplaincy and the Kings Arms, which is a club for young people. The Chaplaincy provides a listening ear to the businesses in the Town and helps with stewarding public events. They were on the street from 7am as part of EHDC's team when the Olympic Flame came through Petersfield in 2012.

Petersfield Evangelical Church

The Petersfield Evangelical Church moved in February 2014 to the Petersfield Community Centre after being formed in 1976. This re-location puts it within 50 yards of the original chapel attached to the 'Old Poor Law Institution' buildings in Readon Close, off Love Lane.

The Evangelical Church, with Christians meeting together for a mid-week Bible Study and Sunday services, is largely served by local visiting speakers from other churches. It is affiliated to the FIEC (Fellowship of Independent Evangelical Churches).

During the early period the church had many children coming through Sunday School. After a fire in 1994, the buildings at Readon Close were put out of use. The church fellowship then met on Sunday mornings in the Day Centre at Bulmer House from 1996 to early 2014.

Over the years some of the staff and many of the residents from the Care Home have joined in with the morning services and enjoyed sharing in worship. Some of the residents came for just short periods, but others came for several years, and one of the church's ministries was to be able to pray for and encourage the Care Home Residents. With the closure of Bulmer House, the residents have moved on to other care homes.

PACT Holiday club

United Reformed Church

The United Reformed Church's minister, Reverend Peter Norris, has been leading the church since 1994 and also serves as hospital chaplain at Petersfield Hospital. The church has links with the other churches in the town through Petersfield Area Churches Together (PACT). Further afield, a group from the church visits remote villages in Ukraine each year providing them with much needed medical support as well as running a programme of activities for both children and adults.

However, the church is really the people who worship there. The church sanctuary, the family centre and the lovely garden are the backdrop for a busy, active and flourishing church with Sunday worship and weekday activities to suit all ages from 0 to 100+. Visitors of all denominations and persuasions are very welcome to all the Sunday services at 11am and 6.30pm, and also to the well-attended special services at Christmas and Easter.

During the week, the premises are put to use to host a wide range of activities. There are groups for parents and babies and toddlers, several groups for women of all ages and, for men with hearty appetites, there is the monthly men's breakfast. For older people, there is the monthly Tea on the Terrace. The Family Centre is also available for hire, both by groups and by private hirers - currently these include a Bereavement Group, a Multiple Sclerosis Group, the Alzheimer's Society and a local Choir.

There has been a place of worship on the site of the United Reformed Church at the north end of College Street since 1795, although the present church was not built until 1883. Much more recently, the old church hall was replaced by the Church Family Centre, which was completed in 2008.

Petersfield Arts & Crafts Society

Petersfield Arts & Crafts Society (PACS) was established in 1934 by Flora Twort and a group of local artists to promote interest in visual arts and crafts in the area. With up to three hundred members, PACS is a thriving community open to anybody with an interest in the visual arts within a ten mile radius of Petersfield. They are passionate about encouraging all skill levels from all disciplines. As a result, they attract amateurs and professionals working in a broad range of media, including ceramics, textiles, wood, stone, metal, glass, multi-media, photography and digital as well as paint and print.

Their demonstrations, workshops, exhibitions and life-drawing sessions encourage confidence and experimentation. This feeds into practice and contributes to high standards of creativity, commitment and workmanship. Regular meetings enable members to contribute to the Society by sharing their ideas, skills and experience. The Society's showcase annual August exhibition, held in the light and spacious Festival Hall, is run entirely by members. They operate a policy of non-selection of works, so every member can experience the satisfaction of seeing their work exhibited in a large gallery space, while the public delights in the vibrancy of five hundred diverse exhibits.

Digital and photographic works have recently been introduced to their exhibition and children and grand-children of members are encouraged to exhibit in the 'budding artist' category. The PACS' public profile has been raised by their new website which has details of exhibitions and workshops for members and non-members.

An innovative 'Create a Collage' charity event invites the whole community to participate in a huge, themed collage at the annual exhibition, which aims to be the artistic hub of Petersfield.

Petersfield Decorative and Fine Arts Society

The Petersfield branch of NADFAS, inaugurated in 1982, is thriving with a membership of nearly 300. They meet 10 times a year, in the Community Centre, for inspiring monthly lectures given by some of the country's top experts, on such diverse subjects as Antonio Gaudi and the architecture of Barcelona to Mad Tracy from Margate - the work of Tracy Emin.

Left to right: Clare Brown - Chairman; *Victoria Puttock - Music student, being partly sponsored by PADFAS; Judy Grill - Young Arts Co-ordinator*

In addition to the monthly lectures, special interest days are held twice a year for a more in-depth study into diverse subjects such as Heraldry or History of Glass. Outside visits are held several times during the year with a recent outing being a private evening visit to Westminster Abbey in the company of The Purcell Singers who related the history of this wonderful atmospheric building through narrative and music. They have an annual tour in which a group of up to 30 members travel to a destination for several days to study the art and related history in that area – the most recent tour was to Lisbon.

NADFAS (the National Association of Decorative and Fine Arts Societies) is a leading arts charity which opens up the world of the arts through a network of 360 local Societies across Britain, in mainland Europe and New Zealand. At a national level NADFAS provides children and young people with exciting opportunities to get involved in creative arts activities.

The Petersfield branch supports a young arts project by sponsoring a local musician studying for a Masters Degree in Performance at the Royal College of Music. Above all, their activities are interesting and fun and in many cases have led to lifelong friendships.

Did you know?

Michelle Magorian lives in Petersfield with her two sons. She was born in Portsmouth, trained to be an actress at the Rose Bruford College of Speech and Drama and after a year at Marcel Marceau's L'École Internationale de Mime in Paris, worked in theatres from Devon to Scotland.

She is best known for her first novel, *Goodnight Mister Tom,* which won the 1982 *Guardian* Children's Fiction Award and has been adapted for screen, stage and radio. Two of her other six novels *Back Home* and *Just Henry* (which won the 2008 Costa Children's Book Award) have also been adapted for television.

Michelle likes Petersfield because there are three lovely bookshops, an orchestra, a wonderful youth theatre, an annual Musical Festival and one of the few costume museums in the UK, as well as friendly places where she can enjoy coffee and a chat.

Petersfield and District Beekeepers' Association

Apiary meetings are held during the spring, summer and early autumn months at the Association apiary at one to two week intervals depending on the time of season, where members gain experience in the handling and management of bees. During the winter, meetings are held in the Petersfield area and include an introductory course for new beekeepers, a programme of lectures on different subjects for the more experienced beekeepers, and the Annual General Meeting. These meetings generally end with refreshments and an exchange of views on beekeeping.

The Association holds its annual Honey Show each September which features exhibits of the first class products of the hives, different types of honey and beeswax, and prizes are awarded. There are also classes for honey-based confectionery. The show is held in a different village each year within the catchment area of the Petersfield and District Beekeepers' Association, and members of the public are always welcome to visit the show where honey is also on sale.

Throughout the season, the association organises the collection of swarms which are hived by member beekeepers. Membership is open to all age groups. Sometimes during the summer months, the association sets up various educational displays at local shows and events as well as visiting schools and organisations in the area, to meet the public and introduce the honey bee and the craft of beekeeping.

Originally formed in 1941 as the Steep Beekeepers' Association, it was encouraged by the movement to grow one's own food during the war years. It was originally based at Bedales School and, for a number of years, meetings were held at members' apiaries in the area until settling at the current apiary on the outskirts of Petersfield.

During the 1950s the name changed to The Petersfield and District Beekeepers' Association. The association started with 10-15 members and has grown to the current membership of almost 200, consisting of about 100 beekeepers with their friends and families. The association is now a registered charity and its purpose is to educate beekeepers in the art of beekeeping and to inform the public about bees and beekeeping.

Petersfield Evening Floral Club

Petersfield is most unusual in having a teaching Flower Club. The club was formed by Myra Banyard, Caroline Parker and Hazel Williams, who had studied for three years to obtain their City & Guilds and wanted to make use of their new qualifications. A Church flower arranger suggested they formed a teaching flower club.

From the start in St Peter's Church in February 1987, the club's aim was to have a limited membership and to get all attending members practically involved, in an informal family atmosphere – imparting knowledge in the mechanics, design and elements of floral art through practical sessions. The first full demonstration was by Lilian Holdman.

The varied programme has ranged from teaching basic triangles and pedestals to abstract, free-form, plaiting, Ikebana and contemporary sessions. Some members have gone on to obtain their City & Guilds qualification. In 1991 the Club applied to become affiliated to the National Association of Flower Arrangers (NAFAS), and it is now a Registered Charity.

Soon after inception, they were asked to decorate two houses in The Spain which were being opened to the public for a few days. When Petersfield's new hospital was opened, the club put up dried arrangements to enhance public areas. Two members went to The Mansion House in London, which was a great honour.

Various churches have benefited from their expertise, St Laurence's RC and the Methodist Church, particularly to commemorate the Millennium. A regular commitment is to create the flower arrangements which grace the stage and the Rose Room at the Festival Hall for Petersfield Music Festival.

In 2001(sponsored by Rams Walk), members were invited to put a floral design in each shop. In 2013, members helped to create a floral spectacular in Winchester Cathedral, a profit of £42,000 was raised for the Cathedral organ. Also in 2013 St. Mary's Buriton was decorated for a Flower Festival and members worked alongside the Church flower arrangers. Members have arranged flowers at Bedales for a Royal Marines Band Concert.

The Petersfield Philatelic Society

Stamps tell the stories of famous people and landmarks, tourist destinations, successful innovations and inventions. These are all brought out in members' displays, exhibitions and competitions. The Petersfield Philatelic Society meets on the first Monday of each month at the community centre.

Philately is now much more than collecting stamps. For those with an interest in geography, stamps are now issued from every country in the world, and they can be found from countries that no longer exist. Postmarks can be found from obscure towns and villages in remote countries.

If your interest is history then stamps tell the story of empire, of the East India Company, of the Russian revolution and everything in between. It is possible to see the evolution of the political scene in every country, the changes in political leaders and governments.

The rare 1852 British Guiana rectangular one cent black on magenta

Here, members are looking at displays of postal history, with stamps and envelopes posted more than 100 years ago. Occasionally on display are real rarities such as the rectangular British Guiana one cent black on magenta, a close cousin to the rarest stamp in the world, the square one cent black on magenta of which only one copy has ever been found.

The Petersfield Pumpkin Growers Association

Each year every member of the Petersfield Pumpkin Growers Association is given 5 seeds from the same packet and variety: British Hundred Weight. Then, on 6 October, the pumpkins are weighed and trophies are awarded for the first three heaviest pumpkins. There are also trophies for the best matched pair and the best all round pumpkin which members present are invited to judge. The record for the heaviest pumpkin was set by Peter Crew in 1996 and weighed 153lbs.

The club was formed in 1976 and originally met at the Bowling Club in St Peters Road. Founder members included locals Norman Bryant, Peter Stevens, Tom Luff, David Fisk, Ray Hill and Phil Sylvester.

The club has a maximum of 30 growing members – there are currently 28 – and meets twice a year: first in April to distribute the seeds and then again on Taro Fair night, 6 October, for the Pumpkin Show. The venue for the competition has varied over the years from the Bowling Club and The Old Drum in town to The Cricketers in Steep. The show is currently held at the Half Moon in Sheet.

Simon Crew has been the club secretary since 2000 and the current Chairman is Andy Anderson. Though the traditions of the club have remained constant, it has kept up with the times and now hosts its own Facebook page. Subscriptions for the club remain low at £5 a year and the club is always keen to recruit new members.

Twinning Association

In 1992 somebody had the idea to link Petersfield with France. The thoughts of long continental holidays combined with empty sunny beaches, cheap rosé wines and luscious pink langoustines were obviously uppermost in their minds. Little did they know they would end up with the one-time textile manufacturing town of Barentin, famous for its hundred statues and the railway viaduct built by the English contractor, Thomas Brassey.

Right, below, and inset: *The twin town of Barentin in France*

The viaduct collapsed soon after its opening, apparently due to faulty lime in the mortar. But since then, everything has been on the up. The viaduct was rebuilt by Brassey with his own personal funds and now forms part of the arms of Barentin. You can see these arms halfway up Ramshill on the wall to the right of Barentin Way.

So 20 years on, Petersfield has friends in Barentin and, while we may not have the rosé wines, there are excellent ciders and calvados, and langoustines abound. To celebrate the 20th anniversary in April 2013 Barentin's mayor came to Petersfield with a delegation and took part in a reception with many members of the twinning association in the Rose Room of the Town Hall. A number of visits and events were organised for our French visitors.

The origin of town twinning comes after the Second World War as part of the effort to build bridges between previous enemies: Barentin entered a twinning arrangement with Warendorf in North Rhein Westphalia in Germany. Petersfield's link with Warendorf, whose town centre is very well cared for and contains many beautiful buildings and churches, originates with its links to Barentin and is approaching its 10th anniversary. Warendorf, the centre for the German Olympic dressage team, lies in a mainly agricultural region and the countryside around is green and relatively flat, in contrast to the hilly surrounds of Petersfield and Barentin.

Above, inset, left and below: *The twin town of Warendorf in Germany*

Petersfield hosts biennial visits from our French and German friends and visits Barentin and Warendorf in return. What started up as a twinning ended up as a tripling!

Petersfield Photographic Society

The Petersfield Photographic Society has enjoyed a varied programme of events that included competitions, speakers and assessment evenings. It meets on most Wednesdays from September through to May, fortnightly for the main meetings and monthly for workshops.

Competitions play a central role in the Society's activities. Three print and three digital projected image competition evenings between members have been held with external judges drawn from across the south of England. Each competition is split into two classes, standard and advanced. Alongside the main competitions there is also a set subject competition. The marks from each are added up at the end of the season and the top scoring member wins the associated class trophy.

A selection of the prints and digital images is selected for entry into Southern Counties Photographic Federation league competitions where they compete against other clubs.

Other interclub competitions have a lighter note. In October we hosted a three way Match an Image competition with Havant and Alton. Each club takes it in turn to put up a start image and the other clubs have to find one that, in the view of the judge, has a similar content. With a set number of images in the pot this becomes increasingly difficult as the evening goes on and the judge is lobbied to accept ever more tenuous reasons to match images.

The highlight of the year was a very successful public exhibition by 27 members of 144 prints and 140 projected digital images at the Community Centre.

The Society is open to photographers of all levels of ability and our aim is to enjoy and share our love of photography and assist in improving photographic skills. The latter is provided through workshops, our website forums or direct contact with other members. New members are always welcome. The current president is Peter Timney who is also joint competitions secretary with John Wigley. The secretary is Pauline Thornhill.

Petersfield Ramblers Club

Most of what Petersfield Ramblers Club exists for can be summed up by four words beginning with F: Fun, Fitness and Friendship in Fresh Air. Their aim is to provide members and potential members with led walks in the beautiful countryside surrounding Petersfield on Wednesdays and Saturdays throughout the year.

Most walks take place within 20 miles of Petersfield and are between 5 and 10 miles in length. They include the South Downs, The Hangers, Iping, Stedham, Woolbeding, Bramshott, Ludshott, Hindhead and Bramdean Commons. The Ramblers venture further afield at times, and in 2012 travelled by coach to Upavon and walked the 'Stones Way' to Stonehenge via Wood Henge. Last year they took a coach to Stockbridge and walked the Test Way down to Romsey via Mottisfont. In 2014 they have walked the Itchen Way in a series of walks, from Cheriton to Southampton.

They have enjoyed walking weekends together, exploring parts of Dorset during the last two years when they were based in Piddletrenthide.

"providing members and potential members with led walks in the beautiful countryside surrounding Petersfield"

In 2014 they have been based in Shanklin enjoying the delights and coastal views provided by walking the Isle of Wight.

Members are encouraged to lead walks, and that involves an annual 'Leaders' Lunch' which is provided to thank those who have led walks in the previous year. The Ramblers have some 40 leaders from their membership of less than 100. Traditionally members turn out in numbers when food is provided and, to this end, the AGM is sandwiched between a morning walk and a communal lunch.

Membership costs £5 a year and you do not need to own a car to join. Members with cars meet at Petersfield Town station and give lifts to those without transport, before driving to the starting place for a walk.

The Petersfield U3A

The Petersfield U3A (University of the Third Age) has a thriving membership of 600 people who are enjoying their retirement in the company of other like-minded people. The various activities are led by the members for the members and there is no limit to the choice of activity.

Three large formal meetings are held each month at the Community Centre attended by between 50 and 120 members. A general meeting on the second Monday of the month attracts about 100 members. Topics are chosen to appeal to a broad audience and those held in 2014 included "Fort Nelson – Palmerston's Folly"; "Pub Signs and their Stories", and "The Life and Times of Tommy Cooper".

There are some 48 groups (always under review), some highly specialised, some intellectual, others educational, but all having a social element. At the monthly arts and heritage meeting speakers talk about various artists with local connections, local historic buildings etc. Occasionally there are organised trips to special destinations such as The Inns of Court in the City of London, or The Globe Theatre, by coach with lunch included. The science and technology group meets once a month with audiences of 35-70, covering topics such as "The Design of Tall Buildings", "Weather by Satellite", "Producing English Wines", and "the Science of Archaeology".

There are seven groups studying foreign languages and seven more dealing with the written word – some read and discuss a chosen book each month while others discuss books in a general sense. Two groups view specially chosen films and then share what they have seen and learned. There is also a current affairs group.

Family history is being studied by two groups, while another group researches the history of Petersfield. More physical groups include walking (short and long distance in the countryside around the town), cycling, table tennis, petanque, and Tai Chi.

Members have special interests in computing, gardening, painting, and competitive board games such as bridge, chess, mah jong and scrabble. On the musical side, there are groups for music appreciation, jazz, recorders, handbell ringing and a choir. Finally, the annual Weekend Away (25-30 people) lasts for 4 days.

Nationally, the U3A is a charitable trust with over 900 independent branches. In 2015 the U3A celebrates its 20th anniversary and there will be a number of events to mark the occasion.

U3A Bridge

The U3A Bridge Club which plays on Tuesday afternoons at the Community Centre has a strong following with up to 10 tables competing. The format is "Duplicate Bridge" where the same hands are played at each table. This means that all the "North – South" players play against all the "East – West" players. It is always fun, always lively and there are always "post-mortae" when comparing how the same games played out at different tables. The expressions on the faces say it all! Concentration, elation or despair, everyone has the same range of emotions; but then it's a new game and it starts all over again!

Phoenix Stitchers

Before the Great British Sewing Bee on TV had got the nation sewing again Phoenix Stitchers had already done it in Petersfield! On the first Saturday morning of most months at Petersfield Community Centre, up to 50 girls aged 7 to 16 come to Junior Phoenix to experience all aspects of working with textiles - stitching, embroidery, dyeing, printing - helped by volunteers who are members of Phoenix Stitchers.

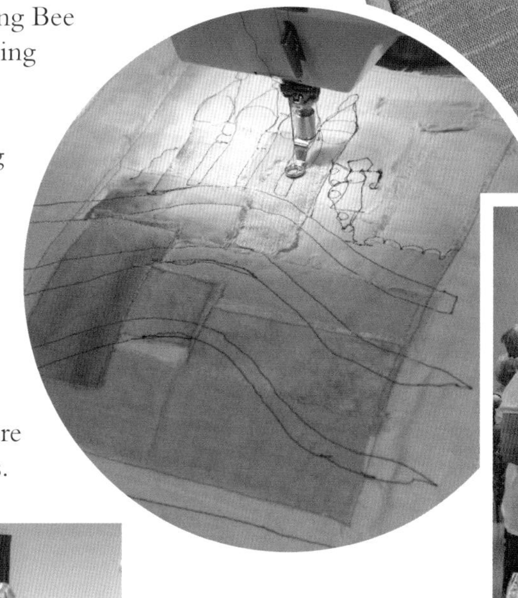

Phoenix Stitchers has more than 100 members who are interested in textiles and stitch. There is a varied monthly programme of lectures and workshops led by visiting tutors – often giving members the chance to try something new! They share a common interest in textiles, learning from each other and being together. Results may be seen on their website and at occasional exhibitions in the Physic Garden – the next is in July 2015.

Did you know?

Comedian and actor Miranda Hart lived with her family in Sussex Road, Petersfield, when she was growing up. The house was bought by Michael Mates, who was then the local MP.

Born in Torquay in 1972, Miranda took a Post-Graduate Acting course at ALRA in London, and then appeared regularly as a stand-up comedian at the Edinburgh Festival from 1994 to 2005. She first caught the attention in *Not Going Out*, a BBC TV flat-sharing sit-com with Lee Mack. Then she wrote and starred in her own comedy show *Miranda*, which started on BBC 2 in 2009, developed from Radio 2's *Miranda Hart's Joke Shop*. This show transferred to BBC1 in December 2012 and the third series had 9.8 million viewers on average. The finale was screened in January 2015. *Miranda* earned her four BAFTA nominations, three RTS awards and three Comedy Awards. She also had a BAFTA nomination for her role as Chummy in BBC1's *Call the Midwife*. Her first big film role – in *Spy* alongside Melissa Mcarthy and Jude Law – was due to come out in May 2015.

Petersfield Bridge Club

Petersfield Bridge Club was inaugurated in 1969 and is a friendly club, affiliated to the English Bridge Union, holding sessions on Tuesday and Thursday evenings at the Community Centre. The hands are duplicated and so printouts are available to see at the end of the session. Bridgemates are used for scoring and therefore the result is ready at the end of the evening.

One member says, "I joined the club when my younger daughter started school and I am still playing 26 years later! It is a very sociable gathering of people from all backgrounds who like to keep their minds active and alert. Our youngest member is a University student who comes along with her lecturer – the oldest member is a lady of 104!

THE ENGLISH BRIDGE UNION
AFFILIATED CLUB

"Bridge is a great 'leveller', with experienced players up against newcomers. But every hand played presents a new challenge and that is the joy of the game. We break for coffee and a (quiet!) chat halfway through the evening – with over 90 members, there is always a friendly or new face to meet".

The club also runs an extensive teaching programme with four teachers tutoring courses at different levels and an 'improvers' session, designed for those who have played before and wish to brush up their bridge before joining the club, and also for students who have just completed the course.

The most popular events for members are the Pairs congress in May and a Teams congress in October each year, when a trophy is awarded to the winners and money prizes to runners-up. The standard of bridge is high and teams from the club enter Hampshire League Competitions and other County and National events.

Petersfield Area Historical Society

Founded in 1973, the Petersfield Area Historical Society's aims are to promote the study and recording of the history of the Petersfield area; to foster interest in research and fieldwork; and from time to time to publish the findings of the Society or of any member.

The Society regularly attracts 70 - 80 members to its monthly meetings with guest speakers during the autumn, winter and spring and, in the spring and summer, it organises visits to places of historical interest. There is also an associated Archaeological Group which holds an additional five meetings a year at the Physic Garden, together with visits to sites of archaeological interest in the area. This group has also held study days and field trips in the summer months.

For residents and visitors to the town, the Society offers regular Town Walks ('Perambulations') throughout the summer months which are led by its members. These have included subjects such as Petersfield in WW1; the Arts and Crafts movement in Steep; historic St Peter's Church; Petersfield pubs, inns and breweries; the archaeology of Petersfield Heath; and 'Murders and Menageries' - a walk geared towards younger visitors.

Above: *A Town Perambulation*

Inset: *Hester Wagstaff's map of Petersfield, 1922*

Left: *An archaeology group talk*

Right: *PAHS publications*

Several members of the Historical Society assisted with the excavation of the Petersfield Heath barrows during the summer of 2014. Working on the three sites, they were involved with a range of tasks from excavation and sieving to recording.

A twice-yearly *Bulletin* is published which contains articles on recent research in the Petersfield area.

The Society has also published many books over the past thirty years, all of which are available at the Museum or the Tourist Information Centre in the Library and at One Tree Books in Lavant Street.

Petersfield WI

The original Women's Institute in Petersfield dates back to 1900, one of the earliest in the country and fifteen years before the national WI movement was founded. Local villages such as Sheet and Stroud have formed their own organisations more recently and the 35-40 members of the Petersfield branch include some who are dual members of two branches.

As is common to all WIs, the group invites to its monthly meetings speakers who talk on a wide variety of topics such as a craft, history, nature, holidays or topical issues of particular interest to women. Meetings are invariably followed by tea and biscuits, giving everyone an opportunity to chat with the speakers.

Celebrating their 20th Birthday. President Linda Sallows with former presidents Florence D'Ath, Ronnie Trenchard, and founder member Shirley Pickup

Interest groups also meet separately to go swimming, hold skittles evenings, run beetle drives, do knitting, enjoy pub lunches, or visit places of interest, including Denman College in Oxfordshire where many types of courses are held for WI members nationally.

In Petersfield, the group connects closely with the wider community and has recently provided props for a production of Calendar Girls, taken part in fundraising activities for the premature baby unit at Queen Alexandra hospital, and they regularly provide bar and cafe staff for events at the Festival Hall.

Women's Institutes are non-political, but they campaign collectively as a pressure group on national and international matters which particularly affect women. The Petersfield branch, for example, recently raised funds for projects in India, while at the national AGM such major topics as Third World social deprivation, organ donation, prostitution or environmental pollution are keenly debated and voted on. It may fairly be said of the WI that there is something for everyone in their programmes and women of all ages, creeds and backgrounds are welcome and encouraged to join.

Community

The Association of Petersfield Businesses

Left to Right: *Dominic Humphries - Chair, Jo Beck, Paul Beck, Rhona Russell, Jaki Ranson, Michael Finch, Shirley Crockford - Treasurer, Tracey Richardson - Secretary, Nicky Curry*

There has been a 'trade' association in Petersfield for as long as most people can remember. The structure and membership has evolved over the years to reflect the changing needs of the town. The Association today is open to all businesses based or operating in Petersfield, whatever size and goods or services it provides.

In this way the membership reflects the diverse business community the town enjoys. The APB is volunteer run, with a committee structure, supported by a modern website, with social media links to ensure news and views are current and relevant. In addition to the Annual General Meeting, open meetings are held during the year and newsletters published regularly.

The APB is established as the 'voice' of the businesses in the town, with strong links to the local authorities, the MP, and other community groups, providing a two-way flow of information and platform to raise issues, make suggestions and challenge decisions.

The APB is very active in looking for opportunities to promote the town as the place to work and visit in the area.

Working in partnership with the local authorities and its chosen charity partner it stages the annual Christmas Lights Switch-On: a family focused, early evening event in the Square, combining entertainment and fundraising culminating with the throwing of the switch for the Christmas Tree to burst into light.

Famous characters have graced the Square, including Pudsey Bear from BBC Children-in-Need, a local Dreams Come True ambassador, our MP, the Mayor and in 2014 Star Wars characters landed in Petersfield.

Inset: *Damian Hinds MP and Town Mayor Sue Harwood*

Below: *Christmas lights, 2014*

Citizens Advice Bureau

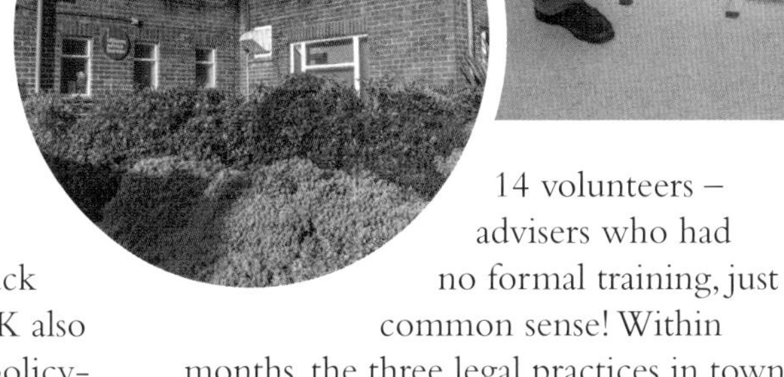

The Petersfield Citizens Advice Bureau (CAB) has 37 advisers to deal with the complex enquiries they receive, which are logged confidentially onto a computer. There are also about 65 volunteers in Petersfield, with outreach bureaux in Liss, Liphook and Horndean.

In the early days, the CAB dealt with families' tax, mortgage, insurance or housing problems. The dominant issue now is debt and the increase in the number of clients needing help.

People are worried about benefits and housing, due to changes in legislation and, in the recession of the early 1990s, many people suffered from negative equity on their property.

The CAB's 'Gateway' system is a filtering process which avoids long queues of people waiting for specialist or generalist appointments. The online 'Adviceline' is another useful tool for the CAB to explain things to clients. Feedback from over 3,000 CABs in the UK also helps to influence government policy-makers.

Formed in 1974, the Petersfield CAB relied for its original organisation on 14 volunteers – advisers who had no formal training, just common sense! Within months, the three legal practices in town had agreed to set up a panel to provide free legal advice to Petersfield residents on a rota basis. Soon after, the number of enquiries being dealt with – over 1500 – was clear evidence of a need being met. Lyndum House in the High Street was the CAB's first home.

Thanks to the leadership of Morag Crawley, followed by Liz Mullenger, 30 years of the CAB were celebrated in 2004. Armed with one Imperial typewriter and one Amstrad computer, in 1990 they moved into their new venue, The Old Surgery in the Festival Hall car park (perfect for allowing the confidentiality of their doctors' interview rooms).

CAB special event charied by Local MP Damian Hinds

Petersfield Counselling Service

The Petersfield Counselling Service has been helping people talk about their problems and feelings in a confidential and dependable environment for 27 years.

Founded in 1987 as an initiative of local churches and caring professions, this is an independently funded, friendly professional organisation offering affordable and helpful counselling to people aged 18 and over.

If people are facing emotional, personal or relationship problems such as loneliness, anxiety, depression, redundancy or job worries, relationship or family issues, loss or bereavement, emotional or physical abuse difficulties, they are advised to ask the Counselling Service for help.

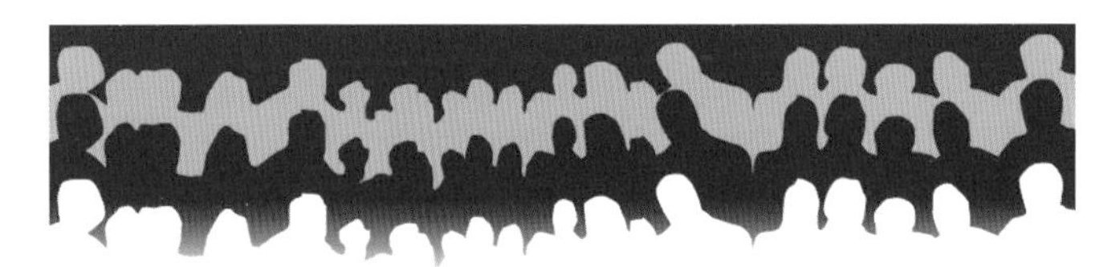

Community First

Community First Havant and East Hampshire (CFHEH) provides local voluntary and community groups across Havant and East Hampshire. It offers a range of support services including volunteering, training, good practice and practical advice, and specialist services and projects including Older People and Youth services, Community Transport, Shopmobility, Community Solutions in Whitehill and Bordon, and Employability Services.

With offices at Tilmore Road in Petersfield and in Havant, Tim Houghton has been the Chief Executive since January 2013. As well as a strong team of staff and trustees, CFHEH has the valuable support of a number of volunteers who help out across different departments and locations.

Community First HEH hosts an annual Celebration of Volunteering Event, and in February 2014 a total of 76 volunteers in East Hampshire were nominated and recognised for their contribution to the local community. They represented a wide variety of areas such as conservation, scouts, guides, sports clubs, community and village groups, National Trust, and various care groups. Volunteers were presented with certificates by Cllr Chris Graham, Chairman of East Hampshire District Council, and Cllr Peter Marshall, the then Petersfield Town Mayor.

Left to right: *Cllr Chris Graham Chairman of East Hampshire District Council, Tim Houghton Chief Executive of Community First HEH, and Cllr Peter Marshall formerly Petersfield Town Mayor*

Inset: *Cllr Peter Marshall presenting the Special Commendation Award to Felicity Mackilligin from Brendoncare Club*

Shopmobility

Founded in 1997 with a shop in Lavant Street, Petersfield's Shopmobility ('freedom to roam') received a generous sum from a will and moved to its present site in the Central Car Park (opposite Waitrose) in 2002, where it was opened by the Lord Lieutenant of Hampshire, Dame Mary Fagan.

It is now run by a team of 27 volunteers, including trustees, and provides an outstanding service for anyone who could benefit from a wheelchair or a motorised scooter for a day, week or month.

With occasional financial help from voluntary organisations in the town, it has over 100 regular members (users of the service) and is a boon for anyone visiting their relatives in Petersfield who have mobility problems. The centre even hires out folding scooters for anyone wishing to go abroad who can take one in the boot of their car.

The scooters are regularly updated, can run up to 15 miles on one charge, and are suitable for all types of terrain. The service is so popular that, since no such facility exists in some surrounding towns or villages, people are attracted to Petersfield for the ease of shopping, visiting or sightseeing here.

Petersfield Fairtrade

Petersfield was awarded Fairtrade Town status in 2008 by the Fairtrade Foundation in recognition of its commitment to trade justice. Every year the Petersfield Fairtrade group organises an event in late February or early March to mark the town's Fairtrade Fortnight. This helps to remind consumers of their responsibility to choose products, whenever possible, that have been fairly traded, ensuring that producers are paid a fair price. And, generally, Fair Trade items do not cost more.

Previous events have included an art competition, Fairtrade quiz, coffee morning, a meal using Fairtrade ingredients for 60 people and a wine tasting. The focus of these events has mainly been food and drink products.

One of the aims of the 2014 event, a Fairtrade Trail, was to make people aware of some of the other fairly traded goods that are available in Petersfield. These include jewellery, toys and clothing. Individuals and families participating in the Trail had to solve a series of clues and spot posters in various Petersfield shops to identify eight fairly traded products. After a draw of all the correct entries, Aimee Redpath, aged 7, was named the winner. She was invited to a special awards ceremony at the Town Hall in March, where the then Town Mayor Peter Marshall presented prizes to her and the three runners-up — Logan Bugh-Brown, the Skrzypczak family and the Thomas family.

Inset: *Aimee Redpath, aged 7, winner of the 2014 Fairtrade trail in Petersfield*
Main photo: *Fairtrade trail Runners-up: Logan Bugh-Brown (9); Sharon, Harry (6) and Ania (4) Skrzypczak; Henry (13), Emily (12) and William (9) Thomas*

What is Fair Trade?

Fair Trade is a partnership between individuals and/or communities and traders aiming for sustainable development for excluded and disadvantaged people in developing countries.
The main aims:

- providing a fair system of exchange "to empower individuals or communities;
- putting food on people's tables, so that they live and work with dignity and develop their communities;
- helping to create "sustainable development";
- returning a higher percentage of the price to those who make the products, as businesses work directly with individuals and communities ;
- developing the business skills of individuals and communities;
- promoting gender equality in pay and working conditions.

Petersfield First Friday

East Hants MP Damian Hinds talking at a typical First Friday Lunch. Inset: Organiser Clive Cook on the left

The First Friday lunches have been a regular feature of business life in Petersfield for some 11 years. Organised by Mike Kirby (Antrobus Accountants), Clive Cook (of Cookson Design), Suzanne Harding (of Premier Properties), and others, First Friday provides an opportunity for business networking as well as hearing an interesting talk by a guest speaker.

First Friday is open to all and there is no membership. A regular visitor to First Friday is the East Hants MP Damian Hinds (above right). Always good value, he can attract a good crowd and provide some lively discussion. Attendees need to pay £19.50 online for a two-course lunch provided by the Folly Upstairs.

Freemasonry in Petersfield

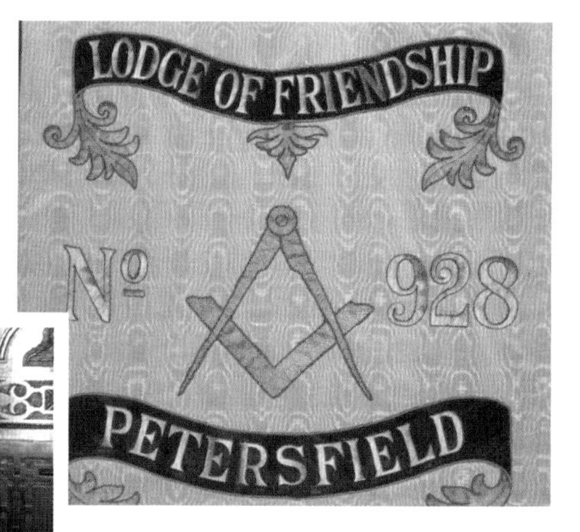

The first Freemasons' Lodge in Petersfield, named 'The Lodge of Friendship', was formed in September 1862. The Lodge met for over 100 years in the building at the rear of the Red Lion Public House in College Street but moved to its present home in Windsor Road in 1964. There are now nine Lodges that meet at the present building, totalling over 250 members.

Freemasonry is one of the largest independent organisations throughout the world and is universally known for the support it provides for charities and deserving causes on a local, national and international level. In recent times, The Lodge of Friendship has given financial assistance to The Rosemary Foundation, Artscape, The Petersfield Stroke Support Group, Stepping Stones Playgroup, Home Start, The Festival for Young People and many more.

Over the years, many of the members of the various Lodges have been local dignitaries, businessmen, schoolteachers, tradesmen, churchmen and those from all other walks of life. Freemasonry prides itself on welcoming members of all ages, creeds, nationalities and occupations. The aims of Freemasonry are to help other people through charitable work and community service, and to share a concern and respect for human values, moral standards, the laws of society and the rights of individuals. Despite its historic reputation for being a secret society, Freemasonry is now much more public and provides a convivial meeting place for men who believe in supporting the community and sharing their approach to life with others with similar values.

Petersfield in Bloom

Petersfield in Bloom is an annual floral competition that has been running for more than 25 years. It began in 1988 as part of a drive to improve the look of Petersfield, called Pride in Petersfield. Its first effort was to persuade business premises in the town to have hanging baskets. The competition began with just one class and one prize – The Picketts and Pursers Rose Bowl. There are now 11 classes, each with an award donated by a business, organisation or individual in the town.

For many years Petersfield has competed in Southern England in Bloom and has won its class three times, in 1992, 2000 and 2002. In 1988 the town represented Southern England in the national competition, Britain in Bloom.

Petersfield Town Council took over the running of the competition in 2013.

Petersfield Library and Tourist Information Centre

The present Library was purpose-built in The Square in 1982 and currently houses approximately 45,000 books, including magazines, spoken word, music CDs and DVDs.

With its central location, the Library acts as an ideal focus for many community activities and services, notably the Tourist Information Centre (TIC), the well-stocked reference library (upstairs), a Register Office with its purpose-built second-floor room for wedding ceremonies and, in the Christmas season, it houses the Cards for Good Causes in the Butser Room.

In July 2014, the whole building was refurbished and, as one feedback comment said, "it is a lovely library in a wonderful town, making for very pleasant outings." Many local residents and others from further afield take advantage of the classes on offer all year round in the Library too, such as reading groups, Baby Rhyme-time, Click and Knit, Warhammer, author talks, evening events and a variety of learning courses.

Although book lending is obviously its core service, the Library also provides computer-based facilities such as Access Research, family history websites, encyclopaedias and e-books, the latter available through 'Overdrive'. Traditional paper-based materials include maps, newspapers, directories, college brochures and local council information, while researchers can access microfilm and microfiche materials.

Many older people cope very well with modern technology and staff are always available to help them if necessary. In addition, the Library staff run courses such as the very successful Getting to Know Your iPad and Basic Computer courses.

Sharing a ground floor front desk with the librarians are the staff of the Tourist Information Centre (TIC), who have an excellent knowledge of the local area. This facility serves as a shop window for local tourism and attractions. Being in the heart of the South Downs National Park, the Petersfield TIC has an extensive collection of local and regional walking and cycling leaflets as well as selling locally made gifts, maps and publications. The experienced staff can offer advice on the latest opening times, easiest transport links, current events and activities so as to provide all the town's visitors with the best experience. They check available accommodation in the area and book rooms for guests. They help with route planning, national coach bookings, public transport information and tickets for events and local theatrical productions.

In short, Petersfield Library is at the heart of the community and it provides a safe, friendly and welcoming place for the public to visit and use.

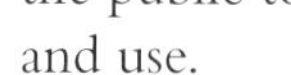

Petersfield Round Table

For Petersfield Round Table 2014 began with the culmination of their year long fundraising campaign for the MS society. Spearheaded by the then Chairman Andy Guest, Secretary Andy Done and numerous other members, the Petersfield Round Tablers took part in marathons, sportifs and even a whole weekend spent on exercise machines in the Square. Together they smashed the £10,000 target and raised over £12,000 for the local MS society.

April marks the start of the Round Table year and this year Andy Guest handed over the Chairmanship to Patrick Glithro along with changes across all the officers of the club, including a new team stepping forward to helm the town fireworks, their biggest event of the year.

July again saw a return of Petersfield Ups and Downs, a charity bike ride around Petersfield and the South Downs. Around 500 riders gathered in the Square on a Sunday morning before tackling the 20 or 30 miles courses or the 5 mile family route.

In addition to raising thousands for charities via Round Table many riders were sponsored for their own causes.

In November 2014, when they ran a fireworks display for the town with a professional display launching over five thousand pounds of fireworks into the skies above Bell Hill, it proved once again to be a memorable night. This single night represents the culmination of many hours of work from the team and every penny of the thousands of pounds of profit is distributed out to local charities.

Looking forward to 2015 and beyond Petersfield Round Table is going from strength to strength. There are now 16 members but they are always on the lookout for new blood. If you are a man aged 18-45 based in the Petersfield area then they would love to hear from you.

The Petersfield Stroke Support Group

Established in April 2011 by Carly Davey, the daughter of a stroke survivor, this thriving group is described as a lifeline for stroke survivors, their carers and families. The warm and friendly atmosphere helps new members to settle in quickly and they are supported by a large team of volunteers.

The 20 or so group members come from all around the South East Hampshire area, Bordon to Havant, and many have Aphasia, a communication difficulty. The volunteers are trained as 'conversation partners' and support communication. There is a monthly seated exercise session by a trained instructor, music sessions, visiting speakers and regular activities such as games and quizzes. Once a month, the carers have a meeting at the same time as the group to share ideas, knowledge and experiences with others.

The group first used The Avenue Pavilion as their venue, and moved to the Petersfield Community Centre in April 2012 to accommodate their growing numbers. When Carly left in September 2012 to take up a job with The Stroke Association, Maureen Gilbert became Chair, assisted by Maryann Hickson as secretary and Jenny Hatfield as treasurer.

In March 2013, the group bid for £1,000 in the East Hampshire 'Approved by You' funding scheme and, following their presentation to over 100 people, won the full amount. The money was used to create a garden on the site of the Community centre. The garden was carefully planned to enable Stroke Survivors to help plant and maintain it, with membrane placed under the shrubs at the rear of the garden to control weeds. Local businesses and organisations provided materials at little or no cost. Stroke survivor Gordon Gilbert, supported by volunteer George Watson and a team of volunteers, worked tirelessly to remove many bags of debris from the area and prepare the garden for planting.

The garden was completed in July, and in September the group had an 'Open Garden' event, attended by the then Town Mayor, Peter Marshall, who cut the ribbon and declared the garden officially open. The garden is enjoyed by the local community and all users of the centre.

Also in 2013, the group won the prize for Best Voluntary organisation by *Life in Petersfield* magazine and were awarded the 'Jenny Turner Scroll for outstanding achievement' by Petersfield in Bloom.

Stroke survivor Gordon Gilbert (left) with volunteer George Watson

Family Firms

Richard Arnold

A fourth generation family business, Richard C Arnold Optometrists has operated in Petersfield for over 85 years. In 1928 Raymond W Arnold leased one of the units in the High Street when the Old Corn Exchange was redeveloped. Richard and Margaret Arnold took over ownership from Richard's father in 1974. Their son Charles is now a director of the Petersfield practice and their daughter Sarah is an optometrist.

Over the last 80 years, advances in techniques and equipment have changed how they operate. They may not fit false eyes any more, but their sophisticated imaging systems allow them to see more of the eye than ever before. For example, standard optical equipment can be likened to looking at your eye through a keyhole, whereas Optomap equipment opens the door and turns on the lights!

Sarah Arnold and Richard Arnold

An independent practice with traditional values, Arnolds are not tied into any manufacturer or supplier. Staff are experienced and highly qualified and all receive extensive training from NVQs to Dispensing qualifications. They do not work on commission and therefore give unbiased advice and recommendations to ensure customers get the right solution for their lifestyle requirements.

All their dispensing opticians and optometrists are registered with the General Optical Council. That means they can legally test and dispense everyone, including children, people with low vision and the partially sighted.

"Such is their loyalty, that some of our customers continue to visit us long after they have moved away from the area"

"We are proud to say that the majority of our customers are recommended to us and for this we would like to thank our loyal clientele, many of whom have been coming to the practice since they were children and continue to bring their families to us," say Arnolds. "Such is their loyalty, that some of our customers continue to visit us long after they have moved away from the area, and so our customer base stretches to Dorset and Devon and other far-flung counties."

Edward Barnsley Workshop

The Edward Barnsley Workshop is tucked away up a narrow country lane in Froxfield near Petersfield. Next to the workshops are the drying sheds, which store carefully seasoned timber.

Unusually for a small furniture-making business the Barnsley Workshop recruits and trains apprentices. David Williams, one of the apprentices who joined in September 2013, has reached the national final of the Skillbuild competition.

One of the most exciting recent pieces was a rocking chair made in oak. With its even black finish and smooth joints this new chair looks as though it might have been sculpted from one large block of wood. In fact, it is made from many pieces of oak skilfully carved by Jouni Heikkinen. He gave the completed chair its open-grained black finish by scorching it with a heat gun and scrubbing it with a wire brush.

"...a workshop that continues today to produce furniture to the highest standard"

Edward Barnsley established his Froxfield furniture workshop in 1923. He spent his life working to commission, making furniture in a wide range of timbers for private homes and public spaces. It was sometimes a financial struggle but he established a workshop that continues today to produce furniture to the highest standards. The Barnsley Workshop has made many notable commissions among them the ceremonial chairs and kneelers for Canterbury Cathedral and the boards for the re-binding of the Domesday Book.

Britannia Reeves of Petersfield

Andy Shotbolt (centre) with staff

The Reeves family have traded from Petersfield for some 100 years. Today four members of the family – Michael, Andrew, Darren and Emma – along with Andrew Shotbolt are the directors of Britannia Reeves of Petersfield, the removal and storage business based in the Causeway.

It all started because John A Reeves, who lived and worked in Chertsey, was advised by his doctor to move closer to the sea because he suffered from ill health. When he arrived in Petersfield, he so liked the area that he decided to live there. He collected and sold fur skins and bought furniture, operating from a small shop in Sussex Road, and as a result he was asked to move furniture. When he died from tuberculosis in 1931 at the age of 52, his widow, four sons and a daughter took the business forward, moving every conceivable item that appeared.

Robert (Bob) Reeves was the eldest and, with the help of his brothers Ted, Sid and Tom, he started to expand into the furniture moving and haulage industry. Bob also died well before retirement age, and his two sons, Michael and Andrew, had to return to Petersfield to help their mother Margaret run the business.

After gradual expansion, the company won a large contract to move and store machinery and office furniture for IBM at Havant. Then Andrew Reeves was asked to advise the National Trust on their moving requirements, and so the firm moved and stored their historic furniture. This work led to a contract with English Heritage, and then The Royal Collection, which involved major work reinstating the rooms at Windsor Castle after the horrendous fire in 1992. This resulted in a letter from the Queen thanking them for their work.

The next major project for Andrew was to plan and empty The Royal Yacht in Portsmouth Dockyard after its decommissioning in 1997.

After the retirement of Michael and Andrew, Andrew Shotbolt joined the family firm in 2002, becoming works manager and then a director alongside the four Reeves family members. "Andrew Shotbolt has steered the company through the demanding recession years," Michael Reeves said, "and his expertise has helped to create one of the best storage facilities in the area with a new self-storage unit. The company continues to expand its fleet and staff. We have to thank our many highly skilled staff for their dedication over the past 100 years that the company has been operating in Petersfield. Without them the firm would never have achieved such a high standard of excellence."

Burley and Geach

Established for over 100 years in Petersfield, Burley & Geach take pride in being a typical High Street firm of solicitors and family mediators. They provide a full range of legal services to the local community, including residential/commercial property work, all aspects of family matters and mediation, dispute resolution, wills, probate, trusts, powers of attorney, employment. They hold the only criminal contract in the Petersfield and surrounding areas.

Being part of a historic market town within a farming community, they have always dealt with agricultural conveyancing. Their Petersfield office has around 15 staff and generally employs local people, most of whom have been with them for over 10 years.

"they provide a full range of legal services to the local community"

They aim to support the local community where possible in Petersfield, as well as Liphook, Grayshott and Haslemere where the firm's three other offices are based. Sponsorship has included the Petersfield Town Football Club, the Petersfield Music Festival and the Rosemary Consort. As well as sponsorship for local causes, the staff and partners raise funds for national charities, such as Cancer Research UK and Breast Cancer Care. Events have included the Race for Life (Guildford), Christmas raffles and a Pink Friday Cake Sale.

Above (top row): *Clare Wells, Diane Duff, Helen McDonald (front row) Anna-Jane Spirit, Richard Baylis*

Inset (from left to right): *Richard Britton, Howard Jennings, Mandy Falzon, Diane Duff, Belinda Brown, Bethia Winter, Elaine Salmon, Angela Church, Richard Baylis, Allison Longhurst.*

Frasers

The firm began life in 1958 when Fraser's was first founded in Reigate, then, twenty years later, a branch in Midhurst was opened. It came to Petersfield in 1987 when the present owner, Stuart Fraser (right), a production engineer by profession, took over the management from his father Thomas.

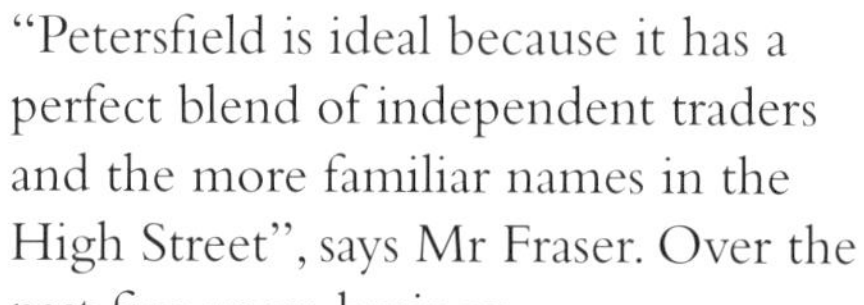

"Petersfield is ideal because it has a perfect blend of independent traders and the more familiar names in the High Street"

"Petersfield is ideal because it has a perfect blend of independent traders and the more familiar names in the High Street", says Mr Fraser. Over the past five years, business has improved enormously, largely due to a rising population in the town, a younger clientele (than in Midhurst) and thanks to the interesting, relatively new demand for pure fibre clothes – in wool, cashmere, silk, cotton and possum!

They say Possum hair is a wonderful product! Although the possum is a protected species in Australia, it has no natural predators in New Zealand and the animals are therefore out of control. Their hair, similar to mohair and very lightweight, is used to provide the raw product for sweaters, hats and gloves.

"Kilts are also now very popular for weddings and other celebrations. We have four of our own contacts in the Highlands for these and we sell both kilts and all the necessary accessories in our Petersfield shop."

Greys Coach Travel

Greys Coach Travel pride themselves on the personal touch so often missing from larger travel companies. Founded by Ray and Sylvia Goodall, the business was taken over by Jamie Munro (pictured below) in January 2002. Since then he has significantly increased the range of places visited with a popular programme of Day Excursions and Holidays taking their passengers far and wide.

Their most popular day trip is undoubtedly the Mystery Tours where the passengers are kept on their toes in anticipation of their destination. With many people making return bookings Jamie needs to keep finding different places to go! With no limit to where they will go for a day, the itineraries have included the obvious seaside/ town destinations and many popular trips into London. They have also been as far as Blackpool and York!

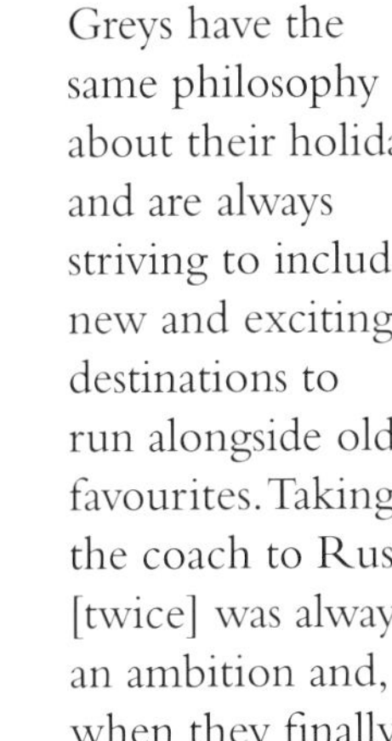

Greys have the same philosophy about their holidays and are always striving to include new and exciting destinations to run alongside old favourites. Taking the coach to Russia [twice] was always an ambition and, when they finally realised this in 2005, it didn't disappoint. Jamie says he could write a book (and may do one day) on the Russian Adventure with so many stand-out moments. Finally crossing the border into Russia was a great feeling although it did need a few bribes along the way! Driving their own bus through the streets of Moscow, and parking by Red Square, were truly memorable as was the time in St Petersburg.

Greys have visited, and continue to go to, all parts of the UK as well as nearly every European country. For a small family company of two buses this is quite an achievement. But they never lose sight of the most important people, their passengers.

"most popular day trip is undoubtedly the Mystery Tours where the passengers are kept on their toes in anticipation of their destination"

Jacobs & Hunt

Jacobs & Hunt is now divided into four separate trading companies having set up as auctioneers and estate agents in 1895. They moved into their prominent, purpose-built premises on the corner of Lavant Street and Charles Street in 1906 where they still are today.

The business remained in the Jacobs family until the founder's grandson, Christopher, retired in 2001. Still trading under the name of Jacobs & Hunt, surveyor Christopher Brockhurst continues the property surveys, valuations, land surveys and agricultural auctions under his Professional Services Company. He and James Dodd own the estate agency, the longest established agents in town. They have sold countless houses in the area, many of them several times, and seeing how prices have risen never ceases to amaze them.

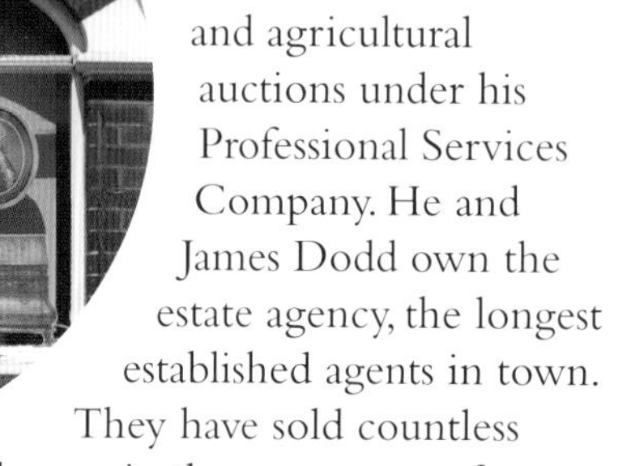

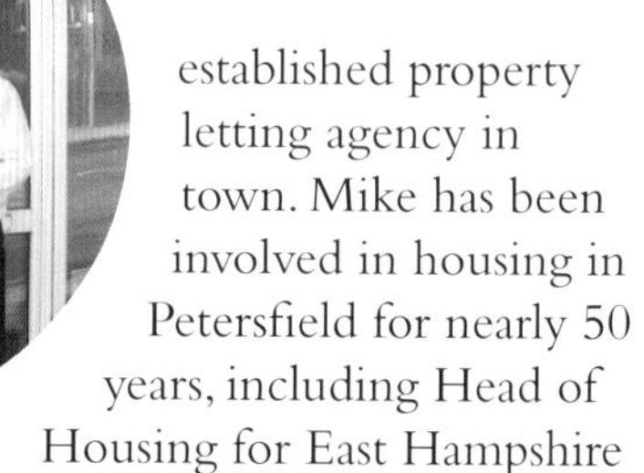

The auction house is a high profile part of the business, attracting long-distance bidders with the introduction of telephone and internet bidding. Auction days are lively, enjoyable and well worth a visit. With 10 sales per year of fine arts and antiques Martin Lawrence, the current auctioneer and owner, is impressed by the range of items they have sold, including a Sedan chair, autographs of the Beatles, and an Inuit North American grease bowl for £56,000 in 2013 (their highest sale).

A distant family link to the Jacobs is retained through Mike Thomas (pictured above) and his family's ownership of the Property Management Services, continuing the longest established property letting agency in town. Mike has been involved in housing in Petersfield for nearly 50 years, including Head of Housing for East Hampshire District Council, and his knowledge and experience are much appreciated by local landlords and tenants.

Littlejohn Bathrooms

The Old Amey Brewery in Frenchman's Road has been the home of bathroom specialists Littlejohn for the past 23 years. Visitors walk upstairs and open the door to the old brewing floor, but instead of beer vats they are sure to be surprised by the superb display of bathrooms in the latest lifestyle settings that now fill two floors of the three-level building.

Above: *Sarah Fascione and Simon Gosney*
Right: *Bill and Pearl Gosney*

The showroom is designed like a department store for bathrooms, with separate sections for showers, tiles, accessories, radiators and lighting. This showroom is one of the secrets of Littlejohn's success and why both their retail and trade customers travel from such a wide area. Littlejohn also say that the knowledge, skill and enthusiasm of their team of 16 is a major reason for their success.

Founded in 1991 by Bill and Pearl Gosney, Littlejohn's current directors are their children, Simon Gosney and Sarah Fascione. This family-run business was one of the first bathroom retailers in the country to offer a designed, managed and guaranteed installation service. Now, with more than 2,500 bathrooms installed, this service remains another cornerstone of their successful business, and for which in the past they have been awarded UK Master Bathroom Retailer

Why do they call themselves Littlejohn? The name comes from the American slang 'small toilet', not that there is anything small about Petersfield's Littlejohn!

MacDonald Oates

Quality of service and loyalty to clients is paramount for MacDonald Oates Solicitors who provide a variety of legal services to individuals and to businesses, making a well-rounded service-based company. Many clients have been loyal for generations, and the firm's reputation is often conveyed through word of mouth recommendations. Clients attest that the 'service was excellent and made the whole process quick and stress-free'.

The office walk that takes place each summer and finishes with supper in a pub. A different route is chosen each year such as Selborne and Hawkley as well as areas near their Midhurst office.

The business is also highly involved in sponsorship and charity work, including the nomination of a charity of the year, and in 2014 they have chosen The Bereavement Counselling Charity. They also have a committee dedicated to fundraising (the MacDonald Oates Charity Events Team known as MOChET). MacDonald Oates are also supporters of other local clubs and societies, such as The Petersfield Ups & Downs Charity Bike Ride and the Petersfield Musical Festival.

"Many clients have been loyal for generations, and the firm's reputation is often conveyed through word of mouth recommendations"

Above: *Karl Smith, Solicitor, at the finish of the PUADS Charity Bike Ride*

Having been in Petersfield since the 1940s, the firm moved from the Square to their current location in St Peter's Road in 2006. As a vibrant and growing firm, MacDonald Oates encourage and reflect their key values of being "open, responsible and fair" in how they treat their staff, in how they work together, and also in the way they provide their services and work with the local community.

Mackarness and Lunt

Mackarness & Lunt celebrated their 120th year in business in Petersfield in 2014. When the firm practised in both Petersfield and Alresford, Arthur Mackarness travelled between the two branches on horseback. The Petersfield branch moved into its present premises at 16 High Street in 1907. Just over a century later, the firm is now without a member of either the Mackarness or Lunt families.

Left: from left to right: Diane Anderson, Kim Maidment, Charlotte Oldham, Michael Parr, Patrick Hunter, Beverley White Below: Roger Petch senior partner

The firm's links with the life of the town have always been very strong: Arthur Mackarness was closely involved with the town's Scout Troop (one of the earliest in the country) and also served as Clerk to the Justices in Petersfield. Nowadays, although there are fewer local staff among the firm's employees, they are to be found participating in such diverse activities as St Peter's Church, the Lion and Unicorn Players and the Town Juniors' football and cricket teams.

"client feedback tells us that we are approachable, efficient and friendly communicators"

There are four partners and a total of 18 staff working principally with private clients and operating, as they have always done, as a market town firm, on personal and commercial legal matters. "Technology plays an ever more important role in our operation" says Roger Petch, senior partner, "which is both an asset and a pressure-inducing feature of our work.

"We find there is still a pleasant village mentality in Petersfield, but we also serve clients who live in, or are familiar with, London. They come to us by word of mouth and like the personal service we offer – and at a cheaper rate than they can get in the capital.

"The fast rail link from London and the Hindhead Tunnel have brought about a closer physical link for them and us, as they give our London clients the chance to come down here to see us face to face in a morning. Indeed, our client feedback tells us that we are 'approachable, efficient and friendly communicators'. We are very proud of this reputation."

Meon Valley Travel

Meon Valley Travel is a prime example of the local and the global combining. Managing Director James Beagrie explains that every time the phone is answered they either "save a life, save a fortune, or sell a dream".

These values reflect the three main aspects to the business: assistance, corporate, and leisure. Despite being such a large and global business, James Beagrie (left) appreciates the community spirit in Petersfield and the way in which local businesses all have reciprocal relationships with each other.

He says that the "warmth of spirit and enterprise are the true heart of Petersfield". His wife, Karen Beagrie, began working in Meon Valley Travel part-time with her father, and is now the Assistance and Leisure Director. The assistance aspect of Meon Valley Travel requires helping customers around the world at any point in time, and their offices are open 24 hours a day, 365 days a year.

"warmth of spirit and enterprise are the true heart of Petersfield"

Meon Valley Travel have celebrated their 50th anniversary in 2014 and Gordon Palmer, the original owner of the company, travelled back from Australia in May to join the celebrations with old and new members of the business. Leisure is the DNA of Meon Valley Travel. Holiday sales were the starting point for the business and still take pride of place in the shop front in Petersfield High Street.

The legacy of the business is also important. Meon Valley Travel is set up to facilitate the takeover of management by the next tier, so that it maintains its family ethos. However, this is not a small business and the company is expanding rapidly, doubling in size every three years.

Morgan's Butchers

There has been a butchers' shop at 12 Lavant Street since 1908. Indeed the original butchers had an abattoir at the back of the shop, which really cut down the food miles. Since then the business has been owned by several people with the current occupants W.Morgan & Sons taking over 40 years ago. In recent years Eric (right), one of the thee original sons, has been in sole charge and he is now joined by his son Colin to ensure a third generation continues the business.

When the Morgans came to Petersfield there were several butchers in the town. But changing shopping habits with the increase of supermarkets have left Morgan's as the sole survivor. This they put down to the quality of their meat and the expertise of their trained butchers, which enables them to offer the service expected of a traditional butchers' shop.

Large and modern refrigerated stores and a preparation area have taken the place of the original abattoir. This space allows prime meat to be aged on the premises. The preparation area is well used for making their own sausages, pies and other meat products. They make their own bacon by selecting and butchering the best cuts from the pigs' carcass and then curing and even smoking the meat on the premises.

"we are still cutting down food miles and retaining a first class independent butcher in the town"

Morgan's say: "It is good to know that after more than 100 years of the butchering taking place in this building we are still cutting down food miles and retaining a first class independent butcher in the town!"

The Petersfield Bookshop

Local artist Flora Twort and Dr Harry Roberts opened The Petersfield Bookshop at No. 1 The Square in 1918. Roberts was an East End doctor who had helped to set up the Panel Scheme, a predecessor of the NHS. In those days members of the staff would come to work on their horses, ride them through the shop and tether them at the back.

In 1956 a young bookseller called Frank Westwood, having learnt his business in the London firm of Francis Edwards came to Petersfield to manage the shop. Two years later he bought the business and moved to its current location in Chapel Street, in those days a stables and a slaughterhouse.

Despite the sad death of Frank Westwood in 2006, it is still a large, rambling bookshop with lots of nooks and crannies and piles of books in every corner. It is one of the few remaining shops of its kind in the region to offer such a volume and breadth of stock with good coverage of all subject areas.

Centre: *John ('Pompey John') Westwood;* Top Right: *Barbara Kelsey and Ann Westwood*

As you enter, two rooms have the look of an old-fashioned library with leather-bound books on all the walls. Off to one side, another room is given over entirely to old hand-coloured prints and maps, many of them dating back to the 17th century.

Further into the shop you come across a warmly lit alcove which displays Ann Westwood's personal collection of antique and vintage dolls, bears and children's toys. This is not far from the display case containing John Westwood's full-sized replica of the FA Cup decked out in the Portsmouth colours following their 2008 win.

A well-known feature of the shop for many years has been its open forecourt with cheap books and paperbacks available to buy 24/7 through an honesty box system in the door. Even with recent renovations the forecourt has been retained and the principle remains.

Petersfield & Reliance Launderers Ltd

A fifth generation independent family-run business, Petersfield Linen Services have provided a laundry service in the South of England for over 100 years. They aim to tailor services to each customer's individual requirements, whether it be by providing a rental service or laundering the customer's own goods.

Their customer base comprises privately owned hotels and restaurants, pubs with rooms, small group hotels, bed and breakfast establishments, conference centres and many other businesses that require a laundry service. Deliveries and collections are made through Hampshire, Surrey, East and West Sussex, Berkshire and Wiltshire, using their own fleet of vehicles from their location in Petersfield.

Now the business is much more focused on the commercial sector and looks to increase production from the site. Robert James (above) continues the family name. There are still a large number of loyal members of staff who have worked at the Laundry for many years supporting Petersfield Linen Services through the changes.

There has been increasing pressure to become more efficient and to process higher volumes of linen through the plant. This has been achieved by introducing more modern equipment and by making significant investment in water and heat recovery. The Laundry has saved over four million gallons of water for re-use in the laundry process and recovers heat at the same time, therefore reducing its carbon footprint.

Picketts & Pursers Ltd

Now in the 165th year of trading, Picketts & Pursers are a fifth generation business, but they know they have to move with the times. Petersfield suits their business and over the years they have served "some fascinating and famous people, many of whom have become our friends as well as customers, and long may this last".

Picketts & Pursers bought the business of Leo Williams at 30 High Street in 1965, on Leo's retirement. This continued the record of having the longest continuity of any trade within the town. Petersfield became the head office of the company in 1972 when its large and prestigious store in Commercial Road, Portsmouth, was sold after a family demerger.

Picketts Staff (left to right): *Jane Emsley; Karen Rogers; Trevor Boyden; Sarah Pickett-Nutbrown; Donna Wilkins; Christopher Pickett [Managing Director]; Henry Pickett; Nicole Chambers; James Taylor; Natalie Wirdnam; Charlotte Lemmon; Lesley Bate*

For the new head office Petersfield was selected as a delightful market town, close to Portsmouth and within striking distance of London and the other branches at Southampton and Salisbury. Michael Pickett moved to Petersfield and he was the third generation since the foundation of the business in 1850.

Picketts & Pursers say: "A good selection of stock at differing price points, coupled with an outstanding service have been our hallmark and has allowed us to prosper over the years. Our customers come from far and wide and some have not even been to the showroom. A truly personal service sees us visit them in their homes or

businesses, our furthest United Kingdom customer living in Scotland. We also have international clients."

"We like to support the local community whenever possible. In 2009 we were awarded the *Life in Petersfield* 'Retailer of the Year' Award."

Rowland's Funeral Services

Cabinet maker Percy Vincent (right) launched Rowland's Funeral Services in 1934, as a department within his father-in-law's furnishing business – Rowland, Son and Vincent. His original philosophy – 'Every client will be cared for as though they were part of our family' – is still the company's core value today.

They are proud of the fact that they are still the only independent Petersfield family-owned and managed funeral directors in the town. Marsha Vincent, the founder's granddaughter, directs the company today, having taken over from her aunt, Mary Vincent, in 2003.

Left: *Michael Vincent*
Bottom left: *Mary Vincent, Tony Thorne and Marsha Vincent*

Rowland's are unique in the town with the facilities of three chapels of rest – two traditionally panelled from English oak and one more contemporary in design – but all offering a dignified, secluded and totally private atmosphere. One of the key services available is 24-hour access for clients to the chapels and rest room. This means clients can visit at any time with no time limit on how long they stay.

"still the only independent Petersfield family-owned and managed Funeral Directors in the town"

They are the only funeral directors in the area with a function room with space for at least 40 guests for a funeral service or a wake. This means smaller groups of mourners can have a service in Petersfield without needing to travel.

All funeral arrangements are made in Rose Cottage, the firm's 200-year-old Grade II-listed building. People often comment that the room and cottage give them a sense of comfort and security in their time of need and this is very important to Rowlands.

The company's roots are firmly in Hampshire but there have been many occasions when they have served much further away. They also looked after the funerals of several high-profile people, including actors, authors and war veterans.

Rowswells

Newspapers and confectionery have been sold in Petersfield under the name of Rowswell for the past 99 years. This means that they are one of the oldest continuous retail businesses in town and their address at number 1 High Street also reflects this.

Descendants of the original Rowswell family sold out in 1976 and since then there have been several owners, the current ones being Amish (below) and Bhauini Master who took over nine years ago. Owners may have changed but Rowswells still retain the same vibrant friendly service selling the same core products.

The shop's Certificate of Registration, 1916

"one of the oldest continuous retail businesses in town"

In recent years, to meet the challenge in competition from supermarkets, they have added new lines including greetings cards and party-related products such as balloons and banners. After a break of many years they have also resumed newspaper deliveries.

Rowswells have played their part in the community by supporting charities, and many organisations have been allowed to set up stalls in Dog Alley, the passageway they own alongside the shop.

Tews Engineering

Tews Engineering has been a sub-contract precision engineering company located on five local sites since 1980, and it has acquired the additional skills and technical capability of other local engineering firms. It merged with Maltby Engineering of Alton in 2000.

Tews Engineering was established in Petersfield in 1910. The founder, Mr WJ Tew, was also the Captain of the Petersfield Fire Brigade, with 15 officers under him. The family name is still visible on a wall advert in the alleyway beside the Bran Tub in Lavant Street. In the Edwardian era, WJ Tew and Sons ran a motorcycle and cycle repairers on the corner with Charles Street (now Chesterton Humberts).

Since 2004 Tews has been associated with Alexander Dennis, the coachbuilders (when the Dennis company merged with Alexander), and it was the new Dennis fire engine of the Edwardian period which the original Mr Tew had experience of driving at the end of his career. He would be heartened to know that his firm was to renew the connection with the Dennis company 100 years after his death.

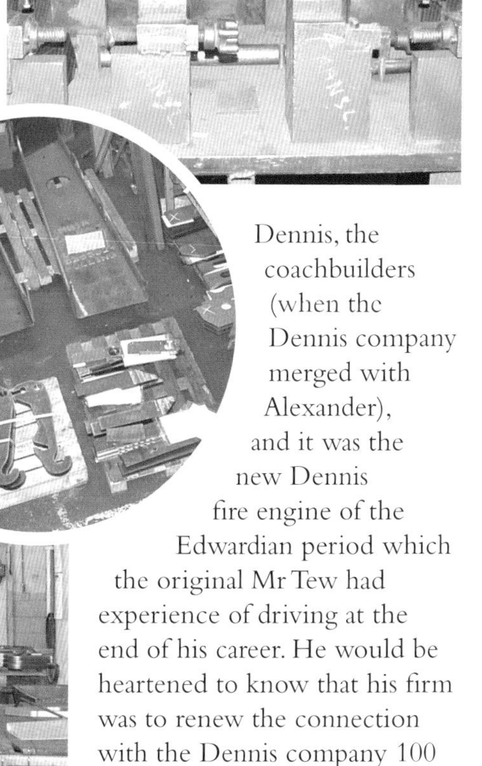

The Petersfield Forge

Repairing cartwheels and shoeing horses was an important part of the business when Joe Smith opened the Forge on the corner of Charles Street and Frenchman's Road in the 1930s. While evidence of the tools and equipment for this work still remains, the business has adapted during the past 80 years to meet changing needs.

What remains constant is the highly skilled workmanship to produce outstanding work with metal and iron. Examples of the Forge's achievements can be seen around the town and in the surrounding counties – such as the gates to Churcher's College, the entrance to Cowdray Park or the superbly restored weathercock on top of the tower on St Nicholas' Church, Arundel.

The current owners are Richard Mason and Lee Richards (above) who took over from Steve Pibworth (left) in 2011.

Both were trained at the Forge by Steve and have spent their entire working lives there, clocking up more than 50 years of experience between them.

Steve Pibworth was a legendary local character, having been born and brought up in Petersfield. He went to Churcher's College and, after National Service, went to work at the Forge for Joe Smith. The site had been the workshop of Ewans Agricultural Engineers, which closed in 1937, and Joe Smith reopened it as the Forge.

Steve told *Life in Petersfield* magazine a few years ago that he reckoned it would be a short-term job and that he might become a doctor one day. But when Joe Smith died, he left the Forge to Steve who remained as chief blacksmith for nearly 60 years until he retired. Sadly, Steve died in 2014. In his working days, he used to be a familiar figure riding round Petersfield on his old bike or in his ancient Mini. "We used to repair and make harrows, trailers and other machinery for local farmers," he recalled. The Forge also worked for British Rail, mending hand tools.

Visiting the workshop is a unique part of the experience of working with Richard and Lee. They have bending and cutting machines, an array of small appliances and hand tools, and a traditional blacksmith's forge and anvil. Their customers are both trade and retail and almost all of their work is bespoke – weather vanes, gates, railings, garden furniture, BBQ grills or simple brackets and much more. With such skill and ability it is understandable that they remain so sought after and busy.

Festivals

Petersfield Festivities

Petersfield Festivals

There are three main Festivals in Petersfield every year: the Spring Festival over the late May Bank Holiday, the Summer Festival covering the August Bank Holiday, and the Christmas Festival on the first Sunday in December. The Spring and Summer festivals both run over three days, and the Christmas Festival has a great one-day Christmas market. These three events are organised by Petersfield Festivals.

The town welcomes many thousands of visitors from all around the local area to these events. Petersfield is very good at coming together and embracing quality events such as these. The festivals, which are free to enter, encourage all ages, faiths, local groups and charities to come together to enjoy themselves and celebrate their amazing community. Petersfield Festivals give local traders the chance to engage with the town and its visitors, who are all delighted with the wide range of quality produce and entertainment: food and drink stalls to suit a variety of tastes; children's entertainment, rides, and petting zoos; competitions; vintage and classic car displays – and a full programme of local live music stretching into the evenings.

Organising the events

In 2010, the Petersfield summer festivities were threatened with abandonment after the previous organisers had decided to stand down. Ben Errey took on the task of organising the summer festivities with only six weeks notice.

Through membership of Petersfield Round Table, Ben teamed up with Steve Jacob (above right), an experienced event organiser and graphic designer. The success of this event led Ben and Steve to rebrand under the name of Petersfield Festivals and include the Spring and Christmas Festivals.

The Spring and Summer Festivals now run from Saturday evening, all day Sunday and for most of the Bank Holiday Monday, so local businesses can reap the rewards of thousands of visitors in the town centre. Petersfield Festivals have won many local awards. They also organise Beer and Cider Festivals in the Festival Hall in February and October, and the Lavant Street Markets on the first Sunday in April and October.

Petersfield Food Festival

The Petersfield Food Festival and the summer Food Awards – dubbed the 'Food Oscars' – are a separately organised event and sponsored by *The Petersfield Post*. They take place on stage in the Square and include cookery demonstrations. Highly prized by the food industry, it is a hard task to choose just a handful of winners.

KORG
Great British Fish & Chips

Taro Fair

Petersfield's mediaeval right to hold fairs was granted to the Lord of the Manor as long ago as the reign of Henry III in the 13th century. The Taro Fair has been held on 6th October at least since the early 19th century, when it consisted of a Cattle Fair (for the sale and purchase of horses, sheep and cattle) in the morning and a Pleasure Fair in the afternoon.

With the agricultural focus of the town's existence, it was important that useful draught horses and colts should be available for sale to farmers as well as the animals which were their raison d'etre. A good Taro Fair was one where there was a good supply of both, after which everyone could enjoy the shows and booths in the afternoon and evening.

Besides the usual swingboats, variety shows and shooting galleries of Victorian times (still in existence today), there were boxing booths, gypsy hawkers, coconut shies, gingerbread and beer stalls, ventriloquists, and even distributors of religious and other tracts taking advantage of the crowds.

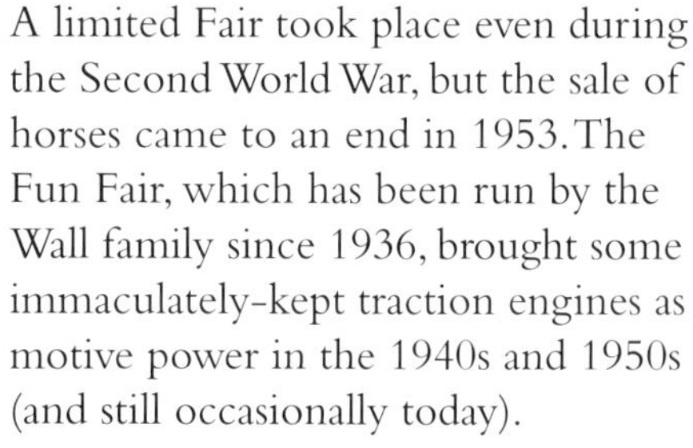

Right: *Steam Traction Engine 'Lady Pride of England' standing in the Fair*

The name "Taro" is believed to derive from the calls of Welsh cattle drovers (the Welsh for bull is pronounced "*taroo*") as they herded their animals along the roads towards this part of Hampshire. Romanies also made their way to Petersfield for the Fair and they parked their caravans in the fields north of the station.

A limited Fair took place even during the Second World War, but the sale of horses came to an end in 1953. The Fun Fair, which has been run by the Wall family since 1936, brought some immaculately-kept traction engines as motive power in the 1940s and 1950s (and still occasionally today).

Today's Fairs cover a fraction of the area they used to and animals are, sadly, no longer in evidence, but Petersfield people are still attracted to the open-air entertainment, enjoy their annual red-letter day (now spread over two or three days), and are generally aware of and appreciate the historic origins of the grand institution that is the Taro Fair.

Above: *The Wall Family with 'Lady', on their 47th wedding Anniversary*

Special Anniversaries

Petersfield has always been successful in organising special events to commemorate a specific anniversary. In earlier days the Square was the focus for the Town Carnival, but more recently we have enjoyed celebrating the Queen's Diamond Jubilee, the inclusion of the town in the South Downs National Park and the 150th anniversary of the railway coming to Petersfield.

This plaque
was unveiled
by
Stewart Palmer
(Managing Director, South West Trains)
to commemorate 150 years
of rail travel between
London and Portsmouth
via Petersfield
Vaughan Clarke,
Town Mayor,
13th April
2009

The railway event gave many people the opportunity to dress up in Victorian costume, ride through town on their vintage bicycle, pony and trap, shire horse, penny farthing or three-wheeler or to display their classic and vintage cars to an admiring and fascinated public. It was a great day out!

The climax of the day arrived when the 'Oliver Cromwell' - a Britannia class steam locomotive which had served British Rail in the 1950s and 1960s – steamed into the station on its way from London to Poole, carrying passengers who were served lunch in the dining car.

The Square also played host to steam driven vehicles of all shapes and sizes, including the 'Victoria, Empress of India' and many veteran cars.

Folly Market

The Folly Market

Chinwags

Chinwags Baguette & Sandwich Bar is in the Folly Market and was established in May 2001 by husband and wife team, Andy, a qualified chef, and Jo Krauze who still own and run the café to this day.

Andy and Jo moved to the area in 1999 from Guildford with their young family and decided to set up a business of their own. They spotted a gap in the market for a sandwich bar offering quality home-made fillings for sandwiches and baguettes, as well as jacket potatoes and home-made quiches, cakes and soups. With Andy's many years' experience as a chef, it was a fantastic opportunity to provide Petersfield with a unique lunch-time service, with superb quality fast food at very competitive prices, to take-away or enjoy eating in, within the charming surroundings of the Folly Market.

The business was an overnight success and, 14 years later, Chinwags is a well-known eatery in the town attracting many loyal local workers, young and older customers, students and tourists alike. They are particularly well known for their generous portions of freshly prepared food, made to order, to the customer's exact requirements.

The team of staff work alongside the owners to provide a friendly, family feel to this special little café while business lunches and a local delivery service expand the café's services beyond the town centre. They reckon that "outstanding customer service, together with extreme value for money is the key to their continued success and customers return to enjoy a 'Chinwags' time after time. Once you've experienced a 'Chinwags', there's just no comparison and you'll be hooked forever!"

The Curiosity shop

The sign above the door says

> *"Browsers make the best buyers: feel free to browse"*

Angie loves her customers to take their time to look around her friendly family-run shop. Step back in time to your childhood! Vintage china, glassware, quirky curios, jewellery and pre-loved furniture await. A new venture but a past passion in all vintage and retro, Angie has been running 'her little shop' since October 2011 and is loving every moment of it!

Dragon Treasures

Dragon Treasures, antiques and collectables, opened in 1994, in a very small shop which, over the next few years, grew like Topsy as one shop wall was demolished into the next one. It is now 3 shops in length and about 20ft wide, offering a diverse range of goods from medals, gold and silver jewellery, paintings, to cut glass, period and collectable china. In total there are seven dealers most of whom started at the beginning.

"We are not only affordable - we try and get you what you want if it is not in stock. We are friendly and helpful and hope to be here another 20 years," says Elizabeth Hayward.

Duncan Eves Jewellers

Petersfield was always the first choice of venue for Duncan Eves Jewellers. The friendly and warm atmosphere that surrounds the town, the loyal and caring community that supports their own people, and its small individual businesses made it an easy decision.

Nestled in the bustling Petersfield Folly Market Arcade, a hive of activity with a host of varying businesses, Duncan Eves Jewellers have been part of this "Folly Community" for more than 15 years.

In today's climate everything is 'manufactured' but Duncan Eves is more traditional with their own workshop, and Duncan will make jewellery to your specifications. You can watch traditional craftsmen working at their benches manufacturing, repairing or indeed remodelling any items of jewellery. Duncan and his wife Elaine are always happy to deal with any aspect of jewellery: whether it's a favourite piece of costume jewellery, or an exquisite precious piece, it will be treated with the care and respect that its owner holds for it.

"The busiest shop in Petersfield!" or, "You are always so busy", are frequent comments made by their valued customers who soon become friends. They often pop into the shop for a chat, where they are warmly welcomed into this family-run and award-winning business.

Rainbows

Positioned in the centre of The Folly Market, Rainbows has tried to create something a bit different. Take a trip to Rainbows to browse a beautiful collection of clothes, gifts, jewellery and accessories, from far away shores and enjoy the relaxed atmosphere and world music.

Whenever possible the stock is from Fair Trade or ethically sourced and much of it is handmade mostly in India, Nepal and Indonesia, often using traditional dyeing and printing techniques on the fabrics to create a wonderful array of styles in beautiful colours and patterns.

Current owner, Ruth Henslow says, "My suppliers often work directly with the producers and crafts people, ensuring that fair trade standards are met, the workers get paid a fair wage, have good working conditions and aren't exploited. We also try to lessen our environmental impact. Some of our products are made from recycled materials. We stock a range of interesting gifts made from coconut shells and bamboo and we have stunning recycled aluminium enamelled table ware. We also have many eco friendly items that are skilfully hand carved from mango wood that is sustainably sourced and we stock various styles of clothing made from beautifully soft organic cotton."

Inz.Pired Boutique

Denize Lloyd-Wickens, a former professional makeup artist, channelled her creativity and flair in a different way when she founded Inz.Pired Boutique at the Folly Market in 2010. Her inspiration came after a battle with cancer and, during her recuperation, she began designing jewellery for her own personal use.

Her designs were made by artisan craftsmen in Andalucia and they were individual and unusual. She knew that wearing her jewellery made her feel special in the dark days when she was struggling with how she looked.

Denize (left) felt sure that others could enjoy them too, so she developed the idea and the Sx.Z range evolved.

Making people feel fabulous about themselves is key to the ethos of the business. How her customers feel during and after a visit to her boutique is important and she has developed her own special customer service.

Her business grew and the opportunity arose to expand into a neighbouring unit in the Folly Market. She introduced a range of clothing to the popular jewellery and accessories, such as Italian leather handbags, Spanish faux leather bags and shoppers, scarves etc.

Her choice of unique, versatile and individual clothing and accessories were very much in demand and admired by the ladies of Petersfield who quickly became loyal customers. Her range is

tailored for 'real women' of every shape and size from small to XXXL, with styles which allow individuality and something different to anything available on the high street. In the past two years Denize has expanded her business and now has boutiques in Wickham, Port Solent and Alton with another planned for Alresford.

Mooka

Mooka offers a wide range of Gelati and sorbets for individuals and trade

using artisan Italian methods and state of the art machinery to give the perfect texture and flavoursome taste that many have come to love over the past two years they have been in the Folly Market.

The main ingredients are whole milk and double cream. It contains only 10% fat which is about half the fat found in commercial ice-cream and, because there is less fat coating the tongue, taste buds can sense flavour better making the flavours seem richer and more intense. Mooka sorbets contain around 50% fruit and all the sorbets are gluten, egg and dairy free, with classic flavours alongside some unique and modern ones.

Owner, Yifat Castle

Overall, there are some 80 different flavours but they can make any flavour to your request, as well as gelati birthday cakes in a selection of shapes and sizes – all hand decorated. For something really special, Mooka offers handmade gelato lollies in different shapes and finishes.

The owner is Yifat Castle who was born in Israel and was a pastry chef for many years, as well as teaching cookery to adults and children. Yifat says, "Having Mooka is an amazing experience; it's a happy and dynamic place which anyone, old or young, can step into and have a little piece of happiness in a cone. I consider myself very lucky to be surrounded (mostly..) by smiling people and joy."

Sweeney Plod

Dave Kerrigan retired from the police force after 30 years at the age of 51, wondering how he could spend his early retirement well away from organised work! It was a friend who suggested that he open a barber's shop and, as Dave's paternal grandfather had had such an establishment, he thought he would give it a go. So, he embarked on a two months' course at Fenchurch Street in London and then, taking a lead this time from his sister's subtly humorous suggestion, decided to call his new shop Sweeney Plod.

When younger members of his family were told of the Victorian literary connection, they were a little anxious for him; however, the concept served him well in setting up his establishment in the Folly Market, which boldly emphasises the Victorian-Gothic horror surroundings which still strike fear in younger passers-by when they catch sight of the row of knives in his window.

Equally, the "Victorian" label suits him well, for Dave has realised that there are many people in Petersfield who appreciate good, old-fashioned service, a real scissors-and-comb approach in the relaxed setting of a Victorian gentleman's club. The Folly Market was the ideal place to practise his art and join his fellow individualists in this part of the town.

An appointments-by-phone system suits all his clients, who do not face a wait, can have their individual styles carried out to their complete satisfaction and enjoy the one-to-one relationship with Dave. Teenagers often bring photos of styles to be copied and, in the privacy of the shop, are not intimidated by onlookers. Dave also offers gift vouchers to give as presents. Sweeney Plod is an unique experience!

Health and Welfare

Back2Health

Since 1995, Jonathan Field (below right) and Mark Christiansen (below left) have run their Petersfield headquarters of Back2Health in Charles Street on behalf of ten practices of chiropractors spread over Hampshire, Herefordshire and Merseyside.

They are not only practitioners of alternative medicine, but clinical researchers publishing papers on the impact of our thoughts, feelings and emotions and how they can affect recovery from pain, an approach to treatment which has been recognised by the Royal College of Chiropractors.

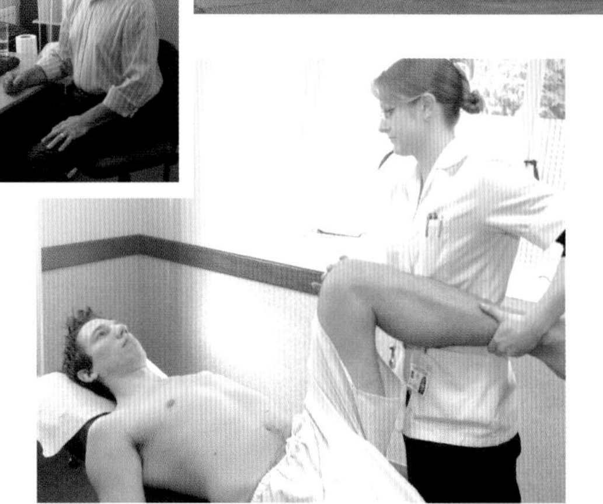

Although Petersfield residents exhibit fewer symptoms of serious muscular pain than many people from other areas – due, says Jonathan, to the proximity of the South Downs and the Heath contributing to their patients' relatively fitter lifestyle – there is clearly a local need for the type of treatment they offer.

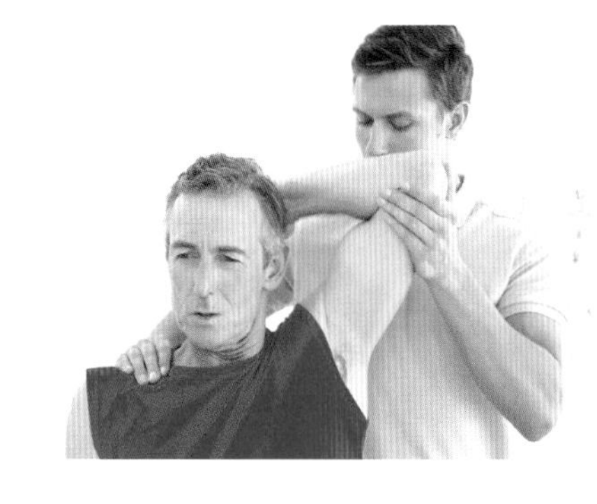

The practice spreads its expertise within and far outside the community and Back2Health takes both private patients and referrals from doctors in the local NHS surgeries, trains GPs for the Wessex Deanery and works alongside health workers at the Taro Centre.

"99.5% of our patients report being either satisfied or very satisfied"

From feedback that Back2Health have received from patients, "99.5% of our patients report being either satisfied or very satisfied with the standard of care they have received with us. The results clearly show that for most there is a real and worthwhile benefit which starts soon after beginning care and that the improvement lasts a long time (at least three months)". Back pain, aching joints, sports injuries and posture problems can all be alleviated by the Back2Health team – and their receptionists receive commendations from patients for their courteous and friendly treatment too!

Beth Svarovska Pilates

A couple in their early 50s contacted Beth Svarovska (right, with Peter Flood, drummer with Bellowhead) after downsizing to Petersfield when their daughters left home. They wanted to be 'in good shape if we become grandparents'. After a series of one-to-two Pilates lessons at their home, she now attends the class on Monday and he comes to Pilates for Men on Wednesday lunchtimes, both at the Methodist Church. Results so far? Skiing went well for him this winter, and she is excited to be establishing her own business in Petersfield alongside lots of voluntary work… no sign of the grandchildren (yet)!

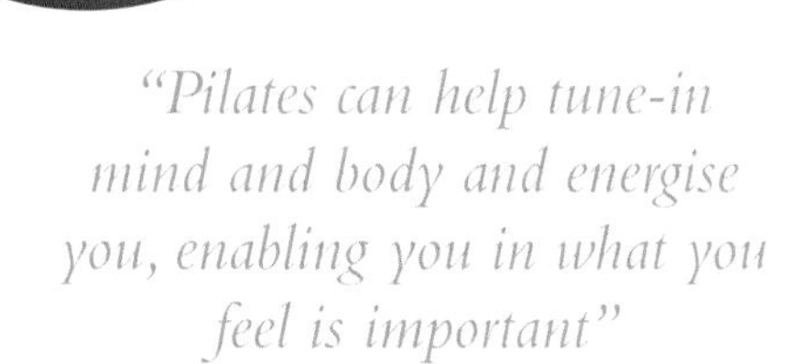

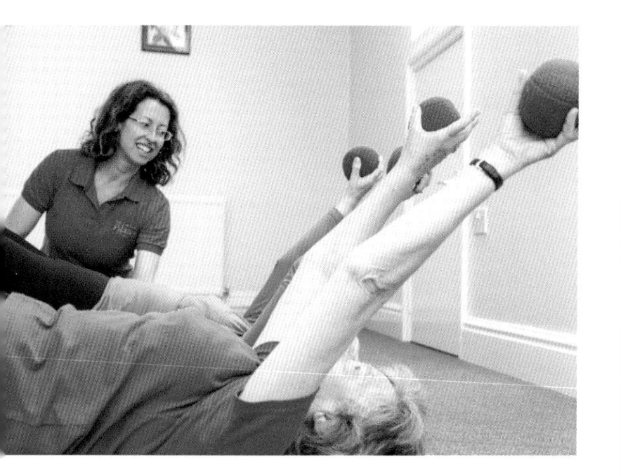

Originally developed by Joseph Pilates (1883-1967) "Pi-lar-tees" is an integrated system of movement, readily adaptable to different needs. It can help you relax, align, strengthen, stretch and have a naturally well-supported spine. "Pilates-based movement is a 'foundation' for life," says Beth Svarovska. "It can help tune-in mind and body and energise you, enabling you in what you feel is important."

Sharing learning with clients is a joy and an honour for her. Particular highlights have included workshops for the King's

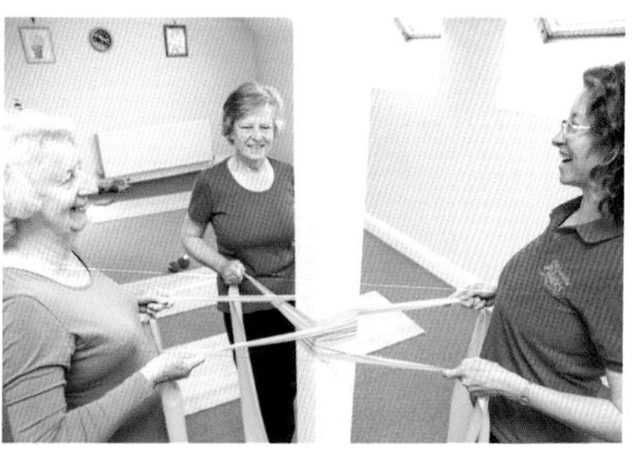

Arms, Inwoods Small School, Liss Forest Ballet School and Peter Pan playgroup. She adds: "I always look forward to my weekly sessions with Chichester & Bognor MS Society. Neurological conditions, osteoporosis and chronic pain are of special interest to me.

"There are many interpretations of the Pilates method," says Beth, "and in this area Petersfield is lucky to have several good teachers. There's a real choice if you are inspired to try Pilates."

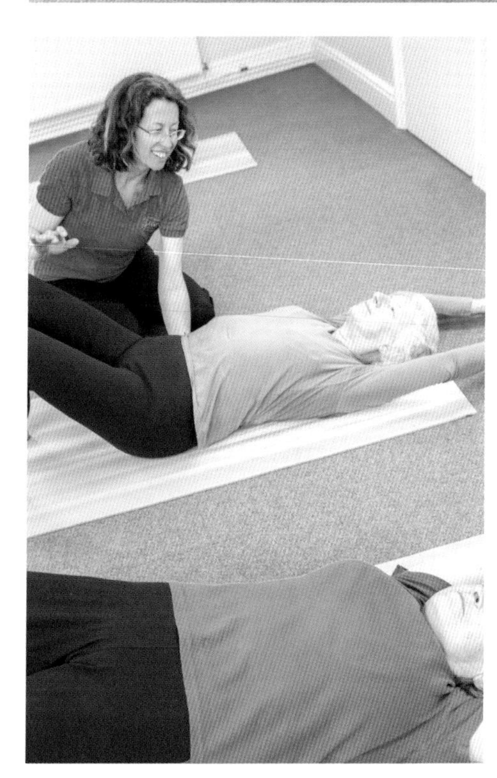

Matheson Optometrists

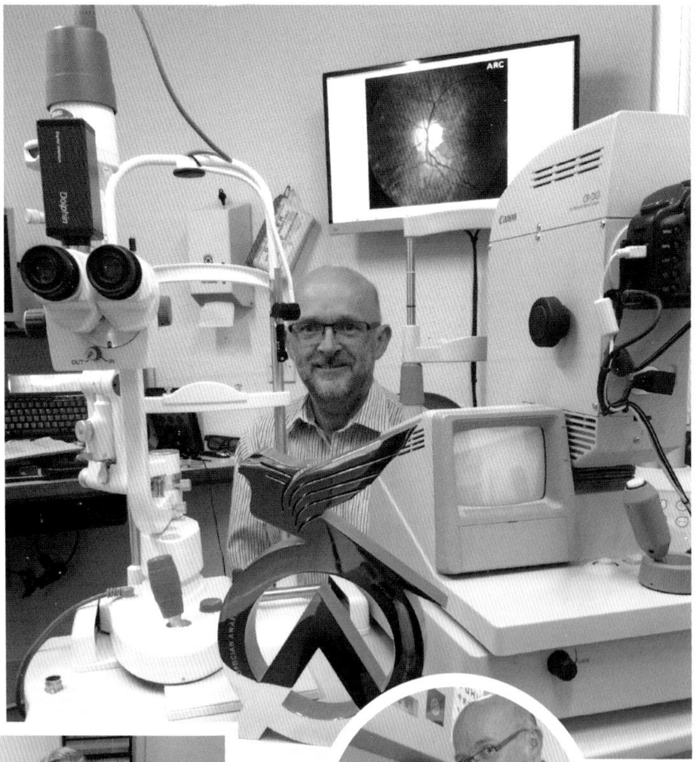

Matheson Optometrists is an independent family business that has been testing eyes in Petersfield for over 30 years and has six practices in the surrounding area. Last year the Macular Society named them as Optometrist of the Year, for their work looking after patients with macular degeneration, and they have just been presented with the National Optician Awards' Optometrist of the Year Award. Andrew Matheson (right) was also the overall winner in the Keeler Retinal Photography Trophy. He was the first Therapeutically qualified Optometrist in the UK and is one of only a handful of optometrists with Specialist Glaucoma Qualifications. Therapeutic Optometrists are qualified to treat as well as diagnose eye disease which greatly improves the service to the patient and helps shorten hospital waiting lists.

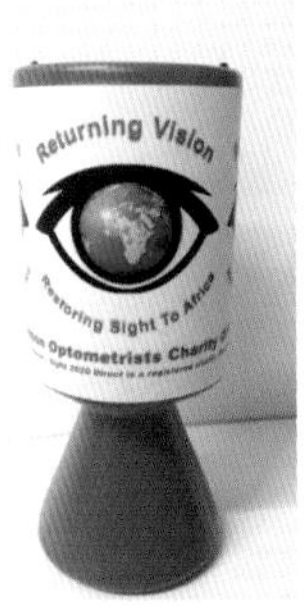

Matheson Optometrists have always been at the forefront of ocular innovation, being one of the first practices to embrace routine air puff tonometry for glaucoma screening in the early 80s. They are involved in research into new technology for eye disease detection, striving to provide the most comprehensive eye-care for their patients. The Matheson practice has had on-site spectacle manufacture since 1986.

They work with local hospitals and private eye specialists, having a high level of equipment used including OCT scanning, retinal photography and Autofluorescence imaging.

Matheson Optometrists are truly a family business with Claire, Andrew's daughter, in her second year of optometry at Cardiff. Andrew and Claire and two of their optometrist staff are also involved in providing eye care services in Africa as well as Romania and Moldova. They collect good condition second hand spectacles which can be reused but also donate over 1000 new pairs each year to these worthy causes. Their patients like the fact that their spectacles as well as financial donations are directly helping visually disadvantaged people.

Additionally, Matheson Optometrists provide all the services you would expect of any quality optician, using high quality lenses and a range of frames from budget to designer. They also specialize in dyslexia, dry eye and colour blindness treatment.

Morgan-Owen & Coates Optometrists

The Lavant Street Optometrists are all about 'vision', and helping people of all ages to make the most of their eye-sight. They focus on family and friendliness, and offer a good value-for-money service. There is a strong and warm team-welcome from the moment anyone steps into the reception areas and the knowledgeable staff are always willing to help.

Left: *(back row)* *Irena Morgan-Owen, Graham Coates, (front) Jo Knight, Elaine Wilkinson*

"We are family oriented", says Graham Coates, "and we see everyone from young children, to their great-grandparents. We would stress our caring and friendly attitude to people of all ages. We also try to keep abreast of the latest technology which is relevant to our patients, and helps us to give a good service.

Irena Morgan-Owen started work in Lavant Street in 1981 when the partners were John Phillips and Brian Edgworth and took over the practice when they retired in the 1990s. As a local family the Morgan-Owens are keen on sport and were founder members of the Petersfield Squash Club in the 1980s. "The daily challenge of trying to make people SEE has become even more rewarding over the years, and I am happy to look after whole families who have been coming to see me for decades!" she says.

With a degree in Biological Sciences, Graham was a sensory analyst for a global drinks company for 10 years, before re-training as an optometrist. He joined Irena and became a partner in the business in 2004. He spends several weeks a year working in Africa, for Vision Aid Overseas, and much of his free time fundraising for the charity by giving talks and raising awareness of the work they are doing.

Vision in Africa

Graham Coates has worked in many parts of Africa, where thousands of people remain blind for the lack of a pair of spectacles. The practice collects old and disused spectacles and recycles them to raise money for eye-care in Africa. Recent trips have taken Graham to Zambia, Burkina Faso, Ethiopia, Uganda and also the Philippines.

Vision Aid Overseas

Petersfield Pilates

Lea Blumlein (right), the founder of Petersfield Pilates, is passionate about the benefits of Petersfield and of Pilates, because of her own personal story. She loves living in Petersfield, and says: "I was born and brought up in the Cotswolds, a beautiful part of the country, with many small towns and villages that help to keep that part of the country unique. Petersfield has a similar feel to some of those special places I visited as a child. Part of its charm, I think, are the people. My husband was brought up here and all his family are around him."

Lea began her Body Control Pilates classes in halls and community centres around Petersfield in 2006 before opening her own fully equipped Pilates studio in the centre of town. Having been an enthusiastic gymnast as a child, then loving high heels in her late teens, she had a prolapsed lumbar disc in her mid-twenties. Suffering excruciating pain, she saw a series of doctors and therapists, one of whom suggested she should try Pilates. "I was soon hooked, as the benefits started to show so quickly," she says. "The damage I had done to my back was only relieved by the increased core strength and flexibility I gained from Pilates." She chose to train with Body Control Pilates because of their high standards and their safety record. "It is vital not to push individuals beyond their individual limitations before they are ready to be challenged.

"I take great joy in knowing that I'm helping someone to recover from an injury or just helping to maintain their fitness"

"Owning and running a busy Pilates studio in the centre of this wonderful town means I meet all walks of life," Lea said. "I take great joy in knowing that I'm helping someone to recover from an injury or just helping to maintain their fitness, and the method can be truly life-changing for people."

Petersfield Walking for Health

The Walking for Health initiative in Petersfield began in May 2004 and has been a runaway success. Initially starting from the Grange Surgery with some half dozen people, it now has over 50 regular walkers setting out from the courtyard behind Winton House.

All walks begin at the same place and time (10am) each Wednesday – and walking is not the only activity; there is the all-important coffee break after the hour's walk.

The social aspects of the group are as important as the exercise, and friendships and companionships have emerged from within the group. An Away Day programme every five weeks or so features walks based in places as far apart as Hindhead, Selborne, East Meon and Warnford. South Downs Park Rangers have enhanced their visits to Old Winchester Hill, and Iping and Chapel Commons. The Petersfield walk has been so successful that it has been split into two, with a short walk, for those who are just starting out on a new exercise regime, and a longer walk for those who feel more energetic.

St Peter's Vets

The St Peter's Veterinary practice is made up of six full-time and two part-time vets. Through an equally-shared rota worked by the vets and nurses the practice manages a 24 hour emergency service for its clients. Over the past 10 years, under the leadership of David Bee and John Wakefield, St Peter's Vets has added services such as ultrasound, digital x-rays, and a comprehensively equipped laboratory.

The practice was founded in 1947 by Charles Foden and Richard Hartley, two vets who had served together in the Royal Army Veterinary Corps in WW2. With its first office in the Square, the practice's farm animal emphasis was expanded by Mike Teale in the 1950s. Over the next 40 years the farm department expanded to serve an area encompassing a 20-mile radius of Petersfield.

The practice moved to its current premises at the corner of Dragon Street and St Peter's Road in 1967. Peter Booth joined the practice in 1972 and spearheaded the development of the small animal side of the practice. In 1992 a new wing was built to include consulting rooms and a larger reception area, allowing the operating theatre and hospital suite to be moved downstairs. For many years, in conjunction with Sparsholt College, the practice has been a veterinary-nurse training centre with one or two veterinary nurses qualifying each year.

By the 1970s equine veterinary work was becoming highly specialised. By the end of the 20th century livestock agriculture saw falling prices and the withdrawal of EU subsidy. In the Petersfield area this was reflected by a steady reduction in the number of dairy herds, traditionally the bread and butter of farm veterinary practice.

In 2004 the practice gave up farm animal work to concentrate solely on small animal practice, the core service it provides today. This had been steadily expanding over the years through the opening of branch surgeries in Horndean in 1978 and Liss in 1986. Under John Whitaker's leadership the work undertaken at the Horndean surgery grew steadily and a new operating suite was opened in 2002.

The Grange Surgery

The Grange Surgery has a splendid nursing team, who won Nursing Team of the Year at the Wessex Faculty RCGP awards in 2014 – a tremendous achievement. Practice Nurses Sue Saxey, Claire Dunn, Julie Port and Healthcare Assistants Katy Smith and Amanda Gardiner have between them offered over 40 years of service to the practice.

Ably run by Practice Manager Paula-May Houghton Clark, the Surgery has grown, but it has not lost its personal touch. The excellent team has continued to be friendly, enthusiastic and dedicated to patient care. It prides itself on getting to know every patient, to enable the best possible care to be provided for each individual person.

The surgery started in 1983 in an old cowshed in the Spain area of Petersfield. Known as the Spain Surgery, it came into being under the auspices of Dr David Wilders, who had left the Heath practice to start out on his own. The essential threads of that friendly, patient-oriented practice still run through its ethos.

Andy Douglas joined David Wilders as a partner in Petersfield in 1988. His wife Madeleine had started working as a locum the year before him, and both are still partners in the Grange Surgery. The surgery changed its name on its move in 2001 to the Grange Building on the old abattoir site on the Causeway.

Andy brings boundless enthusiasm and expertise in cardiology to the practice. Madeleine excels at women's health; babies and teenagers are also among her speciality subjects. On David's retirement in 1999, Andy became senior partner and, soon afterwards, Hugh Coni was appointed as a new partner, and he became very popular with his patients. He kept the surgery up to date with modern technology, and business targets, essential in changing times. Tragically he died from cancer in 2008.

Penny Mileham joined the surgery as a salaried GP in 2002 and in 2011 became a partner, bringing the benefits of her great local knowledge to the practice. Kathryn Bannell joined as a GP Registrar, having achieved a distinction in her RCGP exam. In keeping with Andy and Madeleine, Kathryn is qualified as a trainer and supports the junior doctors that the surgery has working with the team on a regular basis. Hamish Reid joined the practice as a partner in January 2009. His kind and gentle manner has made him very popular with his patients.

Grange Surgery staff from left to right: *Sue Ingram (Secretary), Caroline Frost (Administrator), Dr Kathryn Bannell (GP), Gerard Kavanagh (Assistant Practice Manager), Dr Andrew Douglas (GP - Senior Partner), Dr Penny Mileham (GP), Dr Madeleine Litchfield (GP), Julie Port (Practice Nurse), Paula-May Houghton Clarke (Practice Manager), Nicki Spice (Receptionist), Claire Dunn (Practice Nurse), Amanda Gardiner (Healthcare Assistant), Ony Rogers (Receptionist), and Joy Chapman (Receptionist).*

The Swan Surgery

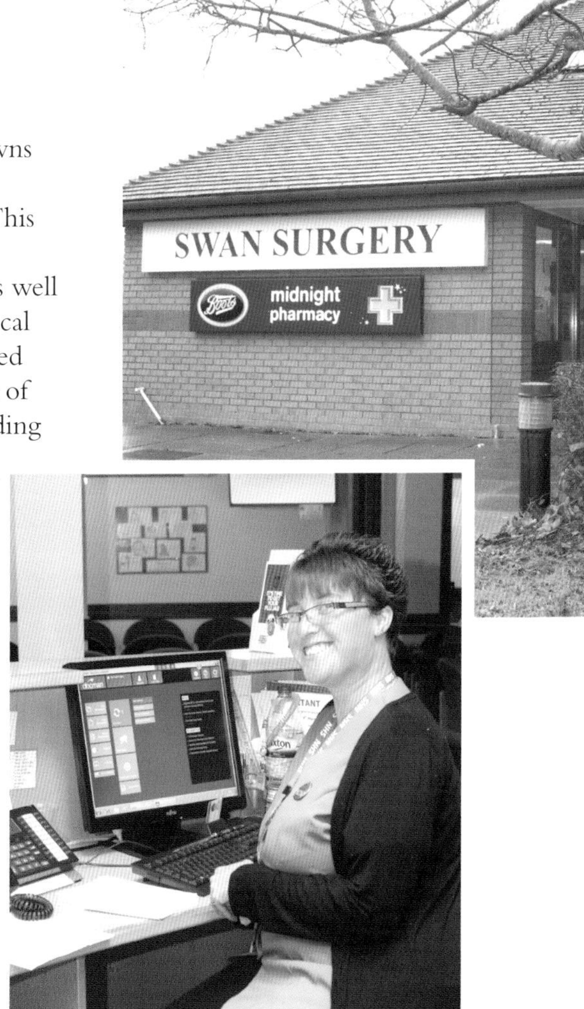

Petersfield was one of the first towns in the country to build a cottage hospital in the late 19th century. This was inspired by the local doctors, funded by generous benefactors as well as the local population, built by local builders and craftsmen, and serviced by the community for the benefit of the townspeople and the surrounding villages.

The origins of today's partnership of six doctors can be found in a small building in the High Street which relocated to the Festival Hall car park in the 1950s. As Primary Care developed, there has been an ever-increasing demand for space and facilities. After a long search, agreement was eventually reached to build new premises next to the Community Hospital and the present surgery was opened in 1991. A major building refurbishment to incorporate a pharmacy and make other improvements was undertaken in 2008.

Modern general practice is the cornerstone of the NHS and the

Swan Surgery is proud to be the largest practice in the town serving approximately 14,000 patients from purpose-built premises with 13 consulting rooms, 4 nursing treatment rooms and a large airy waiting area.

They aim aim to provide personal and holistic care to all patients and the doctors are supported by a dedicated team of practice nurses, health care assistants, receptionists and administrative staff numbering about 40 in all. They are also supported in the community by the district nursing team, health visitors, as well as the Macmillan team and Rosemary Foundation, both of whom are funded by charitable donations. Much more is expected and demanded of general practice today, and the health needs of the population are rising and increasing in complexity.

The Swan Surgery prides itself on seeing everyone who has a clinical need to be seen. They continually monitor and reflect on performance so that they can improve their service to patients. They always welcome comments via their Patient Participation and Patient Reference Groups.

Petersfield Hospital

Petersfield Cottage Hospital, built in 1871, had been the mainstay of the town's medical provision for over a century but, with the steady increase in Petersfield's population after WW2, it became clear that a whole new community hospital was required which would incorporate doctors' surgeries, health clinics, and geriatric and maternity units.

Plans were drawn up in the 1960s, but had to be shelved for lack of money and space on the Swan Street site, where St Peter's vicarage stood. It took nearly 30 years and £4.5 million for the construction of the present hospital to be finally realised, the first such centre in the Portsmouth and South East District Health Authority.

Finished in 1991, with the new Swan Surgery next door a year later, it provided a total of 62 beds for patients in mental health, geriatric and maternity wards, and a whole range of out-patient clinics incorporated into the building.

Today, the hospital is central to Petersfield's life – with a thriving and respected community spirit. Local people are fortunate to have the facilities it provides – the Grange Maternity unit (which survived thanks to a strong, recent campaign) and its new birthing pool; consultants - rather than registrars - available by appointment; less waiting time for patients than at larger hospitals; two rehabilitation wards for stroke patients and others; a geriatric ward for local family members who can visit easily and frequently; and there are units for physiotherapy, X-ray, occupational health problems and a team of community nurses to give advice and treatment. Even outside normal working hours, rooms are available for counselling sessions on a range of health issues.

Duet and Mimosa

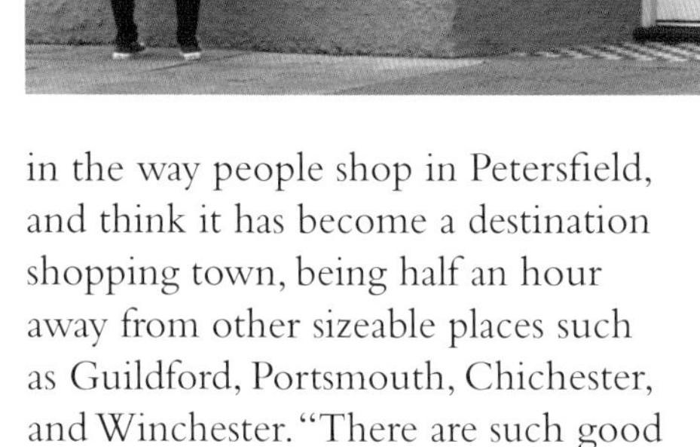

Mimosa

Mimosa in Dragon Street sells European, mainly Spanish and German, shoes that are 'not on the high street'. Owner Sarah Peall buys very carefully, and works hard to find lines that are original and that are not extravagantly priced. She also sells leather handbags and accessories. "We offer customers a unique product, that is affordable," she says. "That is one part of our ethos. The other part is to provide excellent customer service, and our customers are fantastic and loyal."

Sarah used to work as a teacher, but has always had a passion for shoes and dreamed of opening a shoe shop. She greatly values Claudia Riley, who manages the shop, and has been with Sarah since it opened in 2006. Over the years they have noticed a change in the way people shop in Petersfield, and think it has become a destination shopping town, being half an hour away from other sizeable places such as Guildford, Portsmouth, Chichester, and Winchester. "There are such good boutiques and restaurants here now, and many of our customers come here for a day out with a friend to shop and have lunch."

Sarah Peall (left) and Claudia Riley

Duet

Sarah is also co-owner of the fashion boutique, Duet, on the other side of the road. Her business partner there is Rona McTavish. They met when Rona became a regular customer at Mimosa, and she told Sarah she was looking for premises to open a dress shop. "Duet is such a lovely shop," says Sarah, "it is spacious and elegant with high ceilings and great windows. And it is great for me that the two shops are almost opposite each other."

Rona and Sarah run Duet on similar lines to Mimosa, with good customer service being a priority. They feel they pitch the clothes they sell with the right level of sophistication and price for their customers. "Most importantly Duet is all about the shopping experience," says Rona. "We pride ourselves on what we do differently to the high street, and that is why we have such a loyal customer base. We provide a relaxed and welcoming environment for our ladies to spend time in, and that's what I think the Duet team excels at."

There is good cross-over between the two shops with customers often visiting both Mimosa and Duet, and merchandise goes from one shop to the other when they dress the windows. And to the future? "I think we would expand into e-commerce, rather than opening another shop," says Sarah.

The Fabric House

The Fabric House is a traditional fabric, sewing and haberdashery shop. Customers go there to buy curtain and blind fabric, to have them professionally made up, and to seek advice on window treatments, tracks and poles, braids and finials. There's a cosy feel to the shop with its bolts of pretty fabrics, cards of binding and jars of buttons; the smaller items passed to the customer in small, old-fashioned paper bags.

Owner Tracey Jones (below) spends a lot of time in the shop with customers, when she isn't out measuring or fitting curtains. She has customers from Portsmouth to Petworth, Alton and Farnham, and has made curtains for houses in London too. "We get to know our customers, because helping people to decorate their homes is such a personal thing." She puts customer service and the friendly atmosphere in her shop high on her list of priorities for her four part-time staff. "Customers say the shop is friendly and welcoming," she says, "and that is important, whether they are decorating their entire house, or have just come in to buy a few buttons, half a metre of braid, or a ball of wool."

"We get to know our customers, because helping people to decorate their homes is such a personal thing."

Tracey started in Petersfield at Nomad in Chapel Street, in 1999. "I was selling furniture then, and the fabric side of the business developed from there." Since she moved to Lavant Street in 2005 and opened The Fabric House the haberdashery and craft side of the business has grown, due in some part to a growing interest in craft, and TV programmes such as Kirsty Allsopp's *Handmade Home,* and *The Sewing Bee.*

"Petersfield is such a friendly town," says Tracey, "and our customers are a creative lot! And there is a much wider range of exciting fabrics and materials available than when I first started."

The General Wine Company

Alan Snowden (centre) with Damian Hinds and other staff members

The General Wine Company was first opened in Liphook 30 years ago but has had an outlet in Petersfield at the top end of Lavant Street for the last five years.

The owner and proprietor is Alan Snowden and he has built the business into the strong position of being the only independent wine merchant and shipper in Petersfield.

They have a philosophy of providing a range of high quality wine from around the world sourced from small exclusive producers. Not only do they specialise in quality wines but spirits and liquors as well.

Alan holds regular wine tastings each year in the Festival Hall and this year these were attended by over 500 people. A recent visitor to the Petersfield shop was our local MP Damian Hinds, seen here enjoying a glass or two!

Handmade Happiness

Petersfield has many talented artists and creative individuals. Some of them sell their work in Handmade Happiness in Dragon Street.

Shop owner Jenny Stacy (right) says customers come in when they need a special gift. The choice ranges from handmade buttons to stained-glass kaleidoscopes. Everything is made to a high standard. There are ceramic mugs, jugs and bowls, patchwork quilts, silver jewellery, knitted baby blankets and oil painting. Smooth wood bowls and knitted animals. The cards are by local artists too. Even the carrier bags are handmade.

"a shop where local artists and craftspeople are promoted"

Handmade Happiness is a shop where local artists and craftspeople are promoted and their talented work admired. It's inspiring to see what ingenious and beautiful things can be made. In fact customers often want to make some things themselves after visiting.

The Happy Cow

The Happy Cow was conceived by the owners Ian (pictured below) and Georgina Constable-Dakeyne, who knew the name for a couple of years before they opened the shop.

A culmination of ideas collected from far-flung travels, the shop is continually growing and changing. Ian and Georgina have both worked in an animal or farming background for many years and they felt it important to share their love of local produce. They wanted to give producers a fair price and an equal say in how their produce makes it onto your plate.

"...Happy Animals, Happy Farmers, Happy Food"

The reason for the name is simple, say Ian and Georgina. "We have cows, and many will eventually be destined for Sunday lunch at various different locations. However, the life they live, grazing in as natural an environment as possible, with little stress and little interference, leads to Happy Cows."

They found like-minded people to run the shop, so they are free to manage farms, treat animals in a veterinary capacity, and keep a check on their animals. "The Happy Cow is a family," they say. "It couldn't exist without support from those close to us and couldn't continue without the valued customers who come in to share their stories with us." Their beliefs are summed up as: Happy Animals, Happy Farmers, Happy Food.

John Peter

John Peter and Company is one of the longest established hairdressers in Petersfield, having been started by Heinz Naef (top) in 1973. He began – as Heinz of Switzerland – in Station Road, moving to its present location in a new, purpose-built salon along Chapel Street in 1980. Following a change of ownership John Peter Shearman ran the salon from 1990 with the present owner, Nicola Wells (left), who was working as part of the styling team. Nicola then had the opportunity to take the reins in 2005.

All staff work together to offer a wealth of friendly professional services to all ages, as well as extending their services to include wedding parties and balls. Bespoke home or hotel visiting is available along with manicures and make up to complement all hair services for either that special day or just a good reason to treat yourself.

Several of the staff have worked at John Peter for many years and the 20 strong team is made up of five different nationalities, including Holm, from Germany, who came to work in Petersfield from having owned his own salon in Liss in 2003 and, of course, Heinz who remains with the salon to the present day.

Lavant Rowe

When Chris and Stephen Hartshorne Scott opened Lavant Rowe in 2007 they wanted to bring a London-league salon to Petersfield. They recognised the increasing number of people who were moving down from, or commuting to, London. Stephen, Lavant Rowe's principal stylist, has worked extensively in both London and America, and around the world with Steiner Transocean. Chris, once a project manager with IBM, handles the administrative and financial side of the salon, and uses his management skills to develop the Lavant Rowe brand. It's Chris's creative flair that shows in the salon's interior. It is in the ground floor of a Victorian town house with two floors above. In 2012 they opened a beauty salon on the first floor, and still there is space upstairs. "I wanted the salon to look chic and sophisticated without looking over the top in a country market town," said Chris. "We were delighted with the response when we opened," said Stephen, "people were very supportive from the start, and we continue to draw in new clients.

Stephen (left) and Chris

Lavant Rowe won the *Life in Petersfield* Awards 'Best New Business' category in 2008, were highly commended for 'Best Business' the following year, and have been sponsors twice. "We are delighted," Chris says, "that the business continues to grow from strength to strength. Our staff are like our family and we certainly couldn't have done what we have without such a great team."

One Tree Books

One Tree Books arrived in Petersfield in 1994, set up by Tim O'Kelly (right) in what was an old hardware store in Lavant Street. Tim grew up in South Harting and, after seven years in publishing in London and Auckland, Petersfield was the obvious place to return to.

There is no shortage of bookselling in our town, with the nationally renowned Petersfield Bookshop selling antiquarian and second hand books and the chain bookseller Waterstones. However, the assets which makes One Tree Books unique are the friendly staff, deep knowledge of books and its delicious coffee. It is one of the only bookshops in the country to have a licence to sell

alcohol. It certainly helps discussion at the regular book clubs held in the evenings and the many parties to celebrate local authors launch their books!

A number of big names have visited One Tree to promote their books in the last couple of years – David Gower, Jonathan Aitken, Antonio Carluccio, Salley Vickers, Patrick Gale, Michelle Magorian and David Attenborough, who caused quite a stir with queues stretching around the block.

As well as books and coffee, One Tree sells sheet music, CDs, board games, jigsaws and a range of educational games for younger children. It also has reputedly the best selection of greetings cards in town.

One Tree Books achieved national acclaim in 2010 when it won the title of Independent Bookseller of the Year, against stiff competition. It has also won best bookshop in the South on several occasions as well as Business of the Year at the *Life in Petersfield* Awards.

In 2014 it was the 20th anniversary of One Tree Books and they are good for a few more yet.

Petaprint

The business has been established for nearly 50 years. Kevin Povey and Colin Smith have been at Petaprint for the last 20 years, taking over the business from Kevin's dad Barry five years ago, and Lucy Martin has been working with the team for the last three years.

They say, "Printing has changed dramatically with the development of computers and digital printing. It has widened our capabilities so that small colour printing work is much more efficient. We can now offer a wider range of printing services than we could 20 years ago. A lot of our work consists of business stationery covering business cards and letterheads to brochures and leaflets, but we also produce a whole range of personal printing from invitations and correspondence cards to bespoke Christmas cards and service sheets. On top of all the printing we are also very busy with photocopying with over 1 million copies being produced every year.

Colin and Kevin at Petaprint

"There is so much that is special in Petersfield and we get to work with so many excellent businesses, charities, schools, clubs, societies and people"

"There is so much that is special in Petersfield and we get to work with so many excellent businesses, charities, schools, clubs, societies and people that make the town so wonderful to work, live and socialise in.

We are in a very lucky position to be able to see what is happening in and around our town - and there really is so much going on!

"Thank you to Petersfield for keeping us in business and we hope that we can continue to be an important part of our lovely town for many more years."

The Petersfield Cobbler

The Petersfield Cobbler, which opened its doors to customers in 1996, is run by Steve and Moyra White. Steve had been a cobbler for nearly 15 years before taking the plunge and opening his own business.

Driving around Hampshire, Steve (below) and Moyra came across Petersfield and, although there were other cobblers in the town, finding an empty shop on Chapel Street they both had a good feeling that this was where they wanted to trade from. At the time they lived in Portsmouth but, following the success of their business, they moved to Petersfield which has been their home for over 12 years.

The Cobbler Shop also sells high quality leather goods plus a large selection of shoe care products. You can buy suitcases and shopping trollies from this traditional cobbler who moves with the times.

The Petersfield Cobbler advertises with the Petersfield Cam where you can find all the information you need including opening times and an online catalogue for trophies. The shop operates a loyalty system to give something back to returning customers.

Using traditional equipment and a wealth of experience Steve can offer high quality shoe repairs. As well as traditional services Petersfield Cobbler offers high tech engraving with a computer engraver. It has key machines which can cut the majority of keys including chipped car keys.

Petersfield Photographic

Kate Collyer, Gary Boxall and Sophie Andrews with their Fujifilm Shop Of The Year 2014 awards

Local retailer Petersfield Photographic has been named Shop of The Year by Fujifilm. The photo store, which has been in the town for 24 years, picked up the award at the 2014 Fujifilm Digital Imaging Service National Conference.

Owned by Gary Boxall, Petersfield Photographic has been a member of the FDIS group of over 180 photo retail stores across the UK since October 2009. He recently upgraded his processing equipment to the very latest Fujifilm Dry Minilab and also has a 24" inkjet printer and four photo kiosks offering products such as digital prints, photobooks, canvases and mugs.

The new kiosks operate with the latest Fujifilm Imagine. This means that he can offer a full digital print service in store, online and now via smartphones and tablets with the new downloadable Fujifilm Imagine mobile app.

> *"We have always been known in the town for great service when it comes to all things photographic. To have won the FDIS award just proves it."*

Gary has also invested a lot of time and money in re-fitting and merchandising his store to make it brighter and more welcoming to show off its range of photo products and services. He and the shop manager Kate Collyer decided in April last year to participate in the Fujifilm Business Endeavour Awards scheme run by Fujifilm each year and as a result has won the top accolade of Shop Of The Year.

Gary says, "I still can't quite believe it. We have always been known in the town for great service when it comes to all things photographic. To have won the FDIS award just proves it. It wouldn't have happened without Kate and the rest of my fantastic hard-working staff and the support of the Petersfield local community. Thank you."

Plumage

Barbara Carter (below) opened her dress shop in Chapel Street in 1991 and has never looked back. The shop is deceptively small and neat looking but holds a wealth of choice, much of it displayed with matching colours and complementary items hanging next to each other.

As well as high quality clothes and accessories, Plumage has a popular collection of hats and handbags for hire. These are always particularly in demand in the summer, not just for weddings but for events such as Ascot and Goodwood races.

Barbara has eight different collections of garments each year, changing twice with each season. She selects the collections from the four trade exhibitions that she attends annually. The collections are aimed mainly at customers aged over 40 but there is something for everyone and she is highly skilled at colour coordination.

She has loyal customers from a large area – Chichester, Haslemere, Fernhurst and as far afield as Southampton. They say, "I know Barbara is going to know what I like", and can depend on being able to find an outfit for that special occasion or, indeed, just for every day.

Rama

Neil Burnham (below) moved into his ladies' and gentlemen's hairdresser's in Dolphin Court in 1971. That was just three years after the building had received the Design Award for its novel architectural style, following the demolition of the old coaching inn, The Dolphin, in the mid-1960s.

As the first tenant of this property, his establishment is now the longest-surviving hairdresser's in town and some of his present clients still remember these early days. Indeed, some of them may have been the last of the pupils at the old Petersfield High School for Girls which had occupied the old inn from 1919 until 1960.

Neil's hairdresser's and barber's, with the more recent addition of a nail-polishing specialism, has a large number of regular clients from the town and surrounding villages. Word-of-mouth recommendation ensures the success of the establishment and he does not suffer from its slightly hidden position in the building. Neil enjoys working in Petersfield, where, despite its growth since his arrival here, he enjoys the continuing market-town atmosphere and its many facilities.

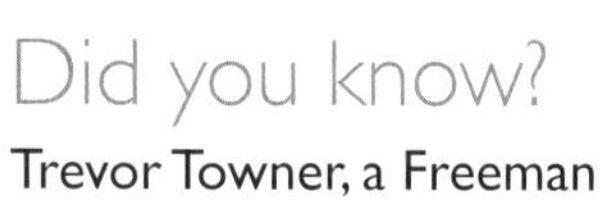

Trevor Towner, a Freeman of the Goldsmiths Company, set up his own business in Petersfield in 1983, the only jewellers with a workshop on the premises. He designed many silver and silver-gilt works : the William III, the Flora Twort, the Hampshire Hog and the Hampshire Rose collections as well as limited edition items, some set with precious stones. Trevor and his wife Jill were active in the town, supporting many charities and trade associations. They retired in 2014.

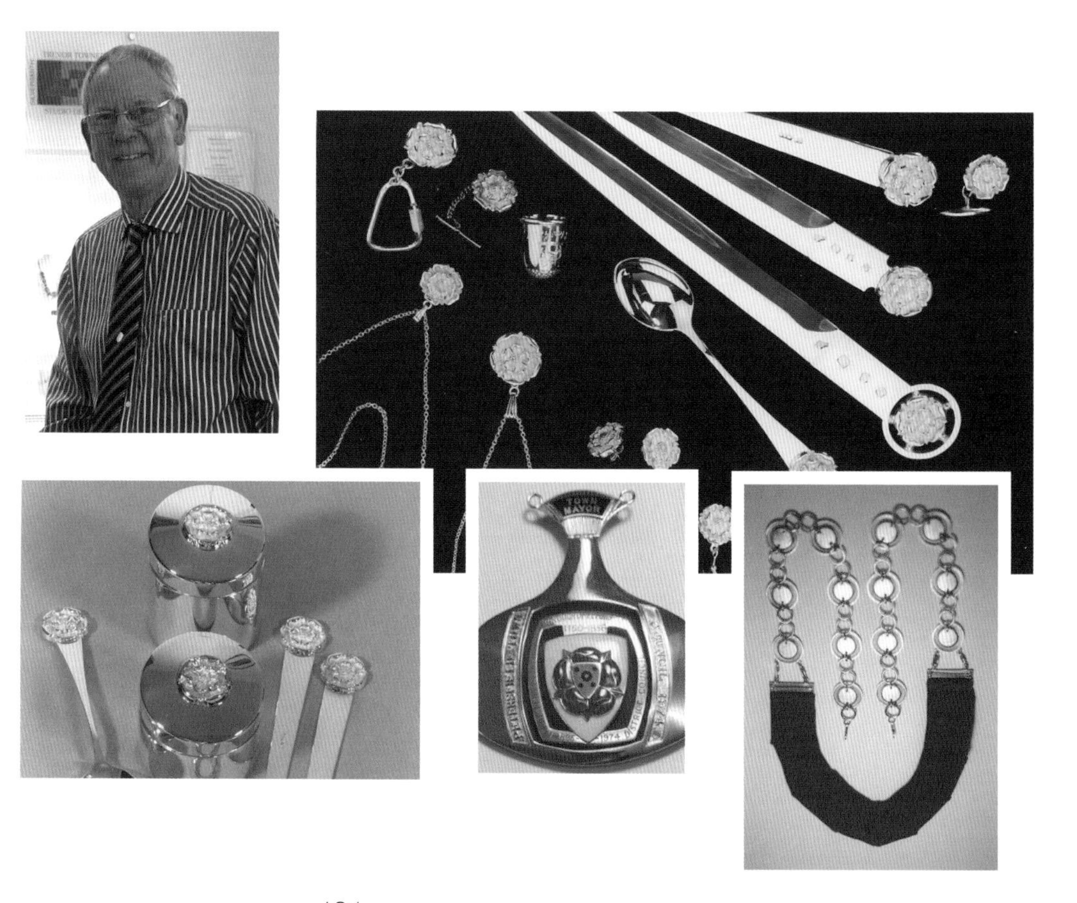

Review

Review directors Elaine Armitage and Paul Hawes have been part of the hairdressing salon's Petersfield journey from day one. In August 1989 they and two staff members first began trading in St. Peter's Road.

The intervening years have seen a stylish expansion of the original flagship premises, and the addition of two more salons, in Waterlooville and Southsea. The team now numbers 42, with most of the home-grown talent taught their trade and life skills in Review's multi-award winning training academy.

Top: Paul Hawes (left) and Elaine Armitage receive the National Training Award from Colin Jackson

Above: Alan Titchmarsh presents Paul and Elaine with the Hampshire Hog Award

Review have been rewarded with many high-profile awards, national and local. These include the British Hairdressing Awards, National Training Awards, British Hairdressing Business Awards, Trend Vision, and Most Wanted Awards.

Giving back to the community has been an important part of their ethos by supporting and fundraising for many charities. In June 2014 Paul Hawes showed his energy inside and outside the salon, by running the three highest peaks in Britain for Macmillan Cancer Support, all within 24 hours.

Review say: "Our main focus still remains our customers, many of whom have remained loyal to us throughout our 25-year journey and who still experience that same welcome and enthusiastic buzz when they enter the salon. Two and a half decades later business is bigger, better, and busier than ever."

Rhona Russell

Rhona Russell (below) took over Square House between St Peter's Church and the Library in 2008. She and her husband, Geoffrey, knew Petersfield well having been weekenders in Rogate for some time. She recalls that when Vaughan Clarke, then Mayor of Petersfield, opened the new boutique that October, "the financial world was collapsing. But there was no going back at that stage."

"It felt the right thing to do; Petersfield felt friendly and safe," says Rhona. "I started trading on the ground floor as a shoe shop, shoes being my special passion. After one year I took the plunge and opened up the first floor with a range of clothing to suit the growing customer base."

"The business has grown to become an established part of the town's retailing scene, employing four local women. It is a stylish ladies' boutique selling an extensive range of clothing, shoes and accessories."

The property has always been an important feature in The Square. In the 1690s it was owned by Richard Churcher, who founded Churcher's College, and in the early 1800s by John Small, the famous batsman and maker of cricket balls. It has been a house, a dentist's, a hotel, a cobbler's (in the cellar, between the Wars), offices and a shop.

"Square House is a wonderful old building," Rhona Russell adds. "Many remember it as Macdonald Oates solicitors, as they spent almost 50 years here. Geoffrey and I sensitively restored Square House – which was a warren of rooms – as well as 25 The Square and 2 Sheep Street, which have been returned to residential use."

"...a stylish ladies' boutique selling an extensive range of clothing, shoes and accessories"

Secret Garden

Sue Brewer (below) has owned the Secret Garden since she took on the lease of her flower shop by the station in 1999. Always interested in flowers and flower arranging she has built a great business by catering to people in Petersfield and a wider online customer base – and her clients include Sir Cliff Michelmore.

The shop's position is ideally suited to customers arriving at and departing from the railway station. Commuters who are late home on the train can buy a peace offering. National and international trade is conducted via "e-flowers" and Sue takes orders through the internet from all over the world.

Fresh flowers are delivered daily from the Netherlands and, although they are not so readily available, English-grown flowers are requested by her clients more and more. Sue likes her busy trade at this central point in the town and, with help from her staff, frequently deals with the growing demand for floral tributes and individually-composed bouquets for local events and many parties, from small to lavish.

Sue Johnson Interiors

Sue Johnson (centre) with her husband Ron and Sarah Marks

Sue Johnson has become part of the fabric of Petersfield since moving into the area some 25 years ago. Having set up in a tiny outlet (13ft x 13ft) in the Folly Market all those years ago, she now operates a top quality home furnishing store in Sheet.

"Sheet is a lovely village and offers the ideal location for my showroom," she says. "There is plenty of parking and clients can easily come and spend some quality time browsing the hundreds of pattern books and samples, with the assistance of helpful, knowledgeable staff. They are welcome to stay as long as it takes, though we can show some long-standing clients the perfect collection in minutes! Anything we don't happen to have we can source, and we cater for every style and budget."

Sue and her husband Rob have worked together for 35 years. "We are a perfect team," she says, "with me mainly in the showroom, and Rob carrying out all the fitting and hanging."

She offers a comprehensive service from supplying fabric, wall paper and paint only, to furnishing complete houses and everything in between. Her business has thrived largely through word of mouth and her clients come from Petersfield and the surrounding area as well as London, the home counties, Sussex, Dorset, the Channel Islands the UK and Europe and even Jamaica.

Sue adds: "We love what we do and we want our customers to be just as enthused with the world of interiors as we are. We are lucky to be working with a great team of curtain-makers, upholsterers, carpet and curtain fitters and the wonderful team in the shop."

Syn-Star

Award-winning entrepreneur Giles Cleverley (top right) was aged 22 when he founded Syn-Star in 2002. He saw an opportunity when he was at university in Portsmouth and opened the first store in Chapel Street, Petersfield, selling music, DVDs and phones. While there are now three outlets, the main branch is in The Square.

Syn-Star provides support for companies and individuals in Hampshire. Giles says: "I have always liked Petersfield; it's a brilliant town. The people are great and they appreciate good, honest service."

Consolidation and growth have come quickly as they have re-positioned their service in IT support. Syn-Star prides itself on always improving and "forever striving to be better", and focuses on supporting local companies of varying sizes. They started a fixed price guaranteed repair service and attracted customers from East Meon to Chichester. Syn-Star look after Macs and PCs, and have become Microsoft partners so that they can repair all kinds of laptop, desktop and server.

In 2004 the business took over the Phone shop in The Square, where it is today. They acquired two companies in 2012 to help with their steady growth into the corporate IT market. In 2013 they won the Sustained Growth Award from Action Coach, a national training organisation. And they continue to grow. "We have had a brilliant year in 2014," Giles said with a smile.

Giles has been very active in many local business networks over the years, and Syn-Star has played its part in sponsoring local charities and events. In 2014 they sponsored Butserfest in the Queen Elizabeth Country Park.

Other awards have included the Business of the Year award at the *Life in Petersfield* business and community awards in 2010, and in 2014 they won the East Hampshire Business Retailer award from Hampshire Chamber of Commerce.

Tara Interiors

The aim of Tara Interiors in Dragon Street is to create classic, contemporary, quirky or functional interior design for the home. Mixing textures and colours, Tara Interiors designs the right space for living, complemented with an individual range of accessories handpicked from Parisian Boutiques, trade shows in Stockholm, London auction houses, and even the odd car boot sale in Buriton.

Services include window dressing, using an extensive range of designer fabrics, sourcing furniture, artwork and unusual objects.

Tara can recommend trusted decorators, electricians, craftspeople, and project managers.

They say: "The shop is a treasure trove, an eclectic mix and, because we believe interior design should not be daunting, your experience will be friendly and welcoming."

The Tile Store

About seven years ago Simon Geddes (below) and David Harden decided to open The Tile Store: location was very important and Petersfield was top of the list. Fortunately, a bike shop had recently moved to a new location leaving the perfect spot to establish the business.

They say, "The ornate brickwork and traditional look complement the tiles and we've never looked back." They enjoy being part of a lovely historic market town and being part of a friendly community of traders.

"The town holds fond childhood memories of visiting grandparents and feeding the ducks at the lake, something I still enjoy doing today," says Simon. "There is always something going on in the town which is great. The various markets and events held in the town draw people in from the surrounding areas."

Did you know?

99% of Petersfield people have never seen this grisly apparition – have you? If not, you'll have to look carefully at the parking area at the back of Chapel Street properties (where the Waitrose delivery trucks go) to catch sight of it on the wall. It signifies the existence of a slaughterhouse at the rear of a shop, once a butcher's. There were many such tradesmen in Petersfield, just as there were many dairies in the town a hundred years ago.

The refurbishment of the International Stores in Chapel Street , fortunately retains its old mosaic entrance step and the monogram relating to its previous owner, Mr DE Hobbs, on its frontage.
In 1876, he was the town's most prominent blacksmith, whose forge was situated in the present bakery at the back of Gregg's. For 15 years, he was also Chairman of the Urban District Council and was appointed a JP for Hampshire. The Lane deserves his name!

This JG&S monogram can be clearly seen high on the front facade of no. 52 College Street. It registers the initials of the owner's company, John Gammon and Son, whose building firm were based there for 50 years in the Victorian era. Thomas Gammon, a well-known carpenter and builder in the town, started the firm in the 1840s and was followed by his son John.

Tiger Rose

Tiger Rose is very much a fashion store. The shop looks colourful and fun, and the price band is wide. "I buy what I love, and people have come to know my style," says owner Josie Ogram (below), "it's fun and a bit boho. This isn't the shop you come to for basic staples, but for something a bit quirky and different."

The shop looked very different when Josie began in the Folly Market in 2004: she started by selling a pretty and eclectic range of jewellery and accessories. Then, after only four months, she moved the shop to its present site on the High Street. "This building had been a gift and accessories shop," said Josie, "and we still sell cards and girlie gifts. Then I started buying a few gilets and cardigans to go with the accessories, and the fashion side really took off."

Josie's background is in buying, for homes rather than clothes, and she clearly has a knack for knowing what people want. She offers a personal styling service to clients who come to her for help choosing a special outfit. "I think probably 80% of the business we do is for regular clients, and 20% are new customers."

Over the years Josie has been involved with various charity events and shows and she plans to do more under the Tiger Rose banner. "My main charity is the NSPCC and I support Women's Cancer. I really look forward to doing more shows for charity while at the same time letting people know what good independent shops we have here and what a great community Petersfield is."

"probably 80% of the business we do is for regular clients, and 20% are new customers"

Vintage & Vogue

After many years of working with her husband at the Petersfield Cobbler, Moyra White decided to open her own shop. With her passion for clothes and accessories Moyra (below) opted to open a dress agency for original and interesting clothing.

In February 2011 Something Blue Dress Agency opened in Chapel Street. Customers brought their clothes for resale, including a number of vintage items. When a vintage clothes shop in Petersfield closed, Moyra bought their stock and re-launched her business in the summer of 2012 as Vintage & Vogue.

With a good customer base Moyra's stock is new, vintage and retro, from original day wear to evening wear. She still operates as a dress agency, and her latest project is an online shop.

White & Rees

White & Rees opened as a shop selling interesting and individual vintage and bespoke furniture in July 2013 - they had been planning to open for around four months while they looked for the right premises. Adam Rees and Neil White (above) wanted the shop to be in Petersfield, as they both love the town.

They spotted a shop premises for rent and immediately knew they had found the right place in Lavant Street with its independent shops such as The Happy Cow, Morgan & Sons and Annie Jones' Tapas bar, and many more. Having acquired the lease they then prepared the shop and on opening day a ribbon was cut by Peter Marshall, the then Mayor of Petersfield.

They say their first year of trading has been "interesting and fun. Having never had a shop before, there was a bit of a steep learning curve, but we seem to be doing well. We won the '*Life in Petersfield* - Best New Business Award 2014', so we must be doing something right!"

Wild Damson

Wild Damson was established in Dragon Street in May 2011. The business was already up and running, and doing well, in a small unit in the Packhouse in Farnham but they felt there was a space for this type of business in Petersfield.

The shop stocks country-style antique furniture as well as old and new home accessories. They have a small onsite workshop where they can transform furniture into more desirable classic pieces using paint from the huge colour range of the Little Greene Paint Company. Demand is high for storage items, bookcases, trunks, cupboards and chests of drawers.

"We regularly receive lovely comments about our customer service – our ethos is to treat people as you would like to be treated," they say. "The Grade II listed shop has lovely large windows and really is our biggest advert – we try to keep the displays updated and interesting."

Did you know?

This mosaic was installed in 1994 as part of the remodelling and enhancement of Dragon Street after the completion of the town's by-pass. It was commissioned by local and county councils and several Petersfield societies and designed by an ex-Bedales student, Rosalind Wates. It celebrates the passing of the Tour de France through the town that year - a first for the town and therefore a pretext for civic celebration and public enthusiasm.

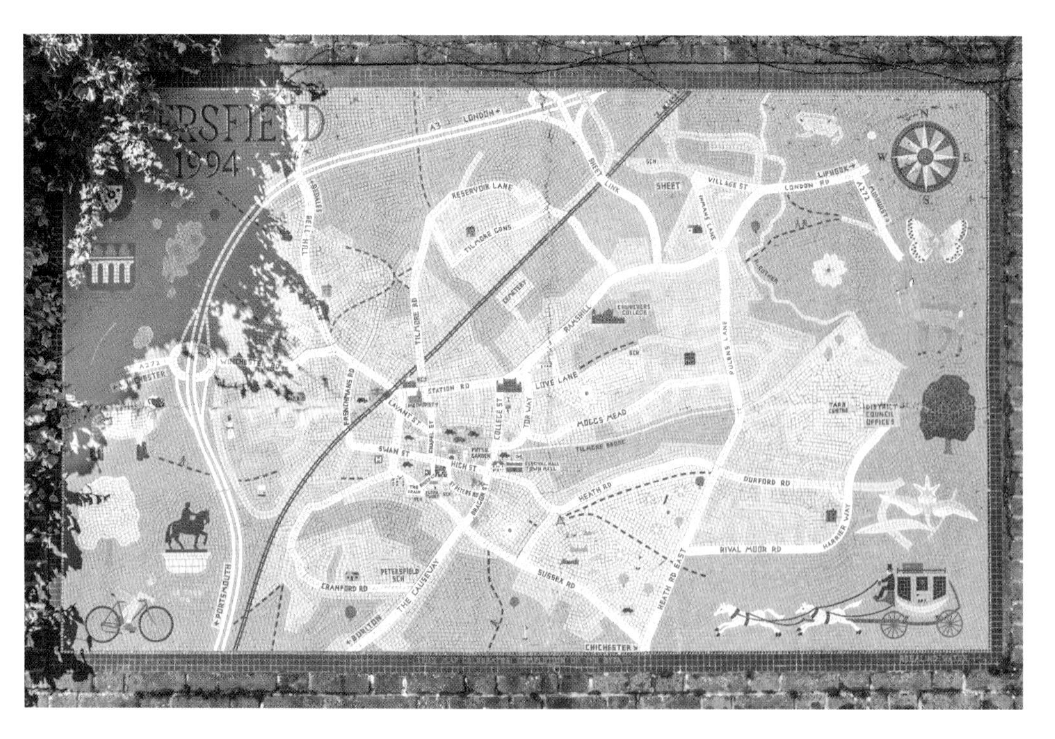

PAGES
YARD
SHOPS
RESTAURANT

Petersfield's Lanes

If Petersfield's High Street largely (but by no means entirely) reflects a national scene with its generic shops and recognisable names, its lanes present a totally separate identity.

If you haven't stumbled across these delightful back alleys, then you haven't reached the heart of the town. Their names are a reminder of prominent past townspeople: Bowen (the donor of our Physic Garden); Crawter (garage owner and local councillor); Hobbs (blacksmith and a Hampshire JP). Or they are pathways to clusters of hidden shops: Folly Lane; Pages Court; Bakery Lane.

Explore these delightful semi-backwaters and you will discover their unique individuality, their old-fashioned charm and their exotic quirkiness. They represent an ideal starting point for first-time buyers into the world of commerce or committed adventurers in the multi-faceted community that is Petersfield. Here, small is not just beautiful, it is positively and richly life-enhancing!

Around Bakery Lane

Fez

What was once a bakery on Bakery Lane is now an intimate, friendly, family-run, traditional Turkish restaurant. Wall hangings, mirrors, lanterns, ceramics, sofas, and carved tables transport you instantly to the Eastern Mediterranean world. The restaurant is called Fez, and it is a hidden gem of Turkish specialties.

Left: *Ebdor* Top Right: *Ayhan*

Although Bilsen and Ayhan buy and use only local products, there is nothing 'local' about the authenticity of their mezzes, coban salad (a favourite) served with pomegranate sauce, or the preparation of their lamb, chicken and fish dishes. These include kebabs, falafel, fish, stuffed aubergine, moussaka and a wide variety of other speciality dishes. Desserts include baklava, kadayif, Turkish delight ice cream, and Turkish coffee and teas.

Established in 2010, Fez immediately attracted attention and has grown to twice its original size since then. There are now three rooms including one upstairs.

The focus of Ayhan and his team is to make customers feel part of their enlarged family, very much as he sees himself as part of the Petersfield community.

Fez is a treat, and customers want to visit this small part of the Eastern Mediterranean again and again once they have been there.

Bakery Lane Barber Shop

Tracy Gould established the Bakery Lane Barber Shop seven years ago. Following her 20-year experience of hairdressing in Liss before moving to the town her enthusiasm has not diminished. She loves the Petersfield clientele and her situation in Bakery Lane, with its intimate and quirky ambience.

Her staff – Dee and Angela, both well experienced in barber's shop demands – ensure the shop is open six days a week, catering for men young and old and providing on-demand styling of all kinds to regulars and newcomers.

Julie's Tearooms

Julie's Tearooms have received excellent reviews since being set up in early 2013. Julie has aimed to create a traditional English tea-room with a relaxed atmosphere, where people can come and chat in an environment where there is no rush.

Most days are very busy, with people waiting for vacant tables. Bookings are also made for individual tables, and afternoon teas are a popular speciality, with everything served in traditional china and with pastries on cake stands. Customers seem to like this old-fashioned touch.

The Sweet Stop

Sally (below) and David Scott-Angell opened the Sweet Stop in April 2014. Having helped out in a sweet shop and then run a mobile sweet shop attending fairs and events around the county, Sally felt confident enough to start a 'fixed' business in Bakery Lane.

She has around 300 varieties of sweets in jars, from the traditional pear drops, aniseed balls and sherbet lemons to modern ones such as Mega Sours. These blast you with a strong sour flavour, followed by the more gentle taste of raspberry or bubble-gum, before returning for a final sour hit. Best sellers are the raspberry bonbons which turn your tongue a startling shade of blue!

All ages of customer frequent the shop, from school children off the morning train, to adults coming in for a personal treat and grandparents bringing in their grandchildren. There are no barriers to a sweet tooth!

The Blacksmiths Daughter

In the last 15 years The Blacksmiths Daughter florist shop has established a strong presence in Petersfield. People have become accustomed to seeing interesting and unusual plants, containers and arrangements displayed outside the shop.

Hands-on owner and Master Florist Kristina (below left) Cousen and her team provide stunning flowers for

weddings, parties and events, sympathy tributes, and hand-tied bouquets and arrangements to suit any occasion. The shop also has a wide selection of vases, candelabras and containers for hire, if anyone wants to go it alone, along with an extensive range of vintage china.

Two members of the team have their say. First, Charlotte, "I have been a florist for some 20 years now. When I moved to Petersfield, I remember so well walking into this amazing flower shop and thinking 'THIS is where I want to work' – and I have now been here 12 years."

Then Olivia, "I have worked for Krissi for 11 years as part of a dedicated team. With the high quality and wide range of superb flowers, my artistic talents are allowed to flourish and progress, thus creating the most wonderful arrangements for our clients, many of whom we have got to know well over the years."

Ann's Pram Centre

Ann's Pram Centre is run by mother and daughter partnership Sue Pellett and Ann O'Rourke, and has been in Chapel Street since 1995, when Sue's son was two. Looking around, she had found it extremely difficult to find out anything about children's car seat safety and so set up Ann's Pram Centre. In the first year the shop dealt in second hand items only, in order to assess the market, but legislation and demand forced a change to new goods. Now they sell prams, pushchairs, buggies, car seats, bedding, high chairs, toys, baby clothes and bath-time products, as well as other items. Ann has recently turned over some space to wool sales. After all, many people like to knit and a lot of knitting is intended for babies!

The impetus to start the shop came from a concern for child safety which has been the basis of the business's success. All staff are fully trained, from folding all the prams and pushchairs, technical information and maintenance to colour ranges and availability. Ann's Prams has been selling the safer extended rearward facing car seats for several years and has chosen never to sell car seats on the internet. Customers are encouraged instead to visit the store for a personal fitting session that makes sure that they get the right product. In an accident this could save a child from serious injury or even save its life. Over the years Ann's Pram Centre has become known for its concern for safety and its excellent customer service. So strong is its reputation that there are examples where three generations of a family have returned to the shop.

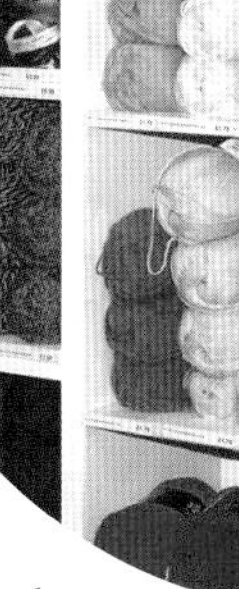

Dower's

Dower's business of creating bespoke, made-to-measure kitchens, bedrooms and studies grew out of Guy Cheeseman's great passion for making pine furniture over 28 years ago. As an increasing number of clients asked for bespoke handmade kitchens, Guy and his wife Pam expanded their business to sell kitchens in pine and all sorts of other timbers and in a variety of finishes.

The team share Guy's enthusiasm and he is always looking for ways to improve the end result. "The greatest reward is when I see the kitchen finished and our clients tell me how truly delighted they are," says Guy. "One of the best compliments paid to us was a client who said that her friends had asked how long the kitchen had been there because it complemented its historic environment so well."

Every Dower's kitchen has units made as individual pieces of furniture, with strong carcases and solid wood doors ensuring long life, as well as good looks. Dower's offer a wide choice of finishes, including painted, oiled, or untreated so people can apply their own finish, and any wood from old pine, new pine, oak, ash and a painted finish.

Dower's also offer all the extras anyone could want from special features, including traditional wood-to-wood drawer runners, slide-out bins, larders, pan and crockery drawers and trays, to cutlery trays, spice racks, wine racks and even ironing boards.

Inside Out

Among a small assortment of shops and businesses on the western side of the central car park is Inside Out. It has just celebrated celebrating 10 years in the town. Set back slightly from the pavement, it is the ideal place to find that individual accessory for your home or a gift for someone for that special occasion.

It was started 10 years ago by Anne Sykes (below) who had previously worked in theatre and television and then fashion. Looking for a change, she decided to create an outlet for something different for the home. A cream picket fence outside and three planters painted in the Inside Out signature turquoise blue lead the customer down to the door. Many of the local celebrities who live in the surrounding area frequent the shop, which is always fun for Anne and her staff.

Jasper, the shop dog, is a great draw too, and many customers pop in just to say hello to him. He is a Jack Russell with a friendly temperament who loves to be stroked; he even has canine friends who call to see him!

Next time you have a moment, pop in and have a look around: you might find just the thing you thought you weren't looking for!

The Garage

The Garage has 'popped up' in many different locations around Petersfield, bringing a wide variety of art, vintage and retro goods to the town. The Garage was established by Cressy Luke (right), a costume designer with a long career in film and TV. She is well known in and around Petersfield for helping to transform Bakery Lane and for running The Name UK, a shop specialising in vintage and contemporary art gifts.

After four years in Bakery Lane, more space and a new location were needed. The Name UK closed in 2013, and a few months later Cressy opened The Garage in the Red Lion's old garage in their car park. The Garage was open for four days once a month with a different theme each month – a mix of vintage and retro collectables in themes such as 'Retro New York loft apartment', kitchenalia, and toys and tools. The Garage has showcased a wide variety of art, including the work of contemporary young photographers.

When the lease ended at The Red Lion, The Garage popped up in the old Lunn Poly shop in Chapel Street on the corner of The Square. In collaboration with Chris Sharples, The Garage's decorative window displays attracted visitors from far and wide.

The Garage found another new site in summer 2014, facing the central Waitrose car park next to Pizza Express. The shop still showcases a collection of art, retro furniture, and carefully sourced vintage items for the home, garden and more. These are one-off items that change on a weekly basis – so there is always something new, even if it's old!

Bakery Lane with its intimate and quirky ambience

Folly Lane

Far Horizons Gallery

Tucked away alongside Folly Lane, where it has been for the last 14 years, Far Horizons Gallery specialises in jewellery, stocking a great selection of work by designers from around the world, and unusual quality gifts. The store is in a beautiful 16th century coaching house and the charm and history of the building complement the goods inside.

The gallery attracts customers from as far afield as Japan and Australia, and Fiona and Hannah McMillan (above left to right) say they have "a genuine enthusiasm for the products we select and hope that this comes across in the store. We only select products that we love – this means that a lot of restraint is required to stop things coming home with us!

"We aim to source perfect gifts for a wide variety of ages and occasions. Our free gift-wrapping service is always popular, especially over the Christmas shopping period. We never mind people just coming to browse; we feel that if we did not own the store we too would so enjoy wandering around, gazing at all of the wares on display."

The gallery finds that the best way to attract new business is through word of mouth. Often customers recommend it to their friends, but they try to maintain a high level of interaction on social media sites such as Facebook and Twitter.

The Gypsy Kitchen

Foraging is the watchword for Nicky Roper and Reece Taylor (pictured below) at the Gypsy Kitchen in Folly Lane, which opened in May 2013. When she was young, Nicky, her sisters and their friends learnt to forage from a gypsy in the Holybourne Downs, who taught them how to differentiate between edible and poisonous mushrooms and wild plants.

They discovered how to stuff apples with elderberries and cook over a fire, and "about the deliciousness of parasol mushrooms simply fried in butter". She has been foraging ever since.

On her first foraging expedition with Reece, who has worked in Michelin-starred restaurants in London, they found wild strawberries and oregano which they served in the café. He cooks breakfasts, lunches and teas every day except Monday when the Gypsy Kitchen is closed. They also offer gourmet supper club evenings on Fridays.

"We create a memorable dining experience using the best local produce married with foraged food prepared to

the highest standards," they proclaim, inspired, they say, by Hugh Fearnley-Whittingstall.

A sample menu on the website offers beetroot goats curd; grilled red mullet; beef shin (locally sourced) with pumpkin dumplings, parasol mushrooms, wilted nettles and braising juices; and, for pudding, blackberry set custard with meringues, hazelnuts and rose-hip and hawthorn syrup.

Pages Court

Bonica

Stephanie Valentine always wanted her own flower shop and in 2007, after successful careers in IT and fashion retailing, that dream came true. As the owner of Bonica – named after a gorgeous pink rose variety – she heads up a team of four florists, all blessed with great creative flair, superb technical skills and a genuine love of flowers.

From traditional English country-garden style to highly structured contemporary designs, they do it all. Daily deliveries mean they always use fresh flowers, giving the best possible colour, scent and longevity, whether it's a bouquet or a buttonhole.

Bonica has a wide selection of gorgeous flowers, plants, Kew pots, gifts and other lovely things to suit every occasion and budget. They also offer a complete range of floristry designs, from bridal flowers to floral tributes, an exclusive range of hand-tied bouquets, and floral decorations for social and corporate events.

Every Bonica creation is handmade with attention to detail and bags of flair. If a customer wants a selection of freshly cut stems the Bonica team will arrange them there and then, ready to take away. If people are looking for a display with an indefinite shelf life, Bonica also has a range of artificial stems that would be arranged with the same flair as the fresh bouquets. Flower selections can be tailored to suit any budget, and Bonica can reproduce any of the designs and arrangements that appear on their website.

Butterflies Lingerie

Butterflies Lingerie has existed in Petersfield for well over 30 years, serving the people in the area with underwear, nightwear, vests, stockings and even bed socks.

In 2007 Sue Love, the current owner, was travelling all over the country for a property developer. Tired of all the driving, she was looking around for something different and noticed that Butterflies Lingerie was up for sale. She got a business plan together, sorted out the finances, and started up with her daughter Helen. Although the opening coincided with the recession, she adjusted her stock to suit the economic climate and more than doubled the turnover.

So many women appreciate Butterflies' personal service. With Helen and the younger assistants they cover three generations, so customers of all ages can feel at home. Over time, people change shape and have different needs, or sometimes people need something for a special occasion, such as a wedding.

Wearing well-fitting underwear ensures confidence, and it can also help with health issues such as backache, neck tension, and headaches, which may be caused by wearing the wrong bra. Sue believes that lingerie is an important part of a woman's life, and buying it should be a pleasant and fun experience.

Cute

Debbie and Amy

Owned by Amy Kinally and Debbie Stevens, Cute opened in October 2004 in Chapel Street. It had a selection of quality baby gifts, continental clothing and traditional wooden toys, something that the owners had found difficult to find in Petersfield since having their children. In 2006, Cute moved to bigger premises in Pages Court just off the High Street and in 2009 opened their online shop.

Debbie and Amy, who met at the local Petersfield NCT group when pregnant with their first children, have got to know their customers very well over the years and say, "One of the nicest things about Cute is hearing about the new babies that have been born and helping excited grandparents and family members choose that special something for the new member of the family," says Debbie.

"One of my most memorable times was when we celebrated our 5th Birthday," says Amy, "We had Fairies and Pirates giving out Cute balloons to the children, free cupcakes, a treasure hunt around Pages Court and even a traditional Punch and Judy puppet show in the courtyard; it really was a magical, memorable day."

Cute have supported the local community as sponsors of the local Winton Players' pantomimes, Petersfield Festivals, and many school fetes in the area: "We need them as much as they need us, and because we both live in Petersfield we take it very seriously," say Debbie and Amy. "We are very lucky to live in such a vibrant busy market town that still has a great number of independent shops and we hope Cute will still be on the High Street in another 10 years."

Monoloco

Now under new management, this small family-run restaurant, licensed cafe and bistro is located in a 200-year old stable block behind what was an 18th century coaching inn in Petersfield High Street.

It is open from Monday to Saturday and serves breakfasts until 11 am, followed by lunches consisting of dishes prepared on the premises. In the summer, meals are served outside in the walled garden courtyard, where the menus change regularly.

Evening meals are available too, and the food, from locally sourced products, is bought daily and cooked fresh. The cuisine is innovative, original, healthy and home-made, changing from season to season.

Nutmeg

Tina Plank set up Nutmeg in 2007. After the birth of her son she had quickly realised that as a new mum with a small child in tow she needed to be able to shop locally, and she still wanted to be able to wear stylish clothes that were well-priced and well-made. And so Nutmeg was born.

Tina contacted the brands she thought would work well together and all were keen to come on board. With her interior design background she enjoyed organising the fit-out of the newly built unit in Pages Court. "Running the business and getting to grips with the buying was a massive learning curve," she says, "not to mention juggling my son and home life - he quickly became a dab hand at redesigning a cardboard box into a serious racing car! Nutmeg retains its core ethos of being a local boutique for local women with a fantastic selection of well-priced, easy-to-wear clothes."

Tina stresses that the shop's success is also down to the back-up of the staff and the wonderful customer service they provide. In recent years Nutmeg has been involved in three charity fashion shows, two of which were organised by Mel Flint, the shop manager.

Following on from the success of Nutmeg Petersfield, Tina moved to Oxfordshire and in 2010 opened Nutmeg in Chipping Norton and, in 2011, Nutmeg in Witney, both to a fantastic response locally.

Petersfieldtube.com

Matthew (right) and Jo-Anne Riley are the people behind the new Petersfieldtube.com. The core of the business is producing videos for business, weddings, and events of all kinds.

The Rileys moved to Australia in 1990, but they always intended to return to the UK. Matthew has worked with video for 14 years and has a passion for anything to do with camera and video. When they returned to the UK in 2014 and with family in the area, they set up Petersfieldtube.com

Matthew has noticed a great difference between the attitude of his Australian and UK clients: British people are shy of being in their videos, whereas the Australians pitch in much more readily. When it comes to business videos, owners try to get staff to take the lead. Matthew states, "People must realise that there's nothing like having the owner of a business in the video, as their knowledge and commitment always shine through! You mustn't feel that it's wrong to promote yourself."

There is also a community element to the Tube, with videos of the events and happenings that bring Petersfield to life. For instance two dogs were lost on Butser Hill: after the owners had searched widely for some days, one of the dogs was sighted on the Hill. Someone suggested putting out their dog baskets on the Hill, and both dogs returned to the baskets and were reunited with their owners.

Rams Walk

Petersfield's central shopping mall with its 22 retail units opened in 1993. It was one of four major developments in the town that year, the other three being the by-pass, the hospital and the Taro Centre.

Rams Walk is a very appropriate name for the mall as the nearby Drum stream was crossed at this point by cattle and sheep going to and from the market in the Square.

The holding company managing Rams Walk, Prudential, had backed the Waitrose bid for their site in 1988 as it doubled the size of the previous supermarket in the High Street. It was a lucky gamble taken during the recession at the time and Waitrose overnight became one of the most successful stores in the country.

Did you know?

'The Downsman' is the official title for this sculpture, beloved by both clambering children and admiring adults as they stroll through the centre of town. The work was commissioned by Prudential in 1999 when they designed Rams Walk – another reminder to the town of its rural heritage. Livestock would be herded across the nearby Drum stream to or from the fortnightly cattle market in the Square.

The sculpture is cast in bronze resin on a metal sub-frame. The sculptor, Andrew Cheese, based the central character on his great-great grandfather, a New Forest cattle farmer, and the sheep portrayed are of the Hampshire Downs breed. To obtain realistic representations of the animals, Andrew temporarily borrowed a sheepdog from a Waitrose customer, but he had some difficulty with the live sheep he brought into his studio – one or two escaped onto the A3!

Petersfield Market

Fancy a hamburger? Need a pair of socks? How about a bunch of flowers for your friend's birthday? The remote control needs a battery? Want an old vinyl record you can't find elsewhere? Shall we get a spare loaf for those people coming over? What about a piece of French cheese for the weekend? Isn't it time for a new school uniform? Anything (and almost everything) can be bought at the twice-weekly market in the Square, the centre of Petersfield life for nearly nine hundred years.

Some of the stallholders are the third generation of their families to have pitches, and some are newcomers. Bryant's have had a fruit and vegetable stall at this market since the 1930s, for instance, while Melanie's hamburger van only came here last October and, she says, "Petersfield is a fabulous place to trade".

All are agreed the market is the essence of Petersfield – after all, the town got its Charter to hold a market in 1181 – and it is the heart and soul of the town. The goods are often seasonal – the flower stall and the cards and handmade gifts outlets are a summer speciality. But the stallholders all find trading successful and, weather-permitting, enjoyable.

Customers appreciate the quality of the products in the market, especially the fresh artisan bread, which far outstrips that available in the supermarkets. And the stallholders appreciate the loyalty, support and friendliness of Petersfield shoppers, as well as the town's beautiful position in the countryside.

The market is old-fashioned enough to attract browsers and casual buyers as well as visitors to the town looking for a bargain or something they cannot find in local shops.

The traders who have stalls in other towns nearby prefer Petersfield for its central position, its cheerful (and relatively prosperous) customers and its variety of goods on offer.

Petersfield Farmers' Market

The Farmers' Market is held in the Square in Petersfield on the first Sunday of every month from 10am to 2pm. Part of Hampshire Farmers' Markets, this offers the chance to buy good, fresh food in season.

Hampshire Farmers' Markets say:
"Our regular Food Comparison Survey's clearly demonstrate that a large proportion of our produce is actually cheaper than the supermarkets, with the savings in food miles and also the middle man costs, passed onto our customers. The public are increasingly looking for assurance regarding the food chain and safety of the produce that they are serving to their families, especially in the light of the recent food fraud scandals. Customers at our markets can be assured of the provenance of each and every item they buy, knowing that it has been locally produced either within the boundaries of Hampshire, or within ten miles of the county border and complies with our own very high standards and criteria."

Family business takes over Petersfield Market

A family business that has worked in the town since 1930 will restore local pride in Petersfield Market after being chosen to run it. Well-known local fruit and vegetable company Bryant Bros are to take over the management of the town's Wednesday and Saturday markets from East Hampshire District Council.

Following an extensive tender process EHDC's Cabinet agreed that the company would be best placed to handle the day-to-day affairs of the market and improve it over time.

The new management agreement will see pitch fees frozen for at least a year, and the extensive use of social media to promote and develop the market. Also, 25% of any profit generated through the management of the market will be donated to local charities and community groups.

Bryant Bros said: "We believe that the market is at the heart of Petersfield and its community. We are delighted to have been given the opportunity to work with EHDC and the other market traders to develop a bustling, vibrant and successful community market for the residents of Petersfield."

Giant Easter and Christmas Charity Markets

The annual Easter and Christmas indoor markets at Petersfield Festival Hall have become a popular tradition in aid of Portsmouth Hospitals Rocky Appeal and other local charities. Petersfield has an abundant number of charities and goodwill which have helped make the markets a success over the years. Traders, craftspeople and charity groups from across the area have richly supported these family-run events.

Organisers Martin and Jeremy Holmes (right) established the Easter Market in 1988 and then, in 2001, took over the running of the Christmas market, which previously had been known as the Mayor's Market. The Christmas Market had been organised by Petersfield Rotaract since 1976 and for a number of years Martin Holmes was Market Chairman in the club. To date, the Holmes family have now held 41 markets, raised over £25,000 for Portsmouth Hospitals and over £75,000 for local charities in total.

The Rocky Appeal started out as a drive to get a body scanner for the QA Hospital. The appeals have continued for advanced, specialist equipment of the future which has included an MRI Scanner, mobile baby incubators, a cancer laboratory and currently a robotic digital keyhole operating theatre. Other charities which have taken part with fundraising stalls have included Petersfield Open Air Swimming Pool, the NSPCC, Age Concern, the Chernobyl Children's Lifeline and Petersfield Musical Festival.

Over 70 stalls are set up in the main hall, on the stage and in the Rose Room. A café is also run in the Rose Room and a Rocky Appeal raffle takes place in the foyer. The profit from stall rents and the raffle, money from the giant book and bric-a-brac stall in the main hall and cash from the café all go towards Portsmouth Hospitals Rocky Appeal. Customers at our markets can be assured of the provenance of each and every item they buy, knowing that it has been locally produced either within the boundaries of Hampshire, or within ten miles of the county border and complies with our own very high standards and criteria."

Did you know?

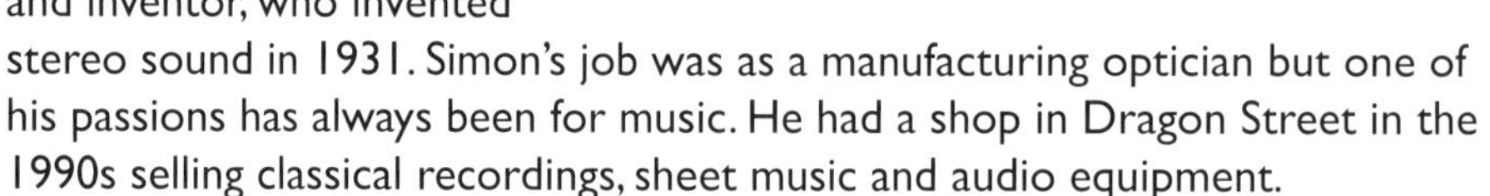

Simon Blumlein, a character well known to many in Petersfield, is the son of Alan Blumlein, an electronic engineer and inventor, who invented stereo sound in 1931. Simon's job was as a manufacturing optician but one of his passions has always been for music. He had a shop in Dragon Street in the 1990s selling classical recordings, sheet music and audio equipment.

Nowadays most of Simon's time is taken up with his enthusiasm for Swiss and German railways. He loves the real thing, and also the models he makes and runs at home.

Petersfield Musical Festival

In the aspirational words of its constitution, the Festival aims to 'promote, improve, develop and maintain the appreciation of music in all its aspects'. For the sisters Edith and Rosalind Craig Sellar, who founded the Festival in 1901, these aims were to be achieved through choral singing. A century later, choral concerts remain at the heart of a programme that showcases the wide variety of music-making in our area.

The 2014 Festival opened with Liss Band, celebrating their 40th anniversary, together with The Choir Company. To end the concert, band and choir joined forces in Leonard Cohen's *Hallelujah* and a rousing medley from *Mamma Mia*.

The Petersfield Orchestra's enterprising programme included a spectacular account of Mussorgsky's *Pictures at an Exhibition*, and Mahler's *Songs of a Wayfarer* with the young South African bass/baritone Njabulo Madlala.

Festival conductor Paul Spicer directed two concerts involving members of five local choral societies. The first featured two modern classics, Leonard Bernstein's rhythmic, tuneful *Chichester Psalms* and John Rutter's reflective *Requiem*, alongside Bernstein songs, enchantingly sung by former Bedales student Sofia Larsson. A week later, we heard Handel's great oratorio *Samson*, a powerful drama with operatic solos and monumental choruses.

Youth Concerts have been part of the Festival since early days. In 2014, two packed audiences enjoyed hearing some 350 young singers and instrumentalists in music ranging from Handel's *Messiah* via songs from the First World War to the latest in Korean pop – an arrangement of *Gangnam Style* for combined wind bands from The Petersfield School and Churcher's College.

From top:

Vocalist and band leader Duncan Galloway with the Pasadena Roof Orchestra – the season's hit celebrity guests.

Soloist Sofia Larsson with pianist Richard Pearce and members of Fernhurst and Petersfield Choral Societies and Midhurst Music Society.

Soloist Njabulo Madlala with conductor Robin Browning and members of the Petersfield Orchestra.

Organist Sarah Baldock at St Peter's Church in the Festival's first celebrity organ recital.

Paul Spicer conducts the Southern Pro Musica Orchestra and singers from Alton, Petersfield and Rogate choral societies in Handel's Samson.

St Peter's Church was the venue for a lunchtime guitar recital, enjoyed by a large audience including pupils from Froxfield Primary School. The next day, Sarah Baldock, organist at Chichester Cathedral, introduced and performed a wide-ranging recital on the newly-refurbished St Peter's organ. In the Friday celebrity concert, the Pasadena Roof Orchestra delighted lovers of swing with their effortlessly stylish performance.

The Festival launched the Michael Hurd Memorial Fund in 2007, to promote music-making among young people through grants and events. In this year's third biennial 'Festival of Young Composers', seven young composers brought their music to The Studio@TPS in February, and the three winning pieces were repeated at the Youth Concerts.

From top:

Liss Band and The Choir Company – both appearing at the Festival for the first time.

Lunchtime recitalists Amanda Cook and Bridget Mermikides with young members of their audience.

Participants in the 'Festival of Young Composers', with adjudicators Philip Young (L) and Jonathan Willcocks.

Helen Purchase, Director of Music at Churcher's College, conducts the College orchestra and young singers from seven schools in Handel's 'Hallelujah Chorus'.

Petersfield: the place to sing

Petersfield is host to lots of choirs, as well as many church choirs! With choral singing gaining ever-increasing popularity, riding on the success of some television programmes, there are plenty of people out there who want to join a choir. They will not only enjoy the music, but can take advantage of the well-known benefits to physical and mental health, and find pleasure in the social aspects of meeting new people and producing results by teamwork.

Three Choirs

Three of the town's choirs – The Petersfield Choir, the Free Radicals and Just Sing – are run by Steve Sargent, formerly Petersfield's police inspector and a life-long amateur musician. Most concerts have free admission, with a charitable collection at the end, making the music accessible to everyone.

The Petersfield Choir was formed in January 2014 and has about 30 members who sing mainstream choral music, mainly without accompaniment. The first concert, of Easter Anthems from the last 500 years, was a resounding success and many more are planned. Membership is open to anyone who has previous choral experience and can read music confidently.

The Free Radicals began in 2007 and has eight or nine members who sing 'anything and everything' including arrangements by The Swingle Singers and The King's Singers and some home-grown music, too. The Free Radicals perform four or five times each year mainly in local churches, raising money for local charities, and has an ambition to travel abroad to sing…if time ever permits.

Just Sing meets in a room above a pub. Pint in hand, the singers (most of whom can't read music) learn new songs every week by ear and sing lustily for pure enjoyment. This is a completely relaxed arrangement; people don't have to come every week and there are no formal concerts. At the end of term, the group meets in the bar and sings to family, friends and whoever else happens to be there.

Community Choir

The Community Choir in Petersfield – open to all, with no auditions, no solos and no requirement to read music – came to fruition in 2007. Seven years on, that ethos remains, interest and enthusiasm continue and the choir flourishes with around 50 members.

They sing songs, unaccompanied, from a variety of different cultures and countries - from a traditional Shetland Isle lullaby to a Russian shape-note hymn and beyond. As Hampshire has such a strong musical heritage, they perform a wealth of traditional folk music.

St Peter's Church provides the back-drop to the choir's twice-yearly concerts led by director Carolyn Robson. An added bonus in 2014 was its donation of £2,000 to PLANETS, the local pancreatic cancer charity. They also participate in community events – and at private functions by request!

Petersfield Choral Society

Petersfield Choral Society was founded in 1903 to take part in the Petersfield Musical Festival which had begun life two years earlier. There were two 'choral societies' in Petersfield for many years, the other being the Thursday Singers, each singing for one of the two choral concerts in the Festival. However, by the 1990s, the two groups were becoming less viable and so a merger took place, with the new joint choir, rehearsing on Thursdays, taken over by Mark Dancer, (right) Director of Music at St Peter's Church, in 1996.

Mark Dancer says "Petersfield Choral Society exists primarily to sing in both concerts in the Festival. This makes for quite a pressurised six months of learning music. The choir is un-auditioned, but because of the fast-moving nature of rehearsals, it tends to self-audition and, luckily, there is no shortage of other choirs in the town which can accommodate enthusiastic amateur singers without that pressure.

"The style of our repertoire hasn't changed hugely over the years: major works continue to be a feature of the Festival; one of the concerts will be a major single work such as the Bach *B minor Mass* or works by Mozart, Haydn or Dvorak; for the other concert, we do shorter works such as opera choruses. In recent years, we have performed Britten's *St. Nicolas Cantata* and Tippett's *A Child of our Time* (which was very demanding for amateur choirs to sing).

"We have a social event just before Christmas which includes a just-for-fun carol sing, while in June, we gather at members' houses to sing madrigals, folksongs or part-songs for our own entertainment, with drinks and nibbles afterwards."

Did you know?

Elizabeth Gotto first launched her children's choirs in Petersfield in 1995. Three different choirs performed at the Petersfield Musical Festival, at Christmas Carol services and with children's choirs from other towns in Hampshire and elsewhere.

Sadly, Elizabeth has retired from her work after 20 years and the Southern Orchestral Concert Society (SOCS), which had featured children's choirs in its concerts, also closed. However, Children's Concerts now operate as a charity and 6,000 local children participate in programmes every year.

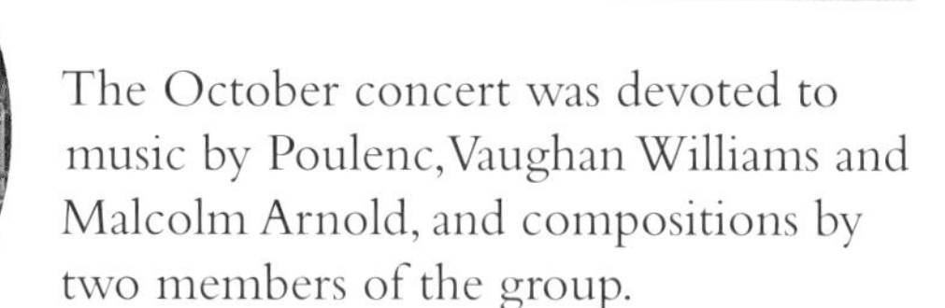

Gemini Consort

Classical music of all kinds has always been an important part of Petersfield life. Ann Pinhey (above) is among those who have played a major role in achieving the very high standard of choral music through the choirs she has organised and trained for a number of years. From her own extensive knowledge, she chooses music from a wide range of often less well-known composers, and both singers and audiences benefit greatly from the experience.

In January 2000 she formed the Petersfield Chamber Choir, which has performed music from the Renaissance to the present day. It appeared twice with the Southern Pro Musica, conducted by Jonathan Willcocks, and performed twice at the Petersfield Music Festival, as well as giving frequent and well attended concerts of its own.

Ann's new choir, the Gemini Consort, consists of 12 experienced singers, some of whom are also instrumentalists. Their first concert, in February 2014, consisted of motets and madrigals by Monteverdi, with recorder music by Frescobaldi and trumpet music by Gabrielli. Their next concert, in April in Buriton, presented a programme of peaceful, reflective music. The summer concert that year, also in Buriton, focused on the music of Purcell, Schubert and Benjamin Britten.

The October concert was devoted to music by Poulenc, Vaughan Williams and Malcolm Arnold, and compositions by two members of the group.

"These concerts are all very popular, and draw in audiences from a wide area," says Ann. "The local availability of music like this is also a great advantage for schools and younger singers and players, showing them what can be achieved and raising their aspirations. We consider ourselves fortunate to have musicians of this quality who are keen to extend the range as well as the superlative standard of music performance in this town."

Music in St Peter's Church

St Peter's Church is central to the Petersfield cultural scene. When the reordering of St Peter's Church was being planned in the early 1990s, it was agreed that the building should be available for use by the wider community for appropriate events.

The church has become an increasingly popular setting for music. The first concert in the reordered church was on 11 December 1999; the following year it held some 10 concerts; and 33 events were held in 2014. More than 200 events have been organised in the past 14 years, many of them for charity. Many thousands of pounds have been raised for local, national and international charities. More than 12,000 people have attended a concert, played or exhibited.

Full symphony orchestras have been squeezed in, as have large and small choirs, octets, sextets, quartets, trios, duos and solo performers. The church has resounded with brass bands, jazz bands, folk bands, recorder bands and guitar bands. Singers from Japan and Russia have been heard, as well as string players from Germany, policemen from Winchester, and bagpipers from Glasgow.

Local schools have played their part, starting with Bedales and TPS in 2005. They were joined by Churcher's College in 2006 and Ditcham Park School in 2009. All contribute to the St Peter's musical scene, and the standard of music-making is breathtaking.

Great credit goes to David Francombe and his committee who have been instrumental in achieving all this. Two other people have made, and are making, important contributions: the indefatigable Ann Pinhey; and Mark Dancer, the musical director of St Peter's, with his series of organ recitals started twenty years ago.

The Petersfield Orchestra

In the sunlit uplands of the Avenue Pavilion – perhaps not so sunlit on a wet and windy Friday night in mid-February – 40 or so intrepid musicians can be found hard at work, in search of their own particular version of spiritual uplift. Their fuel of choice is classical music. Anything from Bach to Brahms, Mozart to Mahler, Schubert to Shostakovitch will do.

It's rehearsal night for the Petersfield Orchestra, and for love of their art and an annual subscription, they allow themselves to be bullied and browbeaten, encouraged and heckled, cheered and goaded by Music Director Robin Browning. Three concerts a year may not sound much. But each one feels like an Everest to climb. So many notes. So difficult too, to find them on a clarinet or a cello, and so tricky to get in tune, and in time.

Originally the orchestra grew out of the Festival's choral concerts. Founded in 1927, by Kathleen Merritt, she ran the orchestra until 1972, when Judith Bailey took over and conducted for almost another 30 years. The members include lawyers, doctors, a surveyor, a submariner (RN, retd.), an industrial chemist, and a generous handful of teachers. For concerts, they bring in 'stiffeners' - professionals from round and about, to beef up the string sound, or who know how to play the bass trombone or the contrabassoon or the flexatone.

Money is always in short supply, and rehearsals are enlivened by a weekly raffle and by the draw for the Supporters Club. The Friends of the Orchestra play a vital part in keeping it alive, particularly when it comes to buying tickets. The county, district and town councils occasionally contribute.

If many of the players are silver-haired, that, they say, is because it takes a lifetime to master an instrument: classical music gets better with age. But there are young faces too, some straight out of school or college. Music knows no age barrier. And when the playing goes well, and the conductor is purring, you can see the joy on the faces of The Petersfield Orchestra.

Natural Environment

Biodiversity and Nature

Dunnock

Migrant Hawker Dragonfly

Robin

Yellowhammer

Whitethroat

Brimstone

Small Tortoiseshell

The Biodiversity Year of 2010 kick-started the need for Petersfield to have its very own Biodiversity Action Plan (BAP). A team of enthusiasts for studying the local ecosystem was born, or, in the terms of nature, it emerged from a chrysalis state and became imago.

What can uplift the mind and soul more than hearing the sweet rhythmic song of the Dunnock? Or spotting the early flight and the yellow flash of the Brimstone butterfly breaking from its winter hibernation? These two and many more signs of nature can bring delight and create an interest to delve further into the wonders of ecology around Petersfield.

The first objective of the project was to promote the importance of a biodiversity plan and raise the level of public awareness to this new development of a local BAP. A stall was held in Petersfield to advertise the intention to have a local BAP and to encourage anyone to join the working group. This was arranged and held on a market day in town displaying numerous photos of local nature and with an explanatory handout leaflet for those who wished to know more.

This gave the best opportunity for a team to come together and form a working group. When established, the team identified the habitats of the town environs, and observed species present, by carrying out a number of surveys. A significant aim was to conserve and improve habitats for wildlife in Petersfield and to advise how it can be supported and protected. One of the many objectives was to enhance, where possible, the large scope of different habitats that exist and this appeared in the action plans. There are river systems to meadows, woodland to heathland, gardens to urban territories, which make up an extensive array of habitats. All of these offer ecosystems of varying character supporting a vast range of nature.

The final work became available in December 2013, published by the Biodiversity Group of the Petersfield Town Partnership, and it was called Petersfield Nature.

Painted Lady

The Good Life Community Garden

In 2013 Petersfield got its very first Community Garden: the Good Life group have demonstrated enthusiasm and dedication in transforming a field into an orchard, vegetable garden, herb bed and, perhaps most importantly, a social space for everyone who labours there and who occasionally needs a cup of tea, some delicious home-made cakes and a gossip (strictly on horticultural matters).

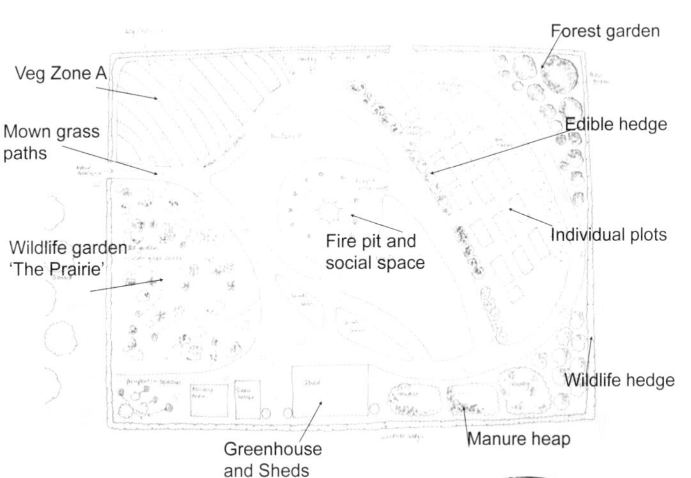

What is a Community Garden? It is what the community decides it should be: this one is a place for making friends, learning about cultivating and planting the land, and contemplating the natural beauty of the area. The space, divided into various zones, allows for a variety of activities, not forgetting picnicking, open days for visiting individuals or groups (e.g. the local Guides) and a general feel-good factor for all.

In the dry weather volunteers have been watering, and harvesting spinach, salads, beans, beetroot and globe artichokes.

A greenhouse has now been erected, bought with a grant from the South Downs National Park. Open days are held throughout the year where volunteers can show what has been achieved and encourage new members into the group.

There are work parties most Sunday afternoons – go along at 2pm to the Garden at Waterworks Road, Sheet. All ages are involved: families, volunteers, those with and without gardens, and those with and without gardening skills.

Petersfield Heath

Petersfield is a fortunate market town, being at the heart of the South Downs National Park and blessed with a heath and a lake. This fine site was bought by the Urban District Council between 1914 and 1927 from three major landowners, and was protected from being sold off in part for the building of 'first-class residences'.

Because of its unique location, combined with the quality of its flora and fauna, the Heath has proved to be a magnet for visitors. People travel from near and far to enjoy its many diverse attractions: archaeology, bird-watching, boating, fishing, cricket, picnicking and dog walking.

These demands impose an enormous pressure on the Heath, which calls for a body to manage and care for it to ensure it is available for all interests. The Friends of Petersfield Heath (FoPH) was formed in 1999 with this in mind after the Golf Club had moved from the Heath to their new course.

Working closely with the Town Council, a group of FoPH members meet fortnightly during the autumn and winter months when they carry out a variety of maintenance and management tasks. To ensure the heathland survives, a war of attrition has to be waged against saplings to prevent the birch and oak trees overwhelming the open spaces, and bracken has to be held in check. The heather, much of which was lying dormant, is spreading with carpets of purple catching the eye every August.

A recent project was the construction of a Raised Path across a boggy section of land on the south east corner of the lake. FoPH volunteers designed the path

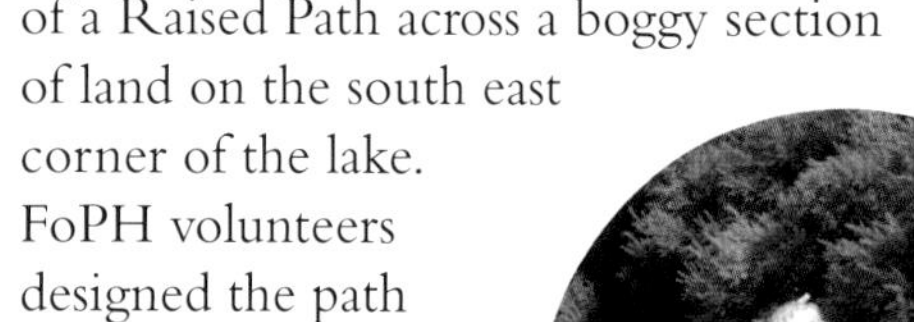

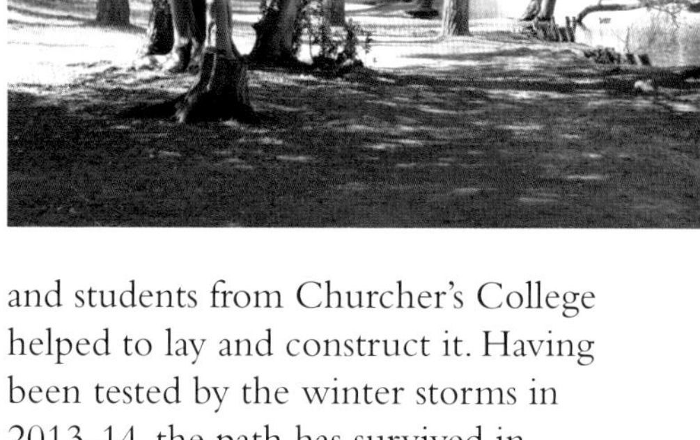

and students from Churcher's College helped to lay and construct it. Having been tested by the winter storms in 2013-14, the path has survived in remarkably good condition. FoPH and Churcher's have combined again this summer to build a second Raised Path over an even wetter patch in the same area.

Another enthusiastic activity is the construction of 'dead hedges', using saplings from clearance work and branches from fallen trees - good recycling practice. The hedges provide a barrier and a habitat for insects and other invertebrates. Over the years the Friends have enhanced the Heath by renovating the rusty Victorian railings and seats, smartening the island with a girdle of green oak panels, and opening up views previously blocked by bushes and trees.

Below: *Friends of Petersfield Heath volunteers and students from Churcher's College undertaking raised pathed laying and construction*

The Heath Barrows

'People of the Heath' is the name given to the four-year project investigating the origin and interpretation of the barrows (burial mounds) on Petersfield Heath which began in 2014.

The first excavations carried out under the leadership of archaeologists Stuart Needham and George Anelay have revealed the remains of a wooden coffin, with worked flints, possibly from arrowheads, and blocks of sandstone inside.

A nearby mesolithic site (close to the present nursery school alongside Heath Road) produced thousands of struck flints, some of which were excavated by local schoolchildren who had been invited to join the search by the organisers, Petersfield Museum.

The Heath Barrows form one of the most impressive Bronze Age cemeteries in south-east England and the sponsors of the project, supported by the Heritage Lottery Fund and the South Downs National Park Authority, are keen to recruit more volunteers over the next three years to continue the excavations.

Petersfield Physic Garden

Peterfield's Physic Garden was a gift from Major John Bowen to the people of Petersfield. He gave his garden behind No 16 High Street to the Hampshire Gardens Trust to be kept in perpetuity as a peaceful green space in the middle of the town for people to enjoy. And they do... When the weather is favourable – and sometimes when it is not – the Garden acts as a mecca for alfresco lunches or just as a place to sit or walk in peaceful surroundings.

John Goodyer, a botanist, and John Worlidge, a horticulturalist, lived and worked in Petersfield during the 17th Century and were the inspiration for the theme of the Garden. It is laid out in the style and with many of the features of a 17th Century garden. All the plants, shrubs and trees are of species known in this country at that time.

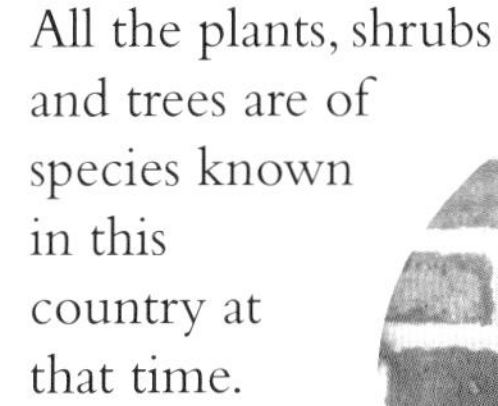

Inset: *John Bowen, donor of the Garden*
Above: *Volunteer gardeners*
Medlar fruit

PETERSFIELD PHYSIC GARDEN
DESIGNED IN THE STYLE OF A 17TH CENTURY GARDEN
ADMISSION FREE

Many visitors are surprised by the number of herbs that exist, also the variety of fruit. The medlar and the quince fruit are the source of many questions to the wardens. They are generally impressed when they see them turned into delicious jellies.

The Garden is open all the year round and admission is free. It is managed and supported financially by the Friends, some of whom also volunteer to work in the garden to keep it attractive to visit. The gardeners produce cuttings and seeds for sale and the Friends organise a major Plant Sale each Spring.

The garden lies within: the only surviving medieval walled burgage plot in the town.

Wednesday afternoons in term time finds the garden full of young people from local schools. On other days schools bring whole classes to study plants and particularly the herbs. It is the herbs which after all justify the title of Physic Garden.

Rotherlands Conservation Group

Rotherlands Local Nature Reserve lies to the east of Petersfield, between Pulens Lane and the Rugby Club. The land was part of Penns Farm which was sold to the local councils in the 1960s. For the next 40 years, the land was unmanaged and the whole site became a wilderness of scrub, brambles and trees. Paths were impassable in summer.

In 2000, concerned local residents formed the Rotherlands Conservation Group with ambitious plans to restore the site as a haven for wildlife and a pleasant riverside walk for the public. Since then, volunteers have cleared scrub and brambles; restored the water meadows and pond; laid gravel on muddy paths; built a boardwalk including a dipping platform and a bridge with railway sleepers; installed bird boxes, noticeboards and benches, and removed immense quantities of Himalayan Balsam.

The group has recently prepared a new management plan covering the next five years. Regular surveys have revealed over 50 bird species, 20 butterfly species, and good numbers of dragonflies, moths and plants. The site was designated a Site of Importance for Nature Conservation in 2001 and a Local Nature Reserve in 2004.

New members are always welcome and no special abilities are needed. Monthly working parties are held on the third Saturday morning of the month and always include time for coffee and a chat.

A healthy member base gives the group a stronger voice in discussions on the future of the site and so they would appreciate support. The group sends a twice-yearly newsletter to members keeping them up to date on what is happening on the Reserve and giving them information on its wildlife.

Did you know?

High Meadow is the land between Petersfield Hospital and Borough Hill.

Footpaths & green fingers

Top Left: *High Meadow*
Top Right: *Path to Buriton from Sussex Road*
Middle Right: *North Field Merritts Meadow*
Bottom Right: *Tilmore Brook*
Bottom Left: *Woods Meadow Railway Bridge*
Middle Left: *Dark Hollow*
Centre: *Tilmore Path*

Petersfields' Green Spaces

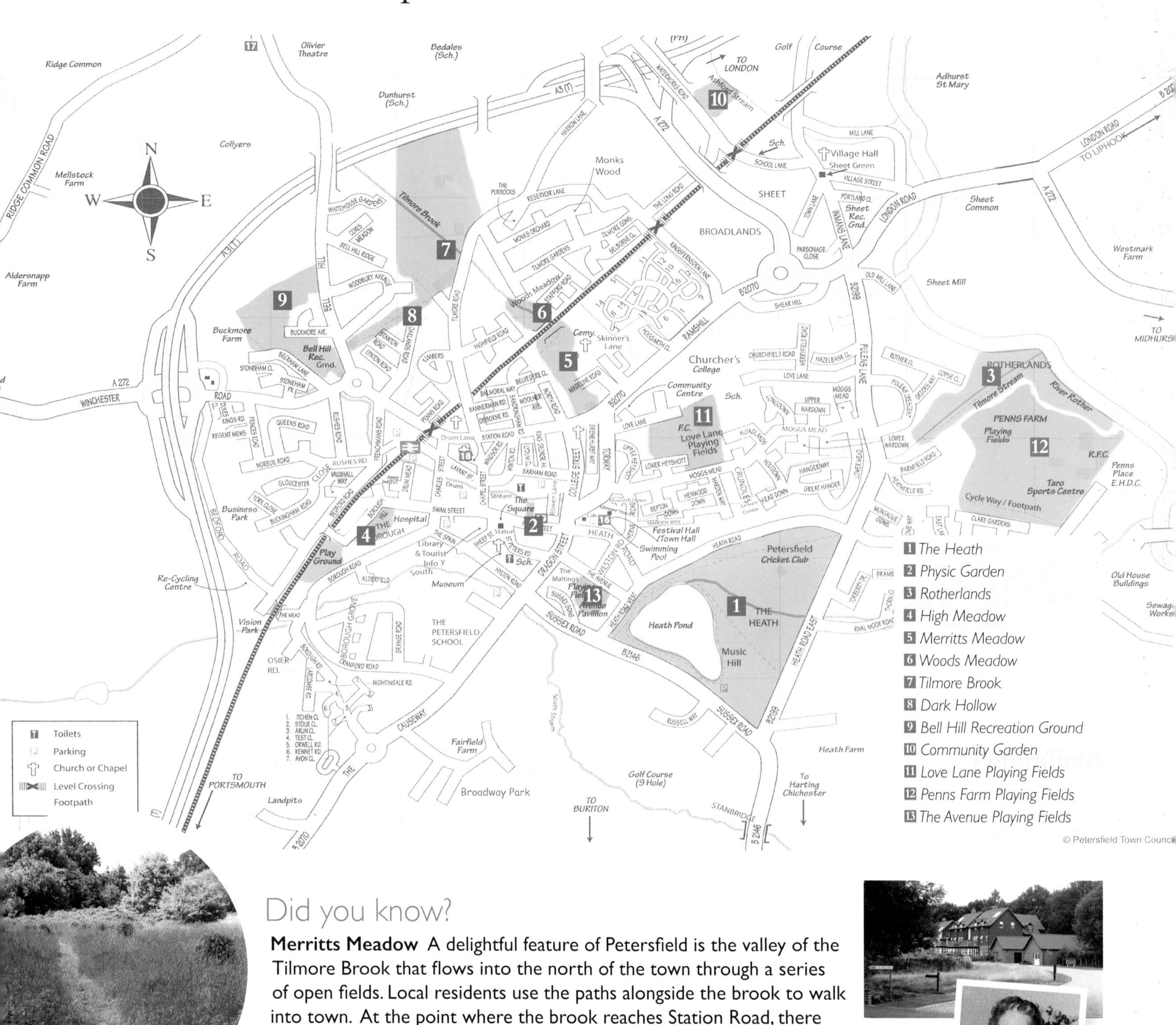

Did you know?

Merritts Meadow A delightful feature of Petersfield is the valley of the Tilmore Brook that flows into the north of the town through a series of open fields. Local residents use the paths alongside the brook to walk into town. At the point where the brook reaches Station Road, there are two water meadows known as Merritts Meadow, named after Kathleen Merritt whose house and garden stood there. She contributed hugely to the musical life of Petersfield, founding and running the Petersfield Orchestra from 1927 until 1972. She was awarded an MBE for her services to music.

Since her death, the meadows have become overgrown with brambles but, as no public money has been available to acquire the land, permission was granted in 2010 for a sheltered housing development on the site. There is hope that public access to the land, across new all-weather paths, will be gained, together with its maintenance in perpetuity.

Out of Town

Out of Town

This section of the book covers the countryside that encircles the town and celebrates our inclusion in the South Downs National Park and our connections with the beautiful rural aspects of East Hampshire.

Features such as the hangers and the sunken lanes are very particular to our locale and these green areas are used by the people of Petersfield for leisure activities, and enjoyed as a refreshing contrast to their life in the town. The green fingers of land and paths radiate out from the town into the countryside, creating strong links between the two, which are complemented by frequent long views to the heights of the surrounding downland.

South Downs Way

The South Downs formally became a National Park early in 2010 and became fully operational in April 2011. Historically, it is believed that there were trade routes along the South Downs going back to the Bronze Age.

In his book on the South Downs Way, Jim Manthorpe gives a good introduction and background, describing it as a 100-mile line of chalk hills stretching from Winchester in the west to Eastbourne in the east.

Initially, the South Downs Way extended 80 miles from Eastbourne to Buriton, on the Sussex-Hampshire border, and was designated a 'Long Distance Bridleway' in 1972. The additional 20 miles through Hampshire to Winchester were added later.

Easily accessible from Petersfield, the South Downs Way passes over Butser Hill, crosses the A3 and winds its way through the Queen Elizabeth Country Park to Buriton and on to Harting Hill and the beautiful escarpments of the South Downs. On the way there is a memorial to Hauptmann Joseph Oestermann, a pilot who flew a Junkers 88 and was shot down over the Downs on the first day of the Battle of Britain, 13 August 1940. The inscription reads 1915-1940, KG54 STAD-g. This refers to Kampfgruppe 54, Bomber Group 54 of the Luftwaffe.

Did you know?

Edward Thomas The poet Edward Thomas and his family were living in Steep in 1914 at the outbreak of the First World War. He was killed at the Battle of Arras in April 1917. Although hardly any of his poems are about the war, he is thought of as a war poet.

His name was commemorated in two windows engraved by Laurence Whistler in All Saints Church, Steep, which were installed (left) in 1978 to mark the 100th anniversary of his birth. The windows are listed as part of a literary walk from Petersfield station.

An established writer, mainly of essays and reviews, Thomas turned from prose to poetry in 1914 largely on the advice of his friend Robert Frost, the American poet (who also lived in Steep briefly).

Queen Elizabeth Country Park

The park contains 1400 acres (6 km²) of open access woodland and downland within the East Hampshire Area of Outstanding Natural Beauty, including War Down (244 m) and Butser Hill (270 m), the highest point on the South Downs, from where the Isle of Wight can be seen on a clear day. The woodland was mostly planted in the 1930s and it consists mainly of beech trees.

Several long-distance footpaths run through the park including Staunton Way, Hangers Way and the South Downs Way bridleway. The park contains over 20 miles of trails for walking, horse riding and mountain biking. There are also adventure areas and picnic areas.

Apart from Christmas and Halloween events there are activities all the year round including The Great Butser Easter Egg Roll, a Vintage Car Show and Auto-jumble, Butser Festival of Flight and the Hill Challenge, the toughest race in the south!

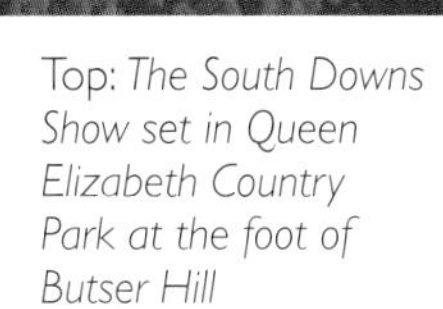

Top: *The South Downs Show set in Queen Elizabeth Country Park at the foot of Butser Hill*

Hangers Way

The Poet's Stone inscription reads:-

This Hillside is dedicated to the memory of EDWARD THOMAS, POET Born in Lambeth 3rd March 1878 Killed in the Battle of Arras 9th April 1917

"And I rose up and knew that I was tired and continued my journey"

Hangers Way was the first long-distance footpath to pass through Petersfield. At 21 miles it is not a particularly long walk which can be completed easily in two days, and in one day by fit walkers.

Starting in Alton the walk passes through East Worldham where there is supposedly an effigy of Philippa Chaucer, the wife of Geoffrey Chaucer. The footpath passes through the villages of Selborne and Hawkley before climbing up the 'Shoulder of Mutton' hill. Here can be found 'The Poet's Stone' (left) which was erected in memory of Edward Thomas who lived in Steep before being killed at the Battle of Arras during the First World War.

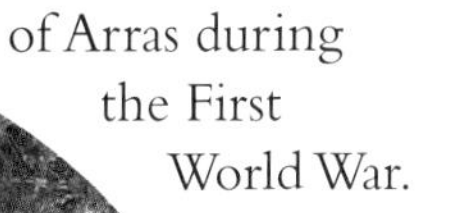

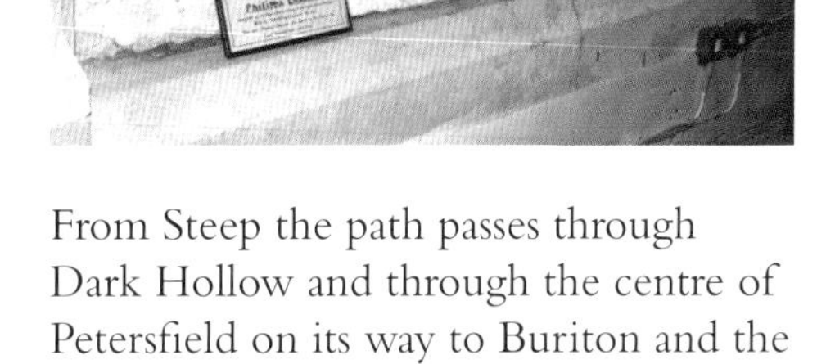

From Steep the path passes through Dark Hollow and through the centre of Petersfield on its way to Buriton and the Queen Elizabeth Country Park.

Butser Ancient Farm

The story of Butser Ancient Farm began with a decision in 1970 by the Council for British Archaeology to establish a working 'ancient farm' where archaeologists could experiment to test their theories on how people lived in Iron Age times.

Work started on a trial site known as Little Butser in 1972 and the first public Open Day was in 1974. The project was run by Dr Peter Reynolds, who combined emerging work in the field of experimental archaeology with teaching classics at Prince Henry's Grammar School in Evesham. Research continued on this site until 1989.

In 1976 a second site, with better public access, opened in the nearby valley of Hillhampton Down. This provided welcome income and an opportunity to construct some ambitious buildings, such as the Pimperne House, based on excavations in Dorset.

In 1991 the project moved to the present site at Bascomb Copse. A vital role was played in the following years by Christine Shaw, who handed the baton on to a new management team in April 2007.

Beltain is a hugely popular festival to mark the start of summer, with a 30ft-high Wicker Man burned as the sun sets. (pictured above right) Craft displays, hot food, live bands and a stunning setting make it a night to remember.

The ancient Quarter Day of 'Mid-Summer' is marked by ancient celebrations of Spring and a Fairy Festival. Samhain celebrates the Celtic New Year in October, with a folk band, story-telling, fire sculpture and ghost tours, while the Great Roundhouse is decorated at the end of December ready for the Tales of Winter Magic round a roaring fire.

Another highlight is Open Night at the Museum, an opportunity to visit the farm in the evening. There is also a 'Dig It' Archaeology Day for children.

Workshops for adults take place throughout the year.

Did you know?

Butser Ancient Farm is an educational resource showing how people lived in Britain 2000 years ago. This world-renowned site is open to visitors all year long and has 15,000 schoolchildren and 12,000 members of the public through the gates annually.

Schools from all over the south of England enjoy a visit to the farm as a highlight in their curriculum topic of Celts and Romans. They become Celts and Romans for a day by taking part in hands on, practical activities that teach them in the most fundamental, far-reaching manner possible what it was like to live in a dark, smoky roundhouse and make mud walls, pottery and jewellery with your bare hands. It is a visit that children remember for their whole lives.

Shipwrights Way

Shipwrights Way is a long-distance path which links villages and towns in East Hampshire. Starting from Alice Holt Forest, the route passes through Bordon, Liphook, Liss, Petersfield, Queen Elizabeth Country Park, Staunton Country Park, Havant, Hayling Island and continues to Portsmouth via the ferry, finishing at the Historic Dockyard. The name reflects the use of oak grown at Alice Holt Forest for Tudor shipbuilding, linking this site with Portsmouth Historic Dockyard, home of the Mary Rose and HMS Victory.

It is open to walkers and cyclists throughout, and as much as possible, the route is off-road, using rights of way and permissive paths. Parts of the route can be used by horse riders and people with disabilities.

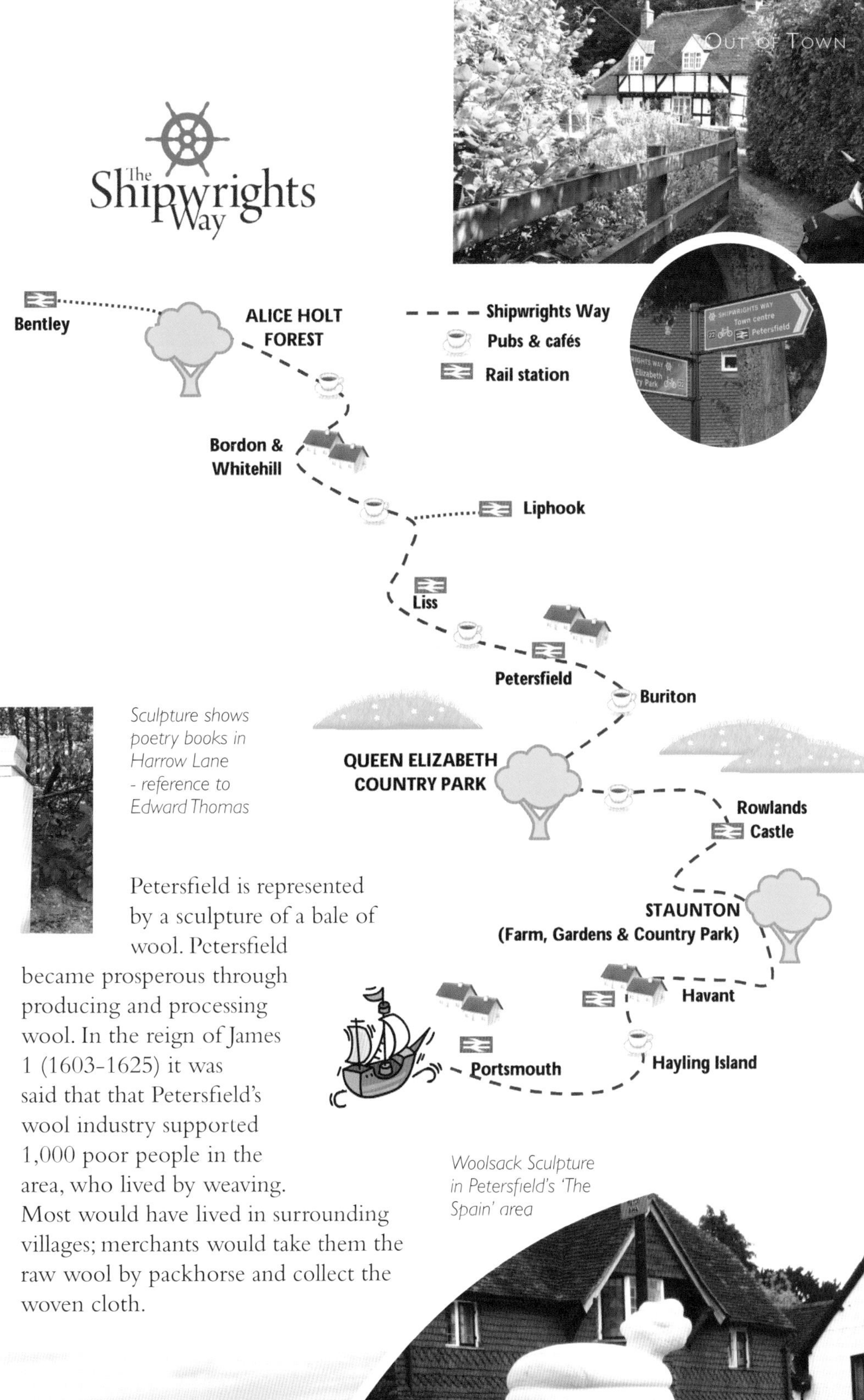

Sculpture shows poetry books in Harrow Lane - reference to Edward Thomas

Petersfield is represented by a sculpture of a bale of wool. Petersfield became prosperous through producing and processing wool. In the reign of James 1 (1603-1625) it was said that that Petersfield's wool industry supported 1,000 poor people in the area, who lived by weaving. Most would have lived in surrounding villages; merchants would take them the raw wool by packhorse and collect the woven cloth.

There are twenty interesting new sculptures along the route of Shipwrights Way, each depicting a story or aspect of the area where they stand. The subjects were suggested by local people and then carved by artist Richard Perry from creamy Portland stone.

Woolsack Sculpture in Petersfield's 'The Spain' area

From rolling hills to bustling market towns, the South Downs National Park's landscapes cover 1,600km^2 of breath-taking views and hidden gems. A rich tapestry of wildlife, landscapes, tranquillity and visitor attractions, weave together a story of people and place in harmony.

Margaret Paren, Chair of the South Downs National Park Authority at the Park's opening ceremony in Petersfield's town square 2011

A dramatic chalk ridge forms the backbone of the National Park and the 160km (100 mile) South Downs Way follows this ridge all the way from the Saxon town of Winchester to the plunging white cliffs of Beachy Head which drop down into Eastbourne.

The South Downs National Park Authority (SDNPA) is the organisation responsible for promoting the purposes of the National Park and the interests of the people who live and work within it – including the people of Petersfield.

"The South Downs is the most populous National Park in the country with more than 112,000 people living here," says Margaret Paren, Chair of the South Downs National Park Authority. "The majority of people live in the bustling market towns of Midhurst, Lewes and, of course, Petersfield, which is an excellent place to start exploring the landscapes.

"Petersfield has played a key role in the history of the National Park, as I know from the work we did together to get Petersfield included, and it was from Petersfield town centre that we launched the National Park Authority on 1 April 2011.

"The town was also the venue of our first anniversary celebration of projects across the National Park supported through our Sustainable Communities Fund – open to any partnership, voluntary group or organisation undertaking a non-profit making project that socially, economically, environmentally or culturally benefits National Park communities. To date, 157 projects have been supported by the fund; of over £1m ranging from food festivals, to community seating, local plays, archaeology digs, pond restoration and even this book.

"I am pleased that The Petersfield Society, in its 70th anniversary year, has been able to create this book celebrating the town and its people and look forward to seeing their dedication to the town and the wider countryside continue."

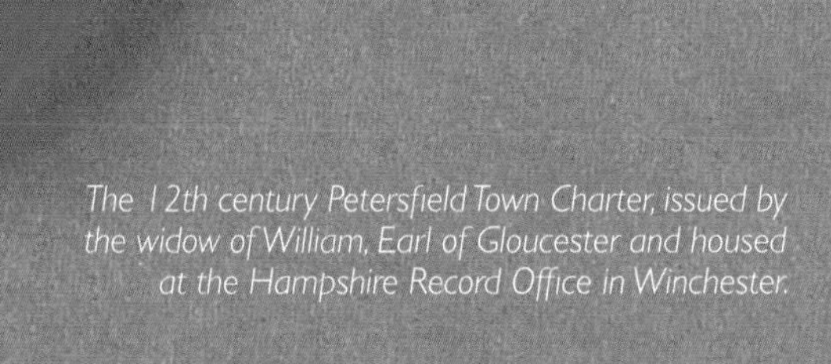

The 12th century Petersfield Town Charter, issued by the widow of William, Earl of Gloucester and housed at the Hampshire Record Office in Winchester.

Petersfield Town Council

Above: Town Council line-up, left to right: *George Watkinson, Bill Organ, James Deane, Anne Church, Neil Hitch (Town Clerk), Sue Harwood (Mayor), Lesley Farrow (Deputy Mayor), Peter Marshall, Vaughan Clarke, Chris Mills, Mary Vincent*

The PTC (Petersfield Town Council) has a four-year lifespan, two councillors being elected to represent each of the six wards: Bell Hill, St. Mary's, Rother, the Heath, St. Peter's and the Causeway. Councillors are occasionally elected according to their abilities rather than their political allegiance; however, within the Council Chamber, politics are forgotten and all Councillors generally work well together. They are all unpaid volunteers who seek to do something worthwhile for the town.

The Planning Committee makes recommendations regarding planning applications to the SDNP (South Downs National Park) or their agents, the EHDC (East Hants District Council) Planning Committee.

Above Five Mayors: *George Watkinson, Sue Harwood, Peter Marshall, Mary Vincent, Vaughan Clarke*
Inset: *Neil Hitch, Town Clerk*
Bottom left: *The chain of Office*

The Halls Committee is responsible for the Festival Hall and the other facilities within the Town Hall: the Rose Room and Garden, the Green Room and the Council Chamber. The Festival Hall is used extensively for theatre and film shows, the annual Musical Festival, visiting artistes and for such events as collectors' and antiques fairs, charity events and art shows.

The Grounds Committee manages the Heath and Heath Pond, playing fields, children's playgrounds and some other green spaces.

The Finance & General Purposes Committee has responsibility for preparing the annual budget and setting the PTC precept for the year.

Every May, the Council elects a Mayor and Deputy Mayor from within its ranks. Councillors serve on one of four committees: Planning, Halls, Grounds, and Finance & General Purposes, and are also actively engaged in cooperating with a number of outside bodies such as The Friends of Petersfield Heath, The Petersfield Neighbourhood Plan, The Open Air Swimming Pool, the Town Football Club, The Rotherlands Conservation Group, The Petersfield Society, The Twinning Association and Petersfield in Bloom.

Petersfield's right to have a Mayor dates from a Charter granted in Tudor times and is symbolised by the Town Mace. The Mayor chairs Council Meetings and also plays a major civic role, which is to represent the Town at a wide variety of functions, such as opening shops or a community garden, attending the AGMs of many community organisations, and being present at the Remembrance Day service and the Christmas Lights switch-on.

The Mayor also raises funds for a Petersfield charity of his or her choice and annually awards a medal and certificate to up to three Petersfield citizens in recognition of their contribution to the Town.

Did you know?

The Petersfield Mace With the engraved date of 1596, it is extremely rare, and was lucky to escape the fate of much other contemporary silver which was melted down by Cromwell in the 17th century to produce money to pay for the troops in the Civil War.

It is just under 24 inches long, made of silver, but has been gilded, with the bowl divided into four panels engraved with the Tudor Rose and Crown below a border of Fleur-de-Lys and Crosses. The sunken centre inset carries the Royal Arms of Queen Elizabeth I. The Town Mace was the property of the ancient Borough of Petersfield. It passed to a body of Trustees when the old Borough was dissolved in 1886, but was retained by Lord Hylton, the last Lord of the Manor of Petersfield, until he was persuaded to hand it over to the Urban District Council in 1923.

Since that time, it has regularly been displayed before the Town Council at its meetings.

The Festival Hall

The Festival Hall is a versatile, multi-purpose venue, suitable for all kinds of events. Perfect for all music, drama and dance performances, it's also an ideal choice for exhibitions, fairs, business meetings, corporate functions, dinner-dances and galas.

Above: *Festival Hall entrance*
Left: *Petersfield Town Hall*
Below left: *Festival Hall and Rose Room function suite*

Located in the heart of Petersfield, next door to the Town Hall it offers flexible space and superb facilities – the perfect setting, whatever the occasion.

Moviola: The New Savoy Cinema

The New Savoy Cinema was established in the Petersfield Festival Hall in 2011 and named after the long-closed old Savoy Cinema in Swan Street. Run by local volunteers who have a keen interest in theatre and film, films shown include classics, action, comedy dramas, thrillers and films for children. Funds raised go towards improving the cinema, the Festival Hall theatrical equipment and other Petersfield Town Council initiatives.

Recent major investment in projection equipment has meant that film quality is excellent and the film supplier Moviola is able to supply a wide selection of up to date films.

Each month there are two films on show, screened the second Tuesday each month, there is a film in the afternoon at 2.30pm and the second is at 7.30pm. In addition to the main feature there is usually a short film which is followed by a break for drinks from the bar or ice creams.

The Petersfield Neighbourhood Plan

There has for a long time been pressure on all Local Authorities in Britain to build more houses. The shortage of houses throughout the country has led to high prices and a situation where it has become very difficult for young people to get on the housing ladder. It has also led to many people becoming stretched financially when interest rates are increased. This has led to Local Planning Authorities losing control of many planning applications as more and more development schemes are refused by the Local Authority only to be overturned by the Secretary of State on appeal.

Above: ***Town Centre map*** *Purple – Cultural or Prominent Buildings; Red – Employment; Orange – Residential; Yellow – Mixed Use; Brown – New Retail; Blue – Multi Deck Parking; Grey – Town Centre Buildings; Pale Yellow – Pedestrian/Cycle priority; Green – Improved landscaping*

Right: ***Overall Site Allocations*** *Pink – New Housing Sites; Purple – Existing Industrial Sites; Hatched Purple – Proposed Industrial Sites; Yellow – Existing Community Sites and Sports Fields; Hatched Yellow – Proposed CS & SF; Red – Reserved for Community Use; Blue – Existing Education Use; Hatched Black – Proposed Cemetery Use (Alternates); Green – Existing Public Green Space; Hatched Green – Proposed PG*

The introduction of Neighbourhood Plans is supposed to make sure that local residents can have a say in where houses are located as long as the agreed numbers of dwellings are met. The Plan could also reflect local aspirations in respect of housing mix, self build opportunities, design criteria and the need to ensure local infrastructure kept pace with development. Petersfield Town Council has been one of the first local councils to recognise the importance of this decision and started the process of putting together a Neighbourhood Plan in May 2012.

It took over two years to understand the process, to put together a team of local residents as well as representatives from the South Downs National Park and local Councils, and to identify all the potential sites around Petersfield. There has been a considerable amount of consultation and engagement with the local community and, from time to time it has been necessary to employ specialist consultants to provide planning advice, and appraisals of each potential site to take account of such things as access, the importance of ecological factors and landscape issues.

The Plan was completed in mid 2014 and then had to receive the approval of the Town Council as the 'owners' of the Plan, the South Downs National Park and the Government Inspector who had to ensure that the number of dwellings met the Government criteria.

A referendum in 2015 gives the people of Petersfield the opportunity to approve the Plan so that it can carry real weight when the Local Planning Authority comes to assess planning applications.

It is hoped that in the future the wishes of the people of the town will be taken into account so that we get the town we want. Time will tell. More details on the website, see Directory.

The Black Sheep

Landlord Nick Eldridge has lived in the Petersfield area all of his life and took over The Black Sheep in late 2013. He and his wife Emma (inset right) run it very much as a good, old-fashioned English pub at a time when this is a diminishing and threatened institution.

" very much a good, old-fashioned English pub"

Located just off the edge of the Square, it is away from the bustle of the town centre but still very much central to the community. Traditional values hold sway in the Sheep – as its many locals know it – with a warm welcome and friendly atmosphere, open fires and good quality 'pub grub' that enhances the fine range of beers on offer.

All of this is further added to by the wide range of TV sports on offer. Nick caters for both the mainstream sports fan – soccer, rugby and cricket – as well as the specialist, with anything from American wrestling to Go-Karting on the two screens.

The Good Intent

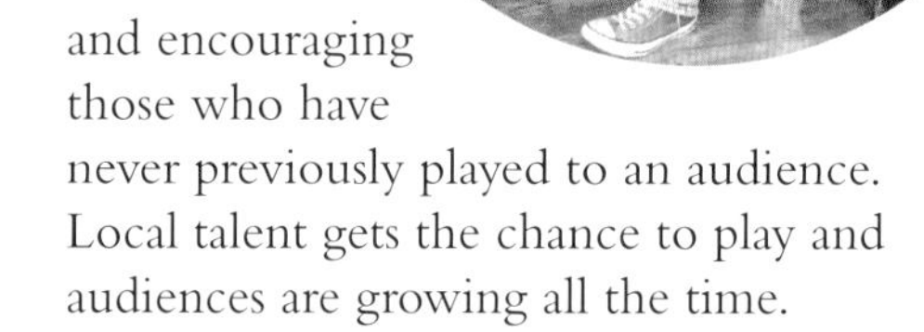

Geoff Smith fell in love with the Good Intent as his local and, when the opportunity to take it over came up in 2010, he leapt at it. The 16th century pub is one of the oldest in Petersfield and the emphasis is on the traditional aspects of the building and its role as a pub and B&B. The pub is aptly named as some of the timbers from the The Good Intent, a Royal Navy vessel of the 1540s, were used in the construction of the building.

Local community, friendly atmosphere, and good beer and food are the focus of this establishment. The food is locally sourced and cooked fresh on the premises.

They run theme nights – in particular the popular around-the-world cuisine nights once a month.

Sunday night music has always been popular and Geoff is spreading this further with folk and acoustic nights, and encouraging those who have never previously played to an audience. Local talent gets the chance to play and audiences are growing all the time.

Geoff reckons he has brought the buzz back to the pub, although this is his first experience of being a landlord. Now he wants to develop the music and events side while retaining its traditional charm and strengths as a good pub with a high quality restaurant.

The George

Joey (Joanna) Rogers, manager of The George in the Square, has no doubt that the pub has the best coffee in Petersfield and beyond – at least that's what regulars say. And she adds, "I have tasted nearly every type of coffee around."

Joey Rogers and Jerry Hicks

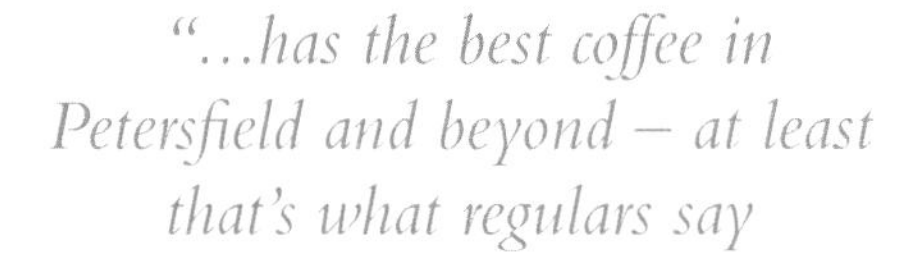

"...has the best coffee in Petersfield and beyond – at least that's what regulars say

But The George, which has a long history, is much more than a good coffee shop – it is one of Petersfield's best-known central eating and meeting places. The pub's Victorian exterior covers an old, large, timber-framed building which was divided into three (two private houses) in the early 19th century.

Jerry Hicks, who lives in Petersfield, became the licensee in January 2014 and brings the same bravura and bonhomie he shows in the Folly Wine Bar and Ale House. The George is particularly proud of the garden area at the back of the pub, which has its own bar. When the weather is not warm enough to sit outside, visitors can enjoy good food and a busy, buzzing atmosphere inside the pub.

The Folly Ale House

Jerry Hicks is one of the longest serving landlords in Petersfield. Having grown up locally and worked in the Folly Ale House bar as a youngster, he saw its potential and took it over in 1993.

He sees his customers "old and young, new and long-term, as mates who have dropped into his front lounge, which just happens to have a licence to serve good beer and wines". In early 2014 he took over the George Inn in the Square and is now looking to establish the same level of welcome, rapport and ambience.

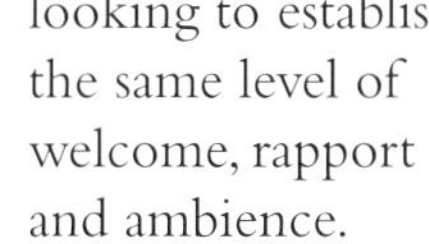

As well as running the Comedy Club at the Folly since 2010, he supports local churches and artists, and the Petersfield Rugby 7s and Outdoor Pool with charity quizzes. He adds that he is "very much an ambassador for the town and community, guiding visitors on places to visit, where to eat and shop etc."

The Half Moon

Colin Baker (right) with his son Paul

The Half Moon attracts a great many of the Petersfield clubs and societies who hold their meetings at the pub in Sheet. They almost certainly enjoy the family atmosphere provided by Colin Baker and his son Paul. Both are chefs, and when one of them is cooking the other is front of house.

Colin acquired the Half Moon four years ago. "I found this pub and bought it for me and my son," he said. "We try to serve traditional British food, on tables with tablecloths.

Local people seem to like this approach and that's why the Half Moon has become a meeting place for people – especially the over 50s. "We are also at the crossroads of Hampshire. On Sundays we can get more than 100 people for lunch."

The Half Moon is a big pub which dates from the 18th century when it belonged to Edward Patrick, a brewer. It has a large garden and a conference area. Now the restaurant has been refurbished, Colin hopes to attract wedding receptions as well as more people for Sunday lunch.

Meanwhile Colin has another pub, the Southsea Marina which is run by his wife and daughter. "Petersfield is for the men, and Southsea for the women," Colin jokes.

The Queens Head, Sheet

Jonathan Berry has found a new home for himself and his family at the Queens Head in Sheet. A much-travelled local pub proprietor and manager, he was born and brought up in Oxenbourne, East Meon, and started his career in local pubs at the Cricketers in Steep in 1996. He has had fruitful associations with the George and later with the Square Brewery and the Black Sheep pubs.

The chance to take over the lease of the Queens Head came in June 2012 when he was approached by Enterprise Inns. So Jonathan (left) and his business partner, Daniele Oliva (the chef), took charge, serving Italian food and a range of special beers, such as Palmer's Copper Ale and Penny Ale, their own brew made by Wells and Young. The Queens Head stages events such as music evenings, an outdoor cinema and a regular Hallowe'en evening in late October as well as hosting functions such as weddings, parties and business meetings.

The building dates back to the 17th century and was rebuilt in the early 1800s. The former London to Portsmouth road used to go right past the pub. The huge tree outside it was planted for Queen Victoria's Jubilee in 1897.

The Old Drum

The oldest surviving pub in Petersfield, The Old Drum in Chapel Street is a pub of two halves. There is a Tudor side, recently dated to around 1580, and a high-ceilinged Victorian addition.

Recently in danger of being demolished for housing it has been lovingly restored and brought back to life by the present landlords Simon and Suzy Hawkins (above)and their partners Robin and Be Canty, not forgetting Digby (right) the pub dog. Decades of brewery neglect was stripped away to reveal Tudor beams, working fireplaces and tongue-and-groove ceilings.

Once the haunt of H. G. Wells, whose mother was in service at Uppark, The Old Drum is now thriving. It has a delightful garden at the back – a quiet haven and, when there is good weather, it is a fantastic sun-trap. The bed & breakfast side of the business is booming with two quiet, luxuriously refurbished rooms in the Tudor side of the pub. There are plans to extend the pub further and include more bedrooms for which there is a pressing demand in Petersfield.

The ethos of the business is to buy as locally as possible and thereby support local businesses. The owners have a nine-acre smallholding which they use to produce their own pigs (for home-cured bacon and hams, sausages and roasts), apple and pear juices, and goose eggs. The pub was recently awarded Silver in The Beautiful South Awards for the best pub in the South-East, a plaudit which was gratefully received as recognition for what they are trying to achieve.

The Square Brewery

The Square Brewery is a traditional town pub, which has stood in the centre of Petersfield for more than 200 years. The pub, which serves freshly prepared food and five cask-conditioned beers, is also known as a 'home of live music in Petersfield'.

The high quality live acts seen and heard at the Square Brewery on Wednesdays and Saturdays cover a wide range of genres – rock, pop, jazz, blues, folk, and country. There are practice sessions upstairs for local bands.

Gemma Watts (general manager) and her husband Cliff (the chef) have worked together for 10 years, first for Gales, then Fuller Smith & Turner (Fullers), who acquired Gales. Their previous pub was the Chairmakers at World's End, near Denmead.

"a great high street pub for locals"

"We want to maintain the Square Brewery's reputation as a great high street pub for locals, serving great food," said Gemma, who grew up in Clanfield. And Cliff adds: "My job is to produce good home-made food on the premises and sourced locally."

The pub is open from 10am, and food is served until 4pm. Wednesdays feature steak nights at two-for-the-price-of-one. Beer-battered haddock and chips are served all day Friday, and Sunday starts with a breakfast club until noon followed by a roast menu until 4pm.

The Cricketers Inn, Steep

The Cricketers' attractions include a gastro pub, 10 letting rooms, a 50-seater restaurant with a wood-fired oven, and outside space for 50 extra covers. The new styling has brought a change of emphasis, and their farm shop sells their own bread and produce from the village gardens and allotments. They have been working with other local food producers of cheese and preserves.

The owner of the Cricketers Inn is a personal friend of Terry Galgy, the current tenant, who moved to Petersfield two years ago. Terry explains: "I was staying with family in Hambledon when I received a phone call from my friend in Switzerland asking me to advise him on what he should do with the Cricketers Inn, as many tenants had passed through its doors." He visited the Cricketers in November 2011, when it was particularly cold, and he was not impressed. "Initially it never entered my mind to take on this pub," he recalls, "but I wanted to come back to England and it seemed to answer the call."

" a vibrant, warm and friendly family pub where visitors can feel at home"

Set in the South Downs National Park and next door to Bedales, the Cricketers has been transformed into what Terry Galgy calls "a vibrant, warm and friendly family pub where visitors can feel at home for a relaxing drink or a good meal with friends".

The Red Lion

Dom Humphries has been the landlord of The Red Lion since it was acquired by J D Wetherspoon and reopened in 2010 after a £3.5 million refurbishment. The pub has a distinguished history, having had a previous life as a coaching inn, as a host to a brewery and as a hotel.

The aim for Dom is that the pub is "a place that encourages conversation". The Wetherspoon brand is famous for being the third highest coffee seller in the UK, having no music, and showing little television. Dom allows TV news when the Red Lion opens for breakfast at 8am, and also for rugby internationals. Having worked for Wetherspoon's for 15 years Dom knows and respects the brand, which has more than 950 pubs, 34 hotels and continues to expand.

The Red Lion serves four guest beers as well as local brews from Ballards and Langhams. The menus are partly specified from HQ, although Dom has some freedom to plan for specials and themed evenings (from grills on Tuesdays to fish and chips on Fridays). The pub stays open until 11pm, and 12.30am on Fridays and Saturdays.

A large establishment covering 3,000 sq ft, with seating for 120 people, the Red Lion has a staff of 30 (23 full time) to match its size. Local organisations, such as the Royal British Legion, hold their regular meetings there.

"There are still places to hide away and put the world to rights over a drink, which is how it should be and what some people want," said Dom, who lives in the town and has been active in the local area as chairman of the Association of Petersfield Businesses for the last two years.

Did you know?

Petersfield Pubs
Petersfield is well-known for its good range of pubs and there are seven* in the centre of town today – with plenty more close by.

In the 19th century Petersfield had some five breweries: Walter Seward brewed at the Royal Oak in Sheep Street; Willam Fitt at the Market Inn; and there was a brewery behind Moreton House in the Spain. Then Amey's (on the industrial estate now occupied mainly by Littlejohn) opened in the 1880s and lasted until the 1950s. Their estate had some 20 pubs.

** The Black Sheep, The George, The Good Intent, The Folly, The Old Drum, The Red Lion, The Square Brewery*

The Red Lion was once a celebrated coaching inn on the road between London and Portsmouth. An alehouse is recorded on the site from the early 17th century and, in 1734, it was acquired by John Jolliffe when it was described as "the Red Lion, lately built, formerly the Sun Inn". The present façade of the main building dates from a modernisation about 1790.

By 1818 the freehold was held by William Jolliffe, and from about 1828-1880 the Red Lion and

The Harrow Inn

The Harrow Inn, one of Petersfield's most celebrated pubs, is a unique family-run 17th Century village hostelry. Set in the Hangers of Hampshire, it offers a range of ales, hearty home-cooked food and a warm welcome throughout the year.

The Harrow has been in the same family since 1929. It is now run by two sisters, Nisa and Claire McCutcheon, (right) both of whom were born and brought up there. Their mother fought and won a well-supported campaign to prevent local council demands for modernisation – and the story can be read in newspaper cuttings round the bar.

The Harrow serves a range of great local beers in the old-fashioned way, straight from barrels behind the bar. The food is legendary for its quality and the size of the helpings. There are huge ploughman's lunches (including home-cooked ham) which would fill the bellies of a whole team of ploughmen and, in winter, you can enjoy their famous soup.

" a unique family-run 17th Century village hostelry"

The two bar areas are best described as 'cosy' but there is plenty of room outside where you can enjoy the sun in the summer. The Harrow is a great stopping-off point for walkers on the Hangers Way. In fact, it is an easy walk from the centre of Petersfield, and there are few traditional pubs like it still operating in the UK.

the Dolphin were under the same licensees, mostly members of the Crafts families, who also were associated with the Railway Hotel and the Harrow. In the late 19th century, the Joliffes sold the Red Lion to Lukers, who built a brewery beside the inn with a huge tower on the corner of College Street and Tor Way. The brewery served eight Petersfield pubs – as well as the Red Lion they included the Dolphin, the Railway Hotel, the Harrow, the Jolly Drover and the Queen's Head in Sheet – and was a well-known landmark until it burned down in 1934.

The Square Brewery, which was first recorded in the 18th century operating under the Holland family, brewed its own beer until the early 20th century. Then George Gale bought the pub and closed the brewery. The pub used to be known as the Six Day House because it was open six days a week on the brewery's working days.

Did you know?

Breweries Petersfield is surrounded by a number of good local breweries. These include Ballards in Nyewood, Bowman Ales in Droxford, Flowerpots in Cheriton, Langhams near Petworth, and Triple fff in Four Marks.

Ballards Brewery is owned and run by Carole Brown, one the few female brewers in the country. Her former husband Mike founded Ballards in 1980. Brewing moved from the family farm in West Sussex to the Railway Inn at Elsted and, since 1988, the beer has been brewed in Nyewood. Head brewer Francis has worked at Ballards since 1981 with brews such as *Midhurst Mild, Golden Bine,* and *Wild*.

Bowman Ales is a micro-brewery based near Droxford. Since 2006 it has produced award-winning real ales such as *Swift One* and *Wallops Wood,* as well as *Quiver, Warbler* and *Nutz*.

The **Flowerpots** Brewery, at the pub of the same name, produces a wide variety of beers which have won lots of prizes, ranging from the regularly brewed *Perridge Pale* (3.6% ABV) to the popular *Flowerpots IPA* (6% ABV). The pub holds a beer festival every August Bank Holiday.

Owned and run by James Berrow and Lesley Foulkes, **Langham** Brewery in Lodsworth was established in 2005. The brewery expanded in 2014 and their award-winning beers include *Hip Hop, Halfway to Heaven,* and *Sundowner.* Visitors are always welcome and the annual Conker Competition celebrated its seventh year in 2014.

Triple fff has brewed many styles of real ale since it was founded in 1997 by Graham Trott, a cabinet-maker and home brewer. In 2012 Graham retired and handed over to Sara Carter. She is responsible for their current beers, with an output of 28,000 pints a week, including *Alton's Pride, Jabberwocky, Moondance*, and the aptly named *I Can't Remember* (6% ABV). Triple fff were voted supreme champions at the 2008 Great British Beer Festival.

Drinkers sampling the produce at Petersfield's Beer Festival in 2014

Annie Jones

Steve has run Annie Jones since 2001, inheriting a quality French restaurant and developing it into a multi-functional unit with three distinct areas: a high quality Anglo-French restaurant with a twist, a coffee shop and an open area for drinking and eating tapas, paella and sharing platters during the day and well into the evening.

Having grown up in the town and regularly eaten at the restaurant, Steve felt it had huge potential for further development and welcomed the opportunity to fulfil these dreams. It is this variety of locations and options, all linked by an ethos of service and customer focus, that gives Annie Jones a special place in the centre of Petersfield.

All the food is sourced locally – most of it from shops only a few yards away.

It is a common sight on a summer's evening to see guests tucking into huge pans of paella and enjoying the garden. The garden comes into its own in the summer when it is regularly packed with drinkers and eaters, and the heating of the outside area means that it is well used even in mid-winter.

" a welcome and ambience that is a bit Mediterranean"

As a Petersfield man through and through, Steve loves the fact that he can bring some of the buzz of the town into his back garden and offer a welcome and ambience that is also a bit Mediterranean.

Café Mezzo

Café Mezzo was established in July 2006 and is an independent family run café by Paresh and Jaineeta Pandya. "As a husband and wife we team we decided to open in Petersfield because we have always lived and worked around this area, which offers both beautiful country surroundings as well as a friendly local clientele. We both have a catering family background and were in Portsmouth before opening Café Mezzo. The name Mezzo means middle in Italian and hence we have a 'midday café'. Petersfield has a lot to offer and the success of our business has a lot to do with people who like Petersfield and describe it as a town with character and charm."

Their goal was to provide Petersfield with a café that provided hot food all freshly prepared to order, as well as a good cup of coffee in a relaxed family atmosphere. Since the opening of the café, the all-day breakfast at Mezzo has become famous with many patrons locally and from out of town. You can come to Mezzo for breakfast, lunch, tea, coffee or delicious free trade hot chocolate and a slice of cake, whilst meeting and chatting with friends and family. There is a good choice of lunch time food from warm French rustique sandwiches to pastas with home-made sauce, as well as Mexican quesadillas and various salads and side orders. All tastes are catered for!

Café Mezzo also takes pride in the coffee they serve and they only use coffee beans that are blended and roasted locally - delivered to order to ensure that the aroma and flavours are present in every cup of coffee they produce. Delicious smoothies & other cold drinks are also on offer.

Did you know?

Dolphin Court One of the town's major coaching inns of the 18th century, The Dolphin, eventually fell victim to Raglan Property Trust in the fateful 1960s, when Petersfield's High Street and Square were transformed by developers. Despite a long-running campaign to save the building - it had been successfully used as a Girls' High School from 1919 until 1961 – the Urban District and Hampshire County Councils approved the Raglan scheme to demolish it in 1965. Two adjacent buildings were razed simultaneously, a Victorian Post Office and an early 17th century family house, leaving the town with 'Dolphin Court' described by the campaigners as "a characterless slab of subtopian masonry" and by a local architect as "like a seaside marine building on an esplanade".

The Dolphin Hotel, 1916

Dolphin Court, 1966

Cloisters Café

With a prime location on a corner of the Square, Cloisters is open seven days a week, 8am to 6pm in summer, closing half an hour earlier in winter, and they aim to offer great food and excellent service. The manager is Jorge (George) Villalon, who is of Chilean origin but sounds as English as an egg, bacon, sausage and tomato.

George, who is a stickler for providing good service, admits, "It is a big commitment, but we are almost always very busy, especially at weekends. People take the trouble to book for breakfast on Sunday to make sure that they get a table."

They like to provide variety by changing their menus seasonally, and they offer outside catering, private parties and functions, such as birthdays.

Cloisters can accommodate 27 people inside and a lot more outside at the tables alongside the Square.

Previously George, who shares the catering with his brother Ricardo, worked at the Crab & Lobster in Sidlesham near Chichester. Having worked freelance at Cloisters for the previous managers, he saw an opportunity when the café changed hands two and a half years ago. Everything is sourced locally – including the staff – and the vegetables come from the Happy Cow in Lavant Street.

The Folly Wine Bar and Restaurant Upstairs

Looking down from the leaded windows onto College Street, the old main street of Petersfield, the Folly Upstairs restaurant is housed in the upper storey of an untouched early 20th century garage. The high-beamed roof reinforces a sense of space while retaining an intimacy that delights eaters and drinkers alike.

The restaurant's reputation is based on high quality and varied food, attracting new custom and retaining the loyalty of their locals and regulars. It is part of the local community, welcoming customers and supporting local businesses and suppliers with locally sourced and seasonal menus. The result is a friendly, family-oriented environment, where unpretentious and delicious food is very much the centre of attention.

"an intimacy that delights eaters and drinkers alike "

The restaurant has also regularly sponsored a team for the Rugby 7s, as well as providing pre-theatre dinners for many of the town's productions. The combination of the best of the old and the new produces great food and service, and serves as a fine advertisement for Petersfield.

JSW

JSW are the initials of Jake Saul Watkins, the restaurant's owner, who set it up in 2001. Jake was new to Petersfield, but not to the area. He was yet to find what Petersfield would hold for him.

Jake explains that "with a good degree of optimism and an enormous amount of hard work", he set out to establish JSW. Even though the restaurant started in a fairly humble site in Heath Road, it quickly began to acquire regular customers. People were thrilled to have food that was not only delicious but also reasonably priced, so they forgave the basic amenities and outside loos.

The restaurant gained a Michelin star within its first year and put Petersfield on the culinary map. The Michelin guide found that JSW was the smallest kitchen in the UK to gain a star!

In 2006 Jake moved to larger and more prestigious premises in Dragon Street, an old 17th century coaching inn that had seen better days. Jake says: "One of the highlights for me, in terms of being part of Petersfield, was getting recognition, and commendation by the Petersfield Society, for the conservation of the building. This meant a lot to me."

Jake is proud and confident that JSW has become an important part of Petersfield, bringing new "foodies" to the town.

La Piazzetta

Set in a charming Grade ll listed 16th century building overlooking the Market Square, and only five minutes walk from the station, La Piazzetta blends traditional Italian cooking and a cosy, rustic ambience. Established in 2006 by two brothers, Nasa and Bekim Shillova, both of whom are energetically involved in their enterprise on a daily basis, this independent and family-owned restaurant was named Petersfield's Best Restaurant in 2011 and again in 2014, and highly commended in 2012 at the *Life in Petersfield* Awards.

Good food at reasonable prices is the key to this establishment, open seven days a week, which serves a range of contemporary dishes and adventurous combinations.

Agnieszka Studzinska and Bekim Shillova

Fresh produce, locally sourced, is used in their pizzas, made with fresh dough. Main courses include veal with wild mushroom sauce and truffle, or Hampshire fillet steak with peppercorn sauce. The menu includes an impressive selection of wines imported from Italy.

Bekim says they love being in Petersfield – "there is such a good community atmosphere here and, although there may be something like 50 places to eat in the town, we know we are different".

Nasa Shillova with two customers

Did you know?

"The Donkey Cart"
The prime position of this medieval house indicates its owners' importance in the town. In 1591, it was occupied by Thomas Osborne, later to become Mayor of Petersfield. In medieval times, it directly overlooked the Square, with its "shambles" (individual market stalls), whose owners held the right to vote in Parliamentary elections.

Within living memory of Petersfield's older inhabitants, it was the workshop and gallery known as "Number One, The Square", run by Flora Twort and her artistic coterie from the 1920s until the 1950s. The old name of "The Donkey Cart" derived from its owner's mode of transport from his house on Oakshott Hanger to Petersfield.

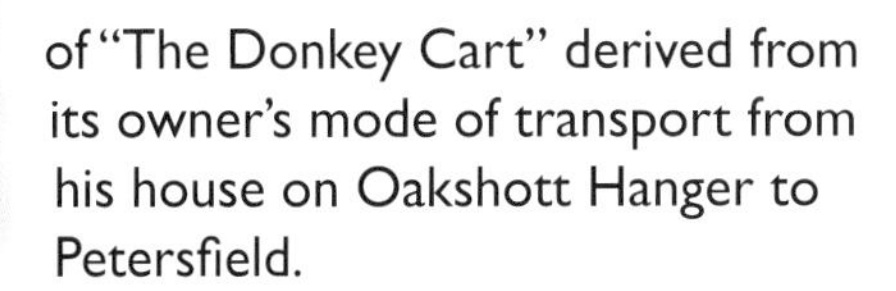

Langrish House

Langrish House is a small country house hotel run by Nigel and Robina Talbot-Ponsonby (below), with a historic past and a reputation for fine dining. It has been home to Nigel's family for more than 150 years.

Built in the 17th century, Langrish House was one of the few Roundhead strongholds in the county during the Civil War. The villagers of Langrish were supporters of Oliver Cromwell, and Royalist prisoners from the nearby Battle of Cheriton in 1644 were imprisoned at the house.

For many years the house was owned by wealthy sheep farmers who used the lake for washing the wool. Then, in 1842, Nigel Talbot-Ponsonby's great-great-great-great-grandfather, bought the house and made major additions to it.

Nigel's father, Edward, inherited the estate in 1937 when he was 19 and, fascinated by machinery, he turned the stables into a factory. By the start of the Second World War the factory was busy making cockpits for Spitfires, and munitions for the war Effort. Later they made steel moulds for the nose cone of Concorde and, as a fine testament to Edward Talbot-Ponsonby, his factory was recognised as one of the finest small engineering works in the world.

The house was sold in 1972 and later was partially destroyed by a devastating fire. It was then bought and restored, and turned into a hotel. By chance, Nigel and Robina, were given the opportunity to buy back the house in 1998, since when it has been home to the seventh generation of Talbot-Ponsonbys.

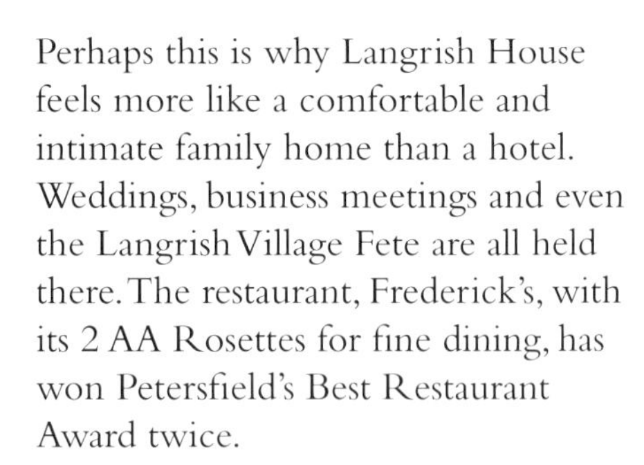

Perhaps this is why Langrish House feels more like a comfortable and intimate family home than a hotel. Weddings, business meetings and even the Langrish Village Fete are all held there. The restaurant, Frederick's, with its 2 AA Rosettes for fine dining, has won Petersfield's Best Restaurant Award twice.

Lemongrass

Lemongrass manager, Sawad Pimpeuk, is delighted with the restaurant's situation in Dragon Street – he finds the town peaceful (no rowdy late-night discos!) and his clientele very appreciative of the Thai cuisine he offers, thanks to his old friend and chef, Wilairat.

With other branches in Horsham, Chichester and Rustington, Lemongrass feels very "local" and their "signature dishes" of rib-eye steaks, stir-fried dishes, lemongrass and seafood have drawn highly favourable comments on Trip Advisor. With such a setting as the old 16th century timber-framed building and its tasteful Thai interior decor, who could fail to be captivated by the experience? Parties and weddings have enjoyed the exotic Asian ambiance – and even the takeaway service is popular with more casual customers.

"Who could fail to be captivated by the experience?"

Petersfield has an enormously wide variety of eating establishments – and Lemongrass must rank among the most exotic and stylish of them all.

The Malabon

The Malabon opened in Petersfield in 2009 – their sister restaurant had been in Liss since 1985, although the Malabon is a separate entity. They chose the town because so many of their customers at Liss came from Petersfield and they saw an opening for a high quality Indian restaurant.

They reckon their special features are the quality and variety of the food - it's not just the standard curry or balti: the atmosphere they create, and the friendliness of their welcome and service is key. Many of the ingredients are sourced locally and they aim for the highest quality.

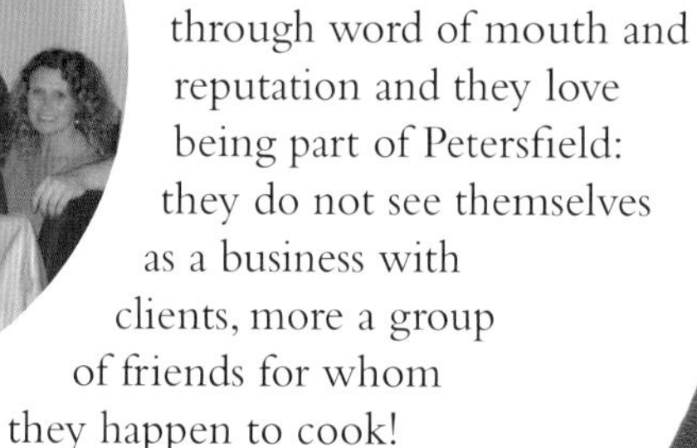

Malabon supports Petersfield Football and Rugby Clubs. The Round Table meets there every two weeks and they support their charitable activities as well. Their business has grown largely through word of mouth and reputation and they love being part of Petersfield: they do not see themselves as a business with clients, more a group of friends for whom they happen to cook!

Did you know?

Dragon Street is sometimes referred to as the first Petersfield by-pass, as it was constructed in the 17th century to allow traffic heading for London or Portsmouth to avoid the town centre.

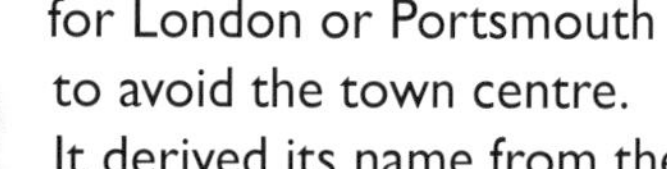

It derived its name from the major coaching inn, *The Green Dragon,* situated where Wild Damson now stands on the west side of the street. In the 18th century, the inn transferred to the east side, in what is now the premises of the JSW restaurant.

Nearby is Dragon House, the elegant Georgian private house, once the home of the Green Dragon's maltster and brewer.

The Natural Apothecary

Owned and run by mother and daughter Carmen and Olivia since 2012, this café and health shop in Heath Road specializes in healthy and innovative food and drinks served in an attractive apothecary-style environment. It is in Heath Road (where JSW once was).

Olivia is a qualified Nutritional Therapist, and the shop section offers a range of nutritional supplements, food, and beauty products, and personal advice as needed.

"The Apothecary was the place to go for libations, curatives, elixirs and potions to help soothe your ailments in the olden days, so we chose this theme for the shop and café," said Olivia. "Of course many of those old potions contained chemicals that did a lot more harm than good, so our customers will be pleased to hear that we don't apply any of those techniques in our kitchen!"

Instead customers can expect healthy breakfast options, simple, interesting and filling lunches, and a daily special, as well as home-made cakes, most of which are gluten-free, coffees and a wide range of teas. Their flowering teas, which bloom in the teapot, are very popular. There is also a wide selection of smoothies and juices that must be made fresh to order because, as Carmen explains, "a juice needs to be consumed immediately before it oxidizes and loses its nutritional value".

Olivia says: "Our customers are simply wonderful and their support has helped make us what we are today: many of them have become good friends. And of course the entire team here at The Apothecary is our greatest asset. Petersfield has such a wide choice of eating establishments so we know that, to be competitive, we must deliver 100% excellence every day."

The Plump Duck

In just over a year, Ian Baker has turned a neglected and dilapidated building in the splendid surroundings of Petersfield Lake, into a vibrant, booming and award winning business. The people of Petersfield obviously agreed with his vision and voted The Plump Duck Café of the Year.

Offering all forms of refreshments, coffees, teas and light meals, Ian has an increasing band of loyal regulars, from fishermen and rowers, joggers and walkers, with and without dogs, to parents bringing their children to the adjacent play area.

With all-weather seating and a brand new covered area, customers can enjoy the view and ambience come rain or shine, along with the locally sourced produce. Plans are already in place to offer bistro style evening meals.

Ian sees himself as blessed by being part of the close-knit community of Petersfield, by the friendliness of his regulars, and by the view from his office window every morning. And who can argue with him?

Schools

Churcher's College

Headmaster Simon Williams with young rugby enthusiast

Just as Petersfield has evolved over the years, so has Churcher's. The last three decades have seen dramatic changes: from an all-boys, boarding school of some 400 pupils to a fully co-educational day school with nearly 850 pupils in the Senior School and 230 in the Junior School in Liphook.

The expansion has been driven by the ever-increasing popularity of Petersfield as a commuter town, and also by a widening catchment area, embracing people from the west, the Farnham area, and north of the Hindhead tunnel. The educational journey for Churcher's students leads them on to some of the most competitive universities in the country.

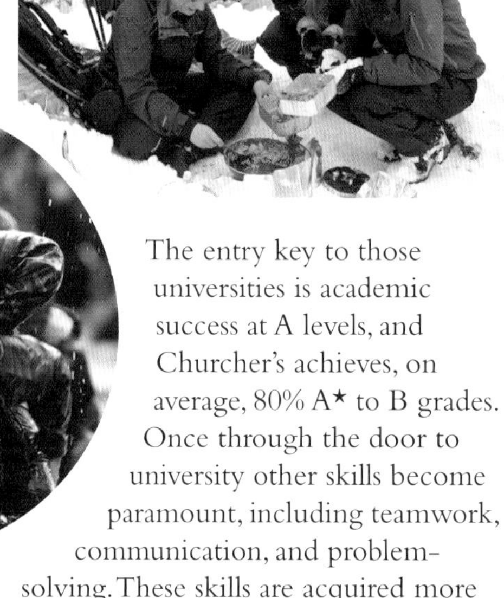

The entry key to those universities is academic success at A levels, and Churcher's achieves, on average, 80% A* to B grades. Once through the door to university other skills become paramount, including teamwork, communication, and problem-solving. These skills are acquired more readily outside the classroom than in, which explains why Churcher's extra-curricular programme is so extraordinary.

The Combined Cadet Force, ever-present since 1905, continues to flourish and is part of an adventurous training programme which sees over 400 enrolled on the Duke of Edinburgh Award Scheme each year. An annual expedition for the Year 9 (aged 14) goes to the Atlas Mountains, the fjords of Norway, and the glaciers of Iceland. And a biennial, senior expedition has seen students on challenges such as paddling dug-out canoes on the rivers of the Amazonian rainforests, tramping through the Himalayas, and climbing from the savannah to the top of Mount Kilimanjaro in Africa.

Exceptional involvement and extraordinary quality in music sees Churcher's involved in supporting many worthy causes in Petersfield and beyond. The prize-winning art in the school graces public galleries well beyond the town's boundaries. Drama, performance, and sport also reach very high levels.

Herne Junior School

In July 2014 the SATS results put Herne Junior School in the top 5% of schools nationally. "Ofsted graded the school as good (in 2013) and recognized the excellent work we have achieved," said Tony Markham, the Headteacher. "We are not perfect but, like all successful schools, we aim to listen to our children, parents, staff and visitors so that we can constantly improve what we provide to our community."

Herne is larger than most junior schools, and it is set in several acres of landscaped grounds "giving space for creative, play, sports, exploration, special reading areas, and adventure". And the school is ambitious, with a £500,000 plan for 2015 to extend it to 16 classrooms.

Headteacher, Tony Markham

The school sees itself as 'firmly in the 21st century'. There are interactive computer whiteboards in the classrooms, a wireless network, and Kindles to promote reading. A new Radio Station launches in 2015. Children can access a range of facilities as well as ICT – a library, music room and a cooking area.

Educational trips, which rely on voluntary donations by parents, take the children to places like Butser Ancient Farm, the British Museum, Weald & Downland, South Downs Planetarium and Ironbridge. They have received the Active Mark for exceptional PE, won Hampshire football competitions, and competed nationally in motor racing and trampolining events. They have awards for international work with UNICEF and The British Council.

"Our challenge at Herne is to make sure that we give each and every child a chance to succeed," Tony Markham adds. "We pride ourselves on being a friendly place where young and old really matter. Last year (2014) we have changed our vision to 'Knowing Every Child – Inspiring Every Mind'. It is our personal challenge that we get to know every family too."

Petersfield Infants' School

The school is a large four-form entry infant school in the centre of the town. This location enables the school to complement many curricular activities with hands-on experiences, which is a key aspect of its philosophy and ethos. The original building is dated 1894 and still exists within today's more modern structure.

Petersfield Infants' School offers all the facilities of a modern school, while retaining many of the more traditional and endearing qualities of the old. The school promotes very high expectations of both achievement and behaviour and is graded outstanding by Ofsted. The curriculum is delivered through a topic-based approach, with literacy and numeracy addressed as separate subjects.

Linda Lee, the Headteacher, says: "Themes are carefully planned to allow for the children's natural pleasure in, and enthusiasm for, practical experiences, their love of investigation and their need to acquire skills, both physical and mental. The skills of working together as a team, and the skills of cooperation and leadership, all add to the completeness of the learning process. The curriculum is tailored towards real life experiences, wherever possible.

Every year, the school steps away from the formal curriculum to immerse the children in focused study experiences. Recent events have included Future Olympians, Sustainability, Performing Arts and Super Citizens.

Linda Lee (left) adds: "The central town location enables the school to maximize the potential of visits to the church, library, heath, lake, local shops and restaurants. In this fast moving, ever-changing world of the 21st century, our children not only become literate and numerate, but they are also able to think for themselves; weigh up evidence and make judgements; care for and about people and things. The school also firmly believes in a strong home-school partnership. Many parents and members of the local community come and work in the school with us to support the children's learning. We think Petersfield Infant School is a very happy place to be!"

The Petersfield School

Officially an 'outstanding Academy' The Petersfield School was awarded Ofsted's highest grade in 2010 and converted to Academy status the following year. "Our standards are always well above average," says Principal Nigel Poole (right). "Our aim now is to move from 'outstanding' to becoming a World Class Academy.

"There is a happy atmosphere and the school is the sort of place where, despite its size, youngsters of every talent and aptitude can thrive and blossom." The strengths of an Academy, he adds, are that it can offer a full range of subjects. "Yet we strive to know every individual well. Classes are kept as small as possible."

The brochure states that the school "stands for traditional values, such as excellent behaviour, courtesy and uniform, but delivered within a dynamic, innovative and warm-hearted context. Every visitor comments favourably on our students' behaviour and attitudes." Outdoor education is another important part of the school's activities, and in

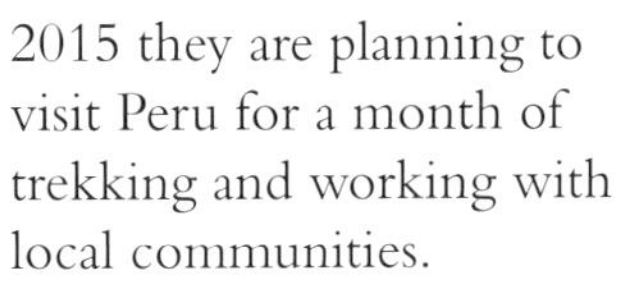

2015 they are planning to visit Peru for a month of trekking and working with local communities.

This 'school with a heart' also has The Studio, opened in 2005 and a great resource for students and for the local area. "The Studio@TPS allows us to work closely with professional performance companies to inspire our students to greater involvement and provide quality experiences within our community." Visiting performers have included English National Ballet, Hull Truck Theatre Company and The Watermill Theatre. The Studio@TPS also serves local community groups and charities as a venue for hire.

The school has been honoured in recent years to have been asked to design the Mayor's official Christmas card. Students have always been extremely enthusiastic

and inspired to enter this competition. Entries have varied from photography to animation and fine art drawings and paintings. The standard has always been high and it has often been a struggle to choose an overall winner.

THE PETERSFIELD SCHOOL

Did you know?

Churcher's Old College This iconic Georgian building in College Street was built in 1729 under the will of Richard Churcher as a school for 12 boys trained in the mathematics of sea navigation with a view to their joining the East India Company.

In the 19th century, more boys were admitted and the curriculum expanded to include the preparation for trades useful to a small, predominantly agricultural, country town like Petersfield. However, living and working conditions in the building were deteriorating, so the Churcher Foundation decided to purchase land at the top of Ramshill, and the new (present) College was opened there in 1881.

The Old College building was taken over for commercial use, then became a private property, was transformed into a hotel in the 1930s and, finally, was a local outpost of the Hampshire County Council.

It has now reverted to private use and serves primarily as a family residence.

Bedales Schools

Bedales comprises three schools: Dunannie (ages 3–8), Dunhurst (ages 8–13) and Bedales itself (ages 13–18), all of which sit within their 120 acre site in Steep village.

The vision of Bedales' founder, John Badley (right), was to create a school which would be profoundly different from the public schools of his day. From 1893, when Bedales began, there was a determination to shape the school around what was considered best for the individual child's educational welfare and happiness. Two strands predominated: breadth ("head, hand and heart") and the cultivation of the individual's intellectual and personal qualities ("intelligence, initiative and individuality").

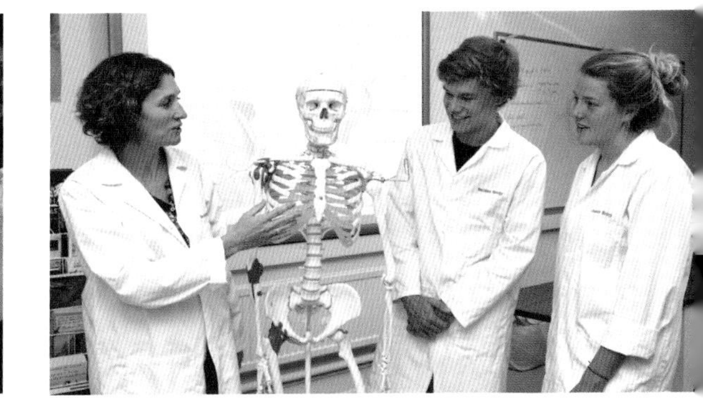

Many of Badley's early innovations are now mainstream: co-educational boarding; the emphasis put on the Arts, Sciences and voluntary service; the importance of pastoral care; and listening to students' views.

The schools' aims include the development of inquisitive thinking with a love of learning and independent thought; the enabling of students' talents to develop through doing and making, including activities such as Outdoor Work; fostering individuality and the encouragement of initiative and creativity; taking pride in the community's distinctiveness and fostering interest beyond the school both in the local community and in national and international awareness. These aims are clearly demonstrated by the students' achievements in all fields.

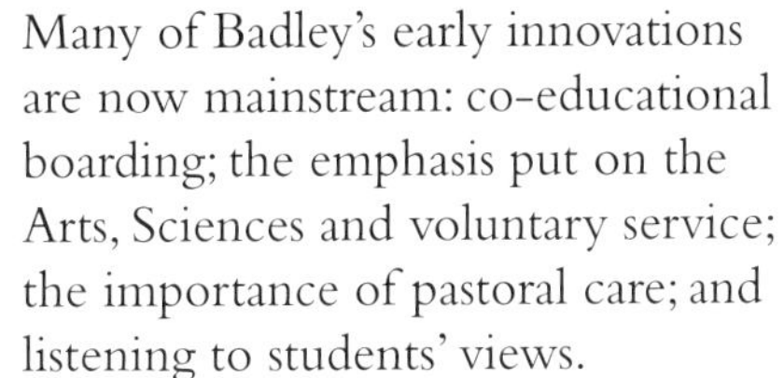

Academic successes are in A levels and the Bedales Assessed Courses, designed as an alternative to GCSEs, and also in the very high quality theatrical, music and artistic performances and exhibitions.

The capacity of Bedales students to think independently and creatively, and to deliver strong A Level grades makes them attractive to a broad range of top universities. Bedales students have a reputation with universities for their independence of mind and have frequently offered unusual academic and personal profiles in their applications for a diverse mix of Oxbridge, Russell Group universities and art colleges. Bedales students therefore arrive at a similar place to those in more formal education settings. They have just taken a different route.

Ditcham Park School

Sitting majestically on top of the South Downs, surrounded by farmland, fields and woods with spectacular views south across the Solent, Ditcham Park is a highly successful independent day school for boys and girls aged 4-16 years. Their mission is "to provide outstanding educational opportunities within a wonderfully supportive and inclusive atmosphere which inspires all of our pupils to tackle new challenges with enthusiasm and confidence."

"Through excellent pastoral support and outstanding teaching our pupils develop a love of learning and achieve success in a wide range of challenging and rewarding academic subjects and extra-curricular activities," says Andrew Rowley, the Head Teacher. "Although not highly selective, the school is immensely proud of our pupils' GCSE results each year, where excellent performance, significant 'value added' and achievement to full potential across the full ability range and beyond is a treasured characteristic of the school's success."

The results over the last 10 years have been consistently impressive with the school near or at the top of the Hampshire GCSE League Tables (Top in 2011 and 2013). These enable each of their pupils to leap confidently into their sixth form A level studies and beyond.

Sport and Leisure

Nomads Badminton Club

Nomads Badminton Club started in the early 80s and has been successfully run by Pat Stocker as the club Secretary and Richard as club Treasurer since 1987. Over the years the club has seen many new faces come and go, and some that just won't leave! In recent years the club has had an average of 25 members per year ageing from 18 to 65. They mainly play doubles and mixed doubles games, with occasional singles games when the numbers allow.

Club nights are held at Bedales School (where they have access to 7 badminton courts) on Wednesdays from 9pm and last for 1½ hours. Having so many courts means that most members play badminton for the whole session. Being a friendly club, some members usually have an after-session drink at one of the local pubs.

Starting in 2015 Nomads are planning to hold an annual tournament, where members are paired randomly and have to play all other teams, accumulating as many points as possible to win the tournament.

Nomads Badminton club is a social club and plan to have one or two social events every year, including the regular Christmas meal and some members host barbecues during the summer months.

Nomads always welcome new members to join the club: all that they ask is that players have a basic understanding of the rules and are able to play to a reasonable level. For a comprehensive view of what Nomads Badminton club has to offer, please see the website for details.

Did you know?

Petersfield-born Calum Chambers hit the newsstands all over the world when he was signed by Premier League football club, Arsenal for £16 million in 2014. Ex-Churcher's College student Calum had joined the Southampton FC academy as a teenager and played in Saints' first team in 2013-14, before moving to Arsenal. Having had a great first season with them, he's also had his first call-up for England, joining Roy Hodgson's squad for a friendly against Norway. He's received high praise from both his manager, Arsène Wenger, and many ex-professional footballers, as well as being voted Man of the Match on more than one occasion by the Arsenal fans.

Petersfield Badminton Club

Petersfield Badminton Club has existed for around 50 years. At its peak, the club made full use of all 7 courts at Bedales School, and had to introduce a waiting list limiting membership to 70. At that time, Petersfield was one of the top clubs in the Alton & District Badminton League, winning most League and Cup competitions over a number of years. Although numbers are now much reduced, recent mergers with Sheet and Liss Badminton Clubs have maintained a competitive core of players and the continuation of a league team in Portsmouth & Havant League.

The club's decision to switch to the Portsmouth & Havant League was in part due to a preference for playing in larger multi-court sports halls, which means that most matches finish in well under two hours. Previously, matches in small one-court halls often continued beyond midnight – and it was quite common for shuttlecocks to hit the low roof beams, sometimes to the advantage of the home team!

Membership is open to anyone over 16 years of age who can play to a reasonable club standard. Club members are affiliated to Badminton England, and are therefore able to access benefits, together with the facilities of the National Badminton Centre in Milton Keynes. The club is very pleased to see a recent increase in younger players, some of whom have taken advantage of local coaching initiatives to progress to a club standard.

Although the main league season runs from October to April, most members choose to play all year round. Club sessions are on Monday evenings at Petersfield's Taro Centre, playing doubles with feather shuttles. Some members choose to finish the evening with a light refreshment at a local hostelry. The club is always keen to welcome new members.

Petersfield Squash Club

Squash is an all-year round sport for anyone and the Petersfield Squash Club (PSC) is well known for friendly members of all ages and standards. As well as Tuesday evening social squash, and Sunday coaching (junior and adult) sessions, there are several annual club tournaments as well as social events including a dinner dance with club Trophy presentations, bicycle treasure hunts, summer barbecues and pub-quizes.

PSC has been established for over 30 years, based at The Taro Leisure Centre. PSC has seven teams in the Hampshire Leagues, and is one of the few clubs in Hampshire that has an annual European Tour to compete in international tournaments.

PSC is proud of their bi-annual charity events and contributions, supporting Children in Need in conjunction with The Taro Centre, even appearing live on the BBC show. Their main sponsor is Morgan Owen & Coates optometrists in Lavant Street.

Petersfield Bowling and Snooker Club

Established in 1908, the club – located almost invisibly in St Peter's Road - has been described locally as 'The Hidden Gem' as it has never been obvious to passers-by but is well known to people for its central location in the heart of the town. The club maintains a warm and friendly atmosphere, which has no doubt contributed to its success over the years. It currently has over 200 members.

It has a well-furnished bar area, a full-sized bowling green with four rinks, and two high-quality full-sized snooker tables. Bowls is played from the end of April to September.

Matches usually take place on weekend afternoons, and regular Three Counties leagues take place every Tuesday evening.

The snooker section has four teams taking part in the Midhurst & District Snooker League on Friday nights through the autumn and winter.

On Tuesday evenings, the club also operates a "3 Reds" handicap knockout which has been popular for over 30 years now, giving all standards of player a fun evening.

The club also boasts some superb modern kitchen facilities, providing support to its bowls and snooker teams when they host matches against rival clubs. It is also now used for the club's busy social events.

Did you know?

Parkrun is an international group, funded by sponsors, that organise free, weekly, 5km runs around the world. They are open to everyone, free, and are safe and easy to take part in and take place in pleasant parkland surroundings – since 2014 there has been a Parkrun at the Queen Elizabeth Country Park. People of all ages and ability are encouraged to take part: from those taking their first steps in running to Olympians, and from juniors to those with more experience.

There is a run every Saturday morning at 9.00am at QE Park with approximately 60 people taking part. The runs are timed and, once a runner has registered, personal records can be tracked on Parkrun's website.

Petersfield Cricket Club

The key objectives of Petersfield Cricket Club are to provide opportunities for young cricketers of all standards to reach their potential, and encourage adults of all abilities to play the game. In 2014 Petersfield Cricket Club fielded five men's senior teams, three competitively in the Hampshire Cricket League (HCL) on Saturdays, one friendly team in Sunday matches and one team in the Ashurst midweek league. One ladies' side played in the Hampshire Cricket League.

Petersfield CC 1895

Petersfield CC Ladies 1895

For colts, the club runs seven boys' sides and one girls' side, from Under 7s to Under 15s. Older colts who have reached the required standard also play in the senior sides. During the winter one senior and two colts teams play the South East Hampshire Indoor Cricket League. There are coaching sessions for all ages, indoors in winter and at the grounds in summer.

Founded in 1751, the club has a long playing tradition and a very picturesque location on the Heath supplemented by a second ground at Penns Place. Recent awards include: in 2013 the HCL award for the most improved ground at the Heath, promotion for the 1st XI and 3rd XI, and the U9A and U15B won their leagues; and the club was voted the EHDC club of the year in 2011.

An English Cricket Board Focus Club and members of the Hampshire Cricket Board, it is run by a large team of volunteers – committee members, groundsmen, umpires, scorers, coaches, those organising social events, and others just helping out when needed. The club is friendly and family-orientated, sometimes with whole families involved as players and volunteers.

Petersfield Town Football Club

Petersfield Town, the town's senior football club, ended a 30-year wait for silverware when they won the Wessex League Division 1 title in April 2014. It was a season full of records for the team, which plays its football at the Love Lane stadium. There were record runs in two cup competitions, three club record victories, 40 goals for top scorer Robbie Tambling and an ending to the campaign full of silverware and promotion.

A season of celebration has followed decades in the doldrums for the club, which was established in 1993. This followed the demise of Petersfield United FC – which was established in 1889 and enjoyed a period at the higher levels of non-league football in the 1980s.

The club adopted a new nickname in 2013 – the Rams was chosen for its historical links with the town of Petersfield. The players proudly sport the town flag on the sleeve of their shirts.

Petersfield Town Juniors Football Club

There are now 32 teams run by Petersfield Town Juniors (PTJ) from Under 8s to Under 18s, and had for the first time in 2013-14 a senior team made up from players that have come through the junior system. There is also a thriving girls section competing from U10 to U16 age groups.

PTJ was formed in 1975 by John Wood. He and another parent David Martin, who were both involved in Cub football, realised their sons were becoming too old to play and needed a club. They set to work establishing the first team of under-12s, with fixtures being played on The Avenue playing field.

In 1980 the growing club moved to new pitches at the Penns Place playing fields, which included facilities for four changing rooms. This was followed in 1989 with the Town Juniors moving to their current home at Love Lane. By 1999 a new building had been built with six changing rooms and a small hall, and remains the home to most of the junior teams to this day.

From its modest beginnings, PTJ are now a FA Community Chartered Standard club, offering the ability to play football to over 500 local children in both a competitive and inclusive environment. The current Chairman is Nick Orr, with Vice Chairman Lee Lloyd and Secretary Julie Butler.

Petersfield Golf Club

Petersfield Golf Club is owned by its members. Currently there are over 700 members made up of full playing members, five-day members, intermediates and juniors. In addition there are social members who use the clubhouse to meet, eat and play bridge.

The gently undulating 18-hole course is 6,437 yards long, and it meanders its way through delightful countryside with some outstanding views. With greens designed by the US Golf Association and free-draining fairways, it offers all-year-round play and a true test for all levels of golfer.

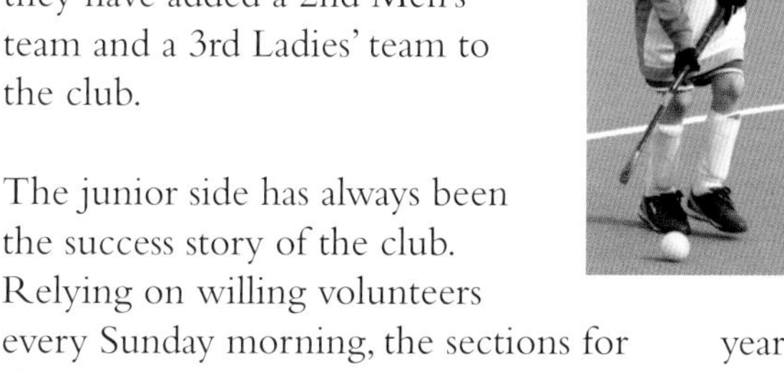

The club was founded in 1892 and until 1997 was based on the Heath in Petersfield. The Adhurst course at Tankerdale Lane was built in 1995, and opened for play in March 1997, with the new clubhouse opening soon afterwards. The Pay-and-Play course in Sussex Road is associated to it.

"The modern and spacious clubhouse has superb views from every window, with an extensive balcony overlooking the 18th green," says operations manager Shaun Manning. "The facilities and the excellent cuisine enable the club to offer exceptional value for society and corporate golf days. The club is now firmly established in its new surroundings and, with an abundance of trees and hedgerows, it looks and plays like a mature golf course."

Petersfield Hockey Club

Formed in 1950, Petersfield Hockey Club (PHC) has risen to the challenge after London 2012. For the season 2014/15 they have added a 2nd Men's team and a 3rd Ladies' team to the club.

The junior side has always been the success story of the club. Relying on willing volunteers every Sunday morning, the sections for the minis (under 8 and 10) and juniors (aged 10-16) have grown to 250 children. The level of coaching provided is significant and better qualified than ever and, in March 2014, the U8's won Gold medals at the prestigious John Wright Tournament.

The club has been bolstered by new blood in the last four years, and the rewards have been reaped in the last two years. The men's 1st XI have won back-to-back promotion going 37 games, and more than a calendar year, undefeated. They have also won the Hampshire Open League Trophy in 2014.

The Vets team has been transformed and has become more than just a fun forum to play with like-aged folk. Now the squad is bulging and the results are impressive: third in the league in the first year after promotion to Wessex Masters Division 1. Even the hitherto invincible Chichester Vets have been defeated in their own backyard. The two Ladies' teams are bolstered by juniors coming of age and ladies returning to hockey after absences of up to 20 years! There are four U15 girls in the Hampshire squad.

Ideally, PHC say, Petersfield should consider having the major sports clubs under one roof.

Petersfield Mountain Bikers

Started in March 2007, Petersfield Mountain Bikers provide an online social network for riders based in and around the local area to chat about and organize rides. The club does not have organised events or a formal structure but rather a gathering of people who like riding bikes off-road.

The network caters for riders of all ages and abilities (minimum age 13) and any member can post up a ride where they would like others to join them. Typically there are two or three rides posted each week and they aim to ride all year round. All rides start from Petersfield Square.

Currently the network has about 280 members, with a core group of 20 or 30 who ride regularly. New members are always welcome and, if you are just venturing into the world of mountain biking, the online forum is a great place to get impartial and local advice about routes, bikes and anything bike-related.

They run introductory rides, suitable for all abilities, from time to time depending on demand. Also each year there is a fancy dress Christmas Eve ride which usually attracts about 30 riders.

The online forum and website are managed by Paul Burt with the overheads covered by about 20 patrons so that membership is free for everyone else.

Out-Fit

Out-Fit sessions are structured outdoor 'boot camp' fitness classes, designed and taught by Bruce Alexander – a former Royal Marine and celebrity Personal Trainer. The 60-minute full body workouts are challenging and fun, and take place on Petersfield Heath on Saturdays, and Monday and Wednesday evenings, throughout the year, come rain or shine.

They are a combination of functional exercises (using your own body weight) and cardiovascular (increasing the heart rate), designed to get the optimum fat burn and toning workout. To help people get the most out of the sessions, they also use a 'colour fitness indicator' system. This involves wearing one of three different colour wristbands that indicate a beginner, intermediate or advanced fitness level.

Fitness assessments are carried out every three months, the results of which suggest the wristband colour and the intensity and difficulty of the exercises performed. Bruce says: "We don't just say you'll get fit, we prove it. No two classes are the same at Out-Fit. It's never boring and, unlike other fitness classes, there's no hiding at the back! As it takes place on the Heath, there are no sweaty gyms and changing rooms – just lots of fresh air and a duck or two."

Body Conditioning

Barry Carter, the man behind Body Conditioning, has lived in or near Petersfield for most of his 31 years. He went to school in the town, and then to university in Chichester. Being passionate about sport as he grew up, choosing a career in sport and fitness was an obvious choice. He has a degree in Sport and Exercise Science, and a Masters in Biomechanics.

He trains his private and corporate clients either at his own studio near town, or at their home or place of work in and around Petersfield. But it isn't all about pumping iron and calorie-counting. Barry has a holistic approach to fitness and believes that his clients' nutrition, exercise and lifestyle requirements are as individual as they are.

His aim is to encourage his clients not to look for a quick fix solution, but to incorporate a better understanding of healthy living. "You need to assess all aspects of clients' lives to create an effective plan," says Barry. "If you are not assessing, you are guessing."

His strong belief is that improving people's understanding and awareness of how to live a healthy lifestyle creates sustainable change and long-term results. "The most important thing," he says, "for people who have never given much thought to their diet and their fitness is to know that it's never too late start."

Petersfield Rugby Football Club

Petersfield 1st XV 2014

Above: *One of Petersfield's Mini Rugby Teams*

In the 2014/15 season Petersfield's 1st XV moved into Hampshire League 1 having been crowned Champions of League 2 in 2013/14, and the club ran three Senior teams plus Veterans and Colts teams, as well as training and fielding some 400 junior players from its Youth and Mini sections.

The highly successful inauguration of a focused Youth Academy in the previous season continued this year, as will the provision of year-round Touch Rugby sessions open to all. Through all of these opportunities the club continued to prove its place as a community asset, providing rugby opportunities for all ages and abilities. To show that it was not standing still, the club approached local schools to help and encourage them to develop a formalised schools rugby programme and provided resources and facilities throughout the year to get teams to play together on a regular basis.

The club has looked to build on last year's tournament success at London Irish, Winchester and Overton for the mini ages – U7 to U12 – which enhanced and added to the Youth team successes of the U13s (Hampshire Vase Winners), U15s (Hampshire Shield Runners Up) and the U16s (Hampshire Shield Winners).

After once again providing a safe venue for county and club competition through the 2013-14 winter which caused many clubs to shut down, the club's fantastic facilities at Penns Place have continued to be recognised as a safe place to host important games and tournaments. The club was hoping to improve last season's statistics when more than 4,000 people visited it, as well as the 800 people who enjoyed the fine dining delights of 1st XV pre-match lunches.

Petersfield 1st XV 1929

Formed in 1927 Petersfield RFC has come a long way since the early players pulled on the red and white shirt and did battle with teams around the county. The club is in rude health, providing the community with first class rugby and social facilities.

Did you know?

Flying international winger Fiona Pocock played rugby for Petersfield minis from the age of 6 to 12, and then the under 16 girls' team at 13. She was selected for the England Under 19 team at 17 before representing the full England XV in the 2010 Women's World Cup.

Taro Leisure Centre

With more than 350,000 visitors a year, the Taro Leisure Centre in Penns Place is undoubtedly the most popular indoor leisure facility in Petersfield. "It's a good community hub," says the manager, Chris Gallagher.

In 2014 the Taro celebrated its 40th anniversary, in a year when its owners, D C Leisure (which assumed management of the facility in 1997), were renamed Places for People Leisure (PFP) Ltd. The Taro has a wide range of facilities for a wide range of people of all ages and all abilities, with an inextricable mix of fun and fitness, and of leisure and pleasure. As well as the central four-lane pool, there is a health suite with a spa pool and steam and sauna rooms for relaxation.

The sports hall holds a variety of activities, from badminton and squash, to basketball, netball and volleyball, as well as gymnastics, karate and tai chi, and indoor archery and trampolining. The fitness and training area provides 105 stations, and the increasingly popular spinning sessions on cycles.

Children are catered for with swimming academy courses, parent and child swim sessions, and an adventure zone. The academy attracts 700 young users aged 2 to 12. And there are programmes and easy accessibility for disabled users.

There is social table tennis and short tennis, and a 'strong and steady' programme for senior users. Wayne Devonald provides physiotherapy and Loretta Burden runs Beauty Matters.

Many clubs use the Taro, home to Petersfield Squash Club and the training venue for the Rugby Club. "Health and fitness are not just about swimming," says Chris Gallagher, who has a staff of 100, full- and part-time. "I have seen a lot of changes in my five years at the Taro and a major investment in the pool, the gym and the changing facilities."

The Taro has introduced recently a wireless wrist-band system for swimming and gym based workouts which monitors and records members' use of the facilities in terms of data for time, endurance, level and cardio-vascular effectiveness.

Petersfield Triathlon Club

Petersfield Triathlon Club (PTC) was formed in 2010 by four local sports enthusiasts. The club has since grown to 120 members, ranging in age from 21 to 63 (with expansion to juniors, aged 8-16 in 2015). They cater for everyone from complete novices to those who compete in triathlon/duathlon for GB in their age group.

The club organised the first Petersfield Triathlon in 2012 to encourage people into the sport and to support local charities. The third annual event in September 2014 attracted over 300 entrants and raised £3,500 for Fitzroy, the national charity based in Petersfield which supports people with learning disabilities. The triathlon was supported by over 50 volunteers from the local community who marshalled the swim, bike and run courses.

The club organises weekly swimming (from September to July at Churcher's College) with sessions alternating between technique, endurance and open water skills. Cycling includes a weekly Saturday cycle ride of approximately 25 miles with routes including many of the local hills! In the summer months the club runs a timed 10-mile ride. Running training is in association with a local running club and there are some coached sessions as well as cross-country runs. The welcome and support for new members are exceptional and swim training sessions are regularly fully subscribed.

The club supports members in becoming qualified triathlon coaches and referees. Club members compete in triathlon and duathlon at local, national, European and world level, at distances from Sprint up to Half and Full Ironman. Local cross-country and cycling time trial events are also supported.

The youth section is led by an experienced triathlon coach who is also the young person's coordinator for Triathlon England's South Central region. In 2015 there is a full programme of junior coaching, training and competitions.

PETERSFIELD TRIATHLON CLUB

Bedales Olivier Theatre

Bedales Schools in Steep are renowned for their arts, drama and music productions, many of them centred in the Olivier Theatre, their award-winning timber-framed structure, finished in 1996.

Co-educational from the start in 1893, Bedales' founder J H Badley wanted the school to be different and to educate the whole person – 'head, hand and heart'. The arts have always been well-supported, and the long list of famous former pupils includes Lily Allen, Sophie Dahl, Daniel Day-Lewis, and Roger Lloyd-Pack.

The theatre offers a full programme of school productions and concerts combined with lively touring theatre, the best in modern jazz, exciting contemporary dance, distinguished classical recitals and poetry readings, and folk blues from the U.K. It has variable stage configurations, with 250-340 seats.

There is free admission to school concerts and school productions, and all exhibitions. Ticket prices for the professional programme aim to promote accessibility wherever possible. There is disabled parking - reserved spaces opposite theatre entrance – and free off-street parking.

Did you know?

The annual Petersfield Shakespeare Festival celebrated its third successful year in 2014 with performances of 'The Merry Wives' and 'Macbeth' in July. Run by Bedales, PSF was founded by Jay Green who was Head of Drama and Head of Sixth Form between 2010 and 2014.

Open-air performances are set in front of Bedales' historic Sotherington Barn on a gentle grass bank. While the company perform al fresco, the audience is covered. There are no seats so people bring their own rugs, seats, and picnics, although there is a bar and light refreshments. The Festival, which Stephen Fry called "a marvellous place to see a marvellous thing", features professional actors from across the UK. The next Festival will be in 2016.

Lion and Unicorn Players

Lion and Unicorn Players celebrated its Silver Jubilee in 1984, gave its 100th production in 2008, and reached its Golden Jubilee in 2009. The Group is fortunate, unlike most 'Am Dram' companies, in having at least as many men as women acting members, and membership is growing. As well as keeping the support of long-standing members, the group continues to attract new and talented people.

Formed in 1959 by a small group of people with a passion for drama, the Players' policy has been to stage good plays of depth and quality from the beginning. Whether they were tragedy, comedy or, occasionally, farce, nothing should be so lightweight that it did not repay the time and effort put in by both actors and audiences.

Playwrights performed over the years have included Shakespeare, Shaw, Ibsen, Christopher Fry (who personally attended several of the Group's productions of his plays), T S Eliot, Arthur Miller, Charles Williams, Noël Coward, Tom Stoppard, David Hare, Robert Bolt, J B Priestley, Harold Pinter, Peter Shaffer, Alan Bennett and Alan Ayckbourn. The Group prides itself on the high quality of its sets and costume designs, both of which have attracted their own accolades. Lion and Unicorn Players came first and second in the final Petersfield Drama Festival.

While most productions have been staged in Petersfield's Festival Hall, the group has also appeared in St Peter's Church, in the intimate surroundings of the Studio at The Petersfield School, and has toured two highly successful productions round the villages of East Hampshire. Each tour culminated in the atmospheric and mysterious space of the Great Round House at Butser Ancient Farm.

Petersfield Theatre Group

"Let's go on with the show" is a line from Irving Berlin's *There's No Business Like Show Business* which sums up the Petersfield Theatre Group (PTG). The company gathers twice a week to prepare, rehearse and present musical theatre, in all its forms. Formed in 2008 from the merger of the Petersfield Operatic Society and Petersfield HiLights, PTG boasts an impressive pedigree of 80 and 40 years respectively from the former societies – a 120 year-old new-born you might say!

The age range of members goes from mid-teens to mid-70s and most get involved in some capacity in most shows – whether it is acting, dancing, backstage, costumes, props or front of house. Although the Group is essentially amateur, it is a source of great pride that a number of former members have progressed to careers in the professional theatre both in the West End and elsewhere. We provide theatrical opportunities to young actors too: the former Petersfield Junior HiLights Society became the acclaimed Petersfield Youth Theatre.

Local personalities feature in our activities; some years ago our then Vice-President would attend all our productions despite his busy film and stage commitments. His name? – Sir Alec Guinness! Recently PTG staged the musical version of *Goodnight Mister Tom*, from the novel by award-winning local author Michelle Magorian. She developed a great interest in our production, attending a number of rehearsals and offering her expert guidance to members of the cast.

The Festival Hall is PTG's spiritual home, but the group does venture elsewhere. We have performed on the back of a lorry in the *Petersfield Festivities*, sung in St Peter's Church and were delighted to be invited to provide the entertainment for the opening concert of the 2011 *Petersfield Musical Festival.*

The Group has been the recipient of a number of Accolades of Excellence awarded by the National Operatic and Dramatic Association - testament to its high performance standards.

With an exciting and varied programme of future productions in the pipeline, PTG will continue to 'strut our stuff' to allow Petersfield people to see top-class musicals, from operetta to classic musicals and more modern productions.

Winton Players

Petersfield's Winton Players is a busy dramatic society with a wealth of talent of many different hues: those who like to act and appear on stage, and those with skills in set design, construction and painting, stage management, costume design, lighting, sound, music, dancing and administration. Every production depends on the support of a large happy team on stage, backstage and Front of House to make the magic happen.

Miss Joan Sare formed the Winton Players in 1947 and initially trained and produced them. Members were drawn mainly from the YMCA mixed youth club. Their rehearsal rooms were in Winton House in the High Street, hence the name of the group. Now 67 years and almost 200 productions later, it is an independent society, registered as a charity, with over 100 members aged from 7 to 80. Three main productions are performed each year: a traditional pantomime in January and plays in Spring and Autumn as well as an evening of one-act plays in the summer and several social events in between.

The Winton Players have their headquarters in Sheet, next to the Half Moon pub. It is partly a 17th century barn which has been extended and converted over the years, and is affectionately known as 'The Hut'. In former ownerships, The Hut has been a coachman's cottage, a breeze-block factory, and, in World War Two, it served as a factory making aeroplane parts. The ravages of time and weather caught up with it a few years ago and extensive repairs and renovations were necessary, at the cost of some £26,000, The money was raised in only 18 months, thanks to the generosity and hard work of members, neighbours and friends to whom the Players will be forever grateful.

At The Hut, members meet for rehearsals and social events, to build scenery and props and to service the extensive wardrobe. With the Annual General Meeting each July, members meet approximately every 10 weeks to discuss items such as future productions. Junior members enjoy a monthly club evening. Each year a proportion of the annual profit is donated to local charities of the members' choice. In recent years, these have included The Kings Arms, The Rosemary Foundation, Friends of Petersfield Hospital, and Canine Partners.

Petersfield Youth Theatre

Petersfield has a flourishing and highly successful theatre group, dedicated to providing opportunities for young people to take part in plays and musicals and to learn theatre skills. PYT (Petersfield Youth Theatre) pushes the boundaries of theatre for young people, offering experiences of the highest possible standard and challenging them with such demanding productions as Les Misérables, Miss Saigon, Cats and West Side Story.

Young people are encouraged to develop their teamwork and communication skills as well as self-discipline, thereby building their self-confidence. All who have taken part in any way have very much enjoyed and greatly benefited from the experience.

Founded in 1990, PYT now has over 260 members with ages ranging from 5 to 25. It is a registered charity with the aim of advancing education in music and theatrical arts among children and young people. The company is run mainly by volunteers who employ theatre and education professionals to direct productions, workshops and projects. It also benefits from the generous sponsorship of its corporate patrons.

Their first permanent home in Petersfield was found in January 2011 and is called 'The Space'. This coincided with the Youth Theatre's 21st birthday year when they were lucky enough to be awarded a 'Jubilee People's Millions' Grant which enabled them to renovate and fit out the building. The Space now houses their ever-growing wardrobe of over 1,000 costumes, with offices, meeting-rooms, and a rehearsal space available for hire by the local community.

As the membership of PYT has grown, so has the variety of its activities. There is now a high quality range of activities throughout the year based on theatre skills. As well as the Autumn Season and Christmas Production, there are workshops during the Spring and Summer terms. In addition there is an annual Easter Project open to non-members as well as members, which usually takes the form of a challenge to produce a piece of musical theatre in four days to perform to family and friends. A Summer School provides further opportunities for members and non-members to build on their theatre skills.

Petersfield Youth Theatre

Young People

Petersfield Air Training Corps

1927 (Petersfield) Squadron Air Training Corps, under the command of Flight Lieutenant Danny Croft RAF, and Flying Officer Lawrence Hughes RAF, is a lively, active group, one of 24 squadrons within Hampshire and the Isle of Wight. Meeting twice each week throughout the year, with many optional weekend activities, it provides a wealth of opportunity for young people aged 13-20. The early weeks of cadet experience are full of activity, from grappling with the intricacies of drill to the finer points of ironing meticulous creases in the correct place on a uniform.

Activity is the word which defines cadet life and this includes target shooting, swimming, and classification training covering everything from the principles of flight to the structure of a jet engine. Fieldcraft training provides the chance to develop leadership skills and acquire expertise in map reading and outdoor survival.

Most cadets seize other opportunities with both hands! Chances to fly in RAF aircraft are the high points of squadron life, most recently in Chinooks. Petersfield cadets have been awarded flying and gliding scholarships and can regularly be found working for Duke of Edinburgh Awards. Week-long residential camps on RAF bases are popular, with opportunities to experience service life at first hand in the UK, Cyprus, Germany and Gibraltar. Cadets have travelled as far afield as Australia and the United States on the International Air Cadet Exchange programme.

Cadets are committed to Petersfield life, regularly providing stewarding and marshalling services at community events, with the seasonal Waitrose bag-packs proving particularly popular with local shoppers. The Squadron joins other uniformed movements at the annual Remembrance Day Parade.

The core aims of ATC are to foster a spirit of adventure, to develop qualities of leadership and citizenship, to provide training useful in either service or civilian life and to promote an active interest in aviation and the RAF. These values are embraced by the amazing young people who form 1927 (Petersfield) Squadron and the community can be justly proud of the part which the ATC plays in Petersfield life.

Petersfield and Liss Girl Guides

In Petersfield and Liss (now classified as a District) there are 2 Rainbow units (5 to 7 year olds), 4 Brownie units (7 to 10 years olds), 4 Guide units (10 +) and a Senior Section unit all of which have a good number of girls in them.

In 2014 the Brownies celebrated 100 years of Guiding and in April 70 girls went to PGL on the Isle of Wight - getting 70 on a ferry did not prove to be too much of a challenge, though the size of the party came as a bit of a shock to other fellow passengers. The Rainbows - the youngest members – had a day at Paultons Park in June.

The units in Petersfield and Liss offer their girls lots of opportunities and challenges that they would not normally undertake, such as international trips, canal boats, trip to Cadbury's World, as well as the usual sleepovers and camps.

The girls are also encouraged to help with local events and, for example, some guides helped out at Petersfield Stamp Auction Day in 2014.

They are very proud to report that some of the Guides have worked towards and completed the Baden Powell Challenge, this award being the highest award that a Guide may achieve, and it can be used as a credit to her on a CV if applying for jobs etc. Older girls may work towards their Gold Duke of Edinburgh award and the Queen's Guide Award.

Festival for Young People

'What do you think of young people?' This was a question put to older people in Rams Walk. Answers ranged from 'out of control', to 'our future'.

'What do you think of old people?' was a similar question put to students from five local schools. 'Grumpy', 'intolerant', 'kind', were some of the answers. In both situations, when the responses were analysed, only 30% were positive.

Festival for Young People (FfYP) believes this is an accurate reflection of our society as the elderly and the young appear disconnected and unable to communicate. As a registered charity they are dedicated to doing things for young people that are not being done by other groups such as scouts and girl guides.

Activities have ranged from sending youngsters to 'Meet the Royal Marines' to organising Art & Craft Exhibitions in the Festival Hall to show off work from local schools: 20 schools took part in 2014. FfYP have sent young people to sea in Tall Ships and to the Calshot Sailing Centre, organised a Saturday morning film club and set teenagers a challenge to ride the South Downs from Winchester to Eastbourne in three days.

Funds have been raised for the Skate Park at Love Lane which the Council were forced to close in 2006 for safety reasons – it was reopened in 2010 when use immediately exceeded all expectations. FfYP are currently seeking to double its size so those confined to wheelchairs or with special learning difficulties can use it.

FfYP is also working on a plan to build a new Community and Youth Centre on the Love Lane Recreation Ground, to be known as 'The CTG Centre' (Connecting the Generations). They would welcome more ideas for activities, volunteers to help, and financial support.

Festival for Young People

Skate Park at Love Lane

In 2006 a hole in a wooden half pipe and a rotting safety barrier at the Love Lane skate park forced the Town Council to remove the structure and consider a new facility. Festival for Young People (FfYP) became involved in the design, planning permission and fund-raising for a new skate park. A Lottery Grant was obtained but this had to be spent before the full design costs could be raised so a decision was made to build in two phases. Construction of Phase 1 was completed in 2010 and has proved to be immensely popular.

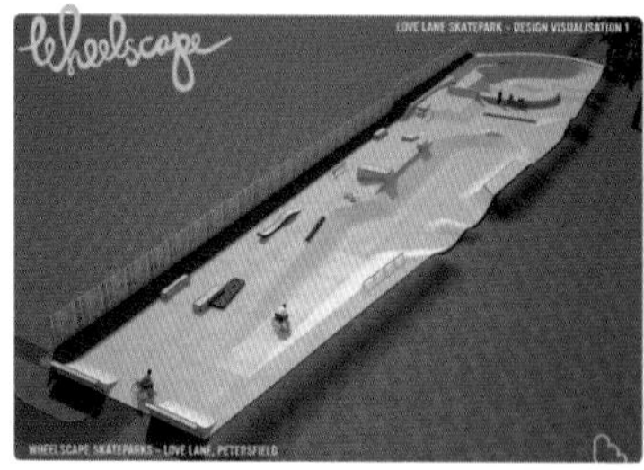

Phase 2 of the park which has been designed for wheelchair and other disabled users

This success prompted FfYP to seek an expansion of the original plan and to consider the legacy of the Paralympics. The Town Council has agreed to double the size of the current park and for the expansion to be specifically designed for use by wheelchair and special needs users. It will be the first such facility in the UK.

Two sisters raised £140 for Phase 2 of the park which has been designed for wheelchair users and other disabled people

Kings Arms Youth Project

The Kings Arms Youth Project has reached thousands of young people locally since the charity first opened its doors in September 2001. Originally set up by local churches, this valuable and sustainable resource has become the biggest of its kind in the area.

It aims to provide the environment and encouragement to bring out the best in young people. Working alongside young people the Kings Arms helps them to develop their potential in life – to take ownership of the club and grow to meet their changing needs. Young people set their own code of conduct, which inspires their adherence.

Left: *Management team - front row (l to r): Meg Lacklison, Caroline Lacklison (operations manager), Mandy May Back row (l to r): Ralph Buckingham, Shelley Brill, Megg Black, Annemarie Woods, Aaron Carr*

There are lots of fun things to do: art and craft, games, cooking, Wii, X-box, table tennis, pool, café/bar, computers suite, graffiti, t-shirt printing, montage, badge making, quizzes, competitions.

The Kings Arms acts as a base for special programmes catering for the needs of young people. The youth centre offers: support for young carers aged 8 to 18 who care for a member of their family; clubs and activities for those with autism; a youth service for those who are NEET (Not in Employment, Education or Training); programmes for pupils who struggle with school or personal challenges. The project also runs open clubs for any young person to attend.

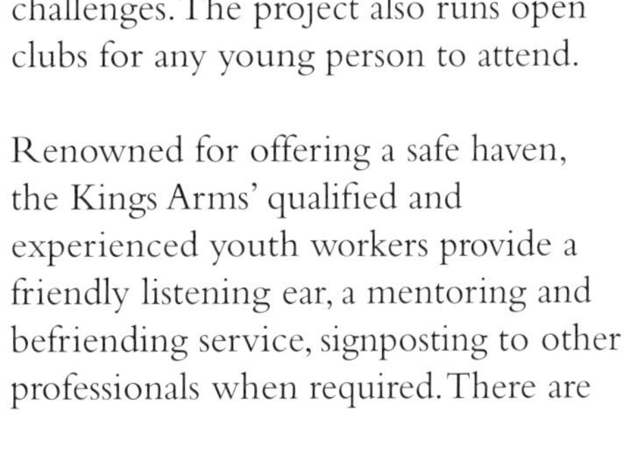

Renowned for offering a safe haven, the Kings Arms' qualified and experienced youth workers provide a friendly listening ear, a mentoring and befriending service, signposting to other professionals when required. There are opportunities for trying and learning new things in a positive setting.

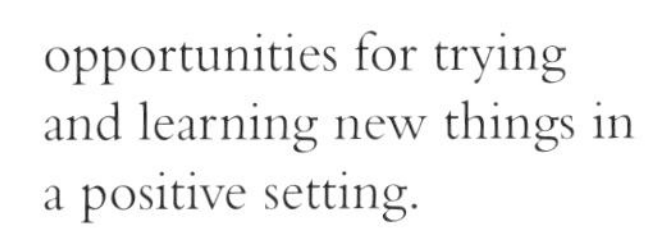

The local community shares responsibility for the care of their young people, by supporting the Kings Arms financially or by giving time and resources to the project.

Local participation is important, and the project is grateful to volunteers. Supporters include schools, councils, police, churches, local businesses and community members who recognise the valuable work being done.

The Petersfield Academy of Dance

Donna Lee Claffey says, "Our aim at PAD is to teach children to dance in a fun and friendly environment and inspire in students a love for dancing and performing."

The Academy has pupils from 3 years through to adults and Donna and her dedicated and experienced team offer ballet, tap and modern classes, as well as Hip Hop/Street and Contemporary dance. Students are prepared and entered for competitions and examinations with the Imperial Society of Teachers of Dancing (ISTD) usually after four or five terms of study. Children's Examinations have been devised to give them a sense of achievement: this is for children who dance for fun and children who may wish to make dance a career.

Classes are held in venues around Petersfield, Sheet, Steep & Liss and the PAD show is held at the Festival Hall. There is also a Summer School and workshops with guest teachers from the dance industry.

Among past students who have wished to pursue a career in dance, some have been accepted at top ballet and stage schools such as the Royal Ballet's school White Lodge, Laine Theatre Arts, Performers, Urdang, Bird, The Place and Masters. Students have also represented England and won medals at the Dance World Cup and the Tap World Championships. Others have performed or worked professionally in the industry in the West End and on cruise ships.

Many ex-students come back to teach or simply help out and give their enthusiasm and experience back to younger students and inspire them.

1st Petersfield Scout Group

The 1st Petersfield Scout Group has provided scouting activities to the local community since 1908 and is one of the oldest groups in the world. The group is an integral part of the Petersfield community, and the Beavers, Cubs and Scouts are involved in all sorts of community projects, from maintaining the Charlie Dickins Community Garden on the corner of Tor Way and College Street to entertaining local residents at the annual OAP Christmas party.

"The group is an integral part of the Petersfield community"

The team of voluntary leaders run weekly sessions for some 100 children aged 6 to14, working to fulfil scouting's aim of developing young people mentally, physically, spiritually and socially. Scouting helps children develop confidence, responsibility and self-sufficiency, and, by enriching their social skills, makes them feel part of their community.

The scouts regularly hike, camp, play wide games on the heath and learn skills such as first aid. They have recently enjoyed shooting, gliding, climbing, visits to the local emergency services and even a fascinating visit to the Chithurst Buddhist monastery. Many scouts are given the opportunity to try sailing in the summer after training from the Petersfield District Scout Sailing club. They have also raised funds to help one of the scouts to take part in the Hampshire contingent at the World Scout Jamboree in Japan in summer 2015.

The Pinewood Derby

One highly popular event over the past 10 years has been the Pinewood Derby: it is a series of model car races for different age groups within the District. Groups buy and make their own cars from wood-wheels-and-axles kits and race them around a 50-foot track in Churcher's College Sports Hall.

The event is locally sponsored and about 600 parents and competitors take part in the race day, which consists of speed trophy races and an F1-style Grand Prix.

Butserfest

Butserfest is a drug and alcohol free one-day music festival for young people which takes place in September in the Queen Elizabeth Country Park. There is no actual age restriction: many attendees are as young as 11, and many more are just young at heart!

The festival launched in 2007 in response to young people in the Petersfield area complaining that there was nothing for them to do. East Hants District Council and Southampton Solent University who organise Butserfest see the festival as an opportunity to impress on young people that they can have a really good time without alcohol and drugs. Its reputation as one of the best festivals for young people is growing year on year.

The Colles Trust

SPONSORS

The Petersfield Society is particularly grateful to these eight sponsors for providing generous support to this publication.

ACKNOWLEDGEMENTS & THANKS

EDITORIAL TEAM:
Nick & Geraldine Keith, David Jeffery, Peter Marshall, Sue McNaughton, Prue Scurfield

CO-ORDINATORS:
John Billington, John Callaghan, Gill Clarke, Bill Gosney, Jill Hancock, Phil Hooper, Isabel Hooper, Tony Struthers

DESIGN:
Neil Pafford, Carol Smith

Photography:
Graham Brown, David Jeffery, Peter Marshall, Chris Pearsall, Prue Scurfield
With special thanks to Michel Focard de Fontefiguieres

Acknowledgements to Henry Ascoli, Ineke Allez (*Barrows*), Ben Errey *(Festivals)*, Andrew Golden *(Petersfield Triathlon Club)*, Marianne Harris (*Butserfest*), Robin Hart (*Biodiversity*), Jonathan Harwood (*Vets*), Phoebe Hiscock, Tracey Howe (*Ramblers*), Andy Owen, Peter Sillick, Paul Soden (*Red Kite*), Tara Taylor, Wendy Wakelin, John Wigley (*Petersfield Orchestra*), Petersfield Photographic Society (*Music Festival*), the Petersfield Post and the Petersfield Museum.

We would also to thank other individuals and organisations who have generously allowed use of photographic material for this publication.

Above *(left to right): Neil Pafford, Nick Keith, Prue Scurfield, Peter Marshall, David Jeffery.*

Southern County Swimmer Adam Massey, carries the Olympic Torch through Petersfield in 2012

DIRECTORY A to Z

Petersfield Society: *www.petersfieldsociety.org.uk*

Architecture and Ambience

Petersfield Museum and Flora Twort Gallery: *www.petersfieldmuseum.co.uk*

Business and Industry

6a Vision: *www.6avision.co.uk*
Agincourt: *www.agincourtcontractors.co.uk*
Antrobus Accountants: *www.antrobus.co.uk*
Cluson Engineering Ltd: *www.clulite.cluson.co.uk*
Corrie, J. B. & Co. Ltd: *www.j.b.corie.co.uk*
Farrow Creative: *www.farrowcreative.co.uk*
Focard de Fontefiguieres, Michel: *www.focard.co.uk*
Kebbell Homes: *www.kebbell.co.uk*
Location Landscapes: *www.locationlandscapes.com*
RAK Ceramics UK Ltd: *www.rakceramics.co.uk*
Whitman Laboratories Ltd: *www.esteelauder.co.uk*

Charities

Artscape: *www.artscapeart.co.uk*
British Legion: *www. britishlegion.org.uk/branches/petersfield*
Fitzroy: *www.fitzroy.org.uk*
Friends of Petersfield Hospital: *01730 263423*
Home Start Butser: *www.homestart-butser.org.uk*
Lions: *www.petersfieldlions.org.uk*
Petersfield Outdoor Pool: *www.petersfieldpool.org*
Petersfield Voluntary Care/Winton House: *www.wintonhousecentre.org.uk*
Probus: *www.petersfieldsdprobusclub.co.uk*
Rosemary Foundation: *www.rosemary-foundation.org.uk*
Rowans Hospice: *www.rowanshospice.co.uk*
Save the Children: *www.petersfield-savethechildren.co.uk*

Churches

Evangelical Church: *www.petersfieldevangelicalchurch.org.uk*
Life Church: *www.lifechurchpetersfield.org.uk*
Methodist Church: *www.petersfield-methodist-church.org.uk*
Petersfield Area Churches Together (PACT): *www.pact.org.uk*
St. Laurence Catholic Church:
www.pact.org.uk/pact_churches-st-laurence_catholic_church.asp
St. Mary Magdalen, Sheet: *www.stmarymagdalensheet.org.uk*
St. Peter's Church: *www.stpeterspetersfield.org.uk*
Salvation Army: *www.pact.org.uk/salvation_army_petersfield125.asp*
United Reformed Church: *www.petersfieldurc.com*

Clubs & Societies

(PACS) Arts & Crafts Society: *www.petersfieldartsandcrafts.org.uk*
Beekeepers, Petersfield & District: *www.pdbka.org*
Petersfield Bridge Club: *www.bridgewebs.com/petersfield*
Petersfield Decorative & Fine Arts Society (PADFAS): *www.hantsiow.nadfas.net*
Petersfield Evening Floral Club: *www.nafas.org.uk/flower_club/Petersfield*
Petersfield Historical Society: *www.petersfieldhistoricalsociety.org*
Petersfield Philatelic Society: *www.petersfieldstamps.org*
Petersfield Photographic Society: *www.petersfieldphotographicsociety.org.uk*
Phoenix Stitchers: *www.phoenixstitchers.co.uk*
Pumpkin Growers Association:
www.facebook.com/PetersfieldPumpkinGrowersAssociation
Ramblers Association: *www.petersfieldramblers.org*
Twinning Association: *www.petersfieldtwinningassociation.org.uk*
University of the Third Age (U3A): *www.petersfieldu3a.org.uk*
Women's Institute (WI): *www.hampshirewi.org.uk/wi-page/petersfield-wi/*
Write Angle: *www.petersfieldwriteangle.co.uk*

Community

Association of Petersfield Businesses, APB: *www.petersfieldapb.co.uk*
Citizens Advice Bureau (CAB): *www.easthantscab.org.uk*
Community First HEH: *www.cfheh.org.uk*
Library: *www3.hants.gov.uk/library; 0845 603 5631*
Fairtrade: *www.fairtrade.org.uk*
First Friday: *www.first-friday.org*
Freemasons, The Lodge of Friendship: *www.lodgeoffriendship928.org.uk*
Petersfield Counselling Service: *www.petersfieldcounsellingservice.co.uk*
Round Table: *www.petersfieldroundtable.co.uk*
Shopmobility: *petersfieldshopmobility@gmail.com*
Stroke Support Group:
www.stroke.org.uk/support/petersfield-stroke-support-group
Tourist Information Centre (TIC): *www.visit-hampshire.co.uk*

Family Firms

Arnolds Optometrist: *www.rcarnold.co.uk*
Britannia Reeves: *www.reevesremovals.co.uk*
Burley & Geach: *www.burley-geach.co.uk*
Edward Barnsley Workshop: *www.barnsley-furniture.co.uk*
Frasers: *www.frasersformen.co.uk; www.frasersonline.co.uk*
Greys Coach Travel: *www/greyscoachtravel.net*
Jacobs & Hunt, Auctioneers:
www.jacobsandhunt.com; Estate Agents: *www.jacobshunt.co.uk*
Littlejohn Bathrooms Ltd.: *www.littlejohn.co.uk*
MacDonald Oates LLP: *www.macdonaldoates.co.uk*
Mackarness & Lunt Solicitors: *www.macklunt.co.uk*
Meon Travel: *www.meonvalleytravel.com*
Morgans Butchers: *www.morgansbutchers.co.uk*
Petersfield Linen Services: *www.petersfieldlaundry.com*
Picketts & Pursers Ltd: *www.pickettsandpursers-southampton.co.uk*
Rowswells: *www.mynewsagent.co.uk/7464/*
Rowland Son & Vincent Ltd: *www.rowlandsfuneralservices.co.uk*
The Forge: *www.petersfieldforge.co.uk*
The Petersfield Bookshop: *www.petersfieldbookshop.com*
Tews Engineering Ltd: *www.tews.uk.com*

Festivals

Hometown Festivals: *www.petersfieldfest.com*
Petersfield Food Festival: *www.petersfieldfoodfestival.com*

Folly Market
Chinwags: *01730 710038*
Curiosity Shop: *mycuriosityshop@hotmail.co.uk*
Dragon Treasures: *07810 184511*
Duncan Eves: *www.duncanevesjewellers.co.uk*
InzPired: *01730 261413*
Mooka: *www.mooka.co.uk*
Rainbows: *01730 269991*
Sweeney Plod: *www.sweeneyplod.co.uk*

Health & Welfare
Back2Health: *www.b2h.co.uk*
Beth Svarovska Pilates: *www.bethpilates.com*
Body Conditioning: *www.bodyconditioning.info*
Grange Surgery: *www.thegrangesurgery.org.uk*
Matheson Optometrists: *www.matheson-optometrists.com*
Morgan-Owen & Coates: *www.morganowencoates.co.uk*
Petersfield Hospital: *01730 263221*
Petersfield Pilates: *www.petersfieldpilates.com*
Swan Surgery: *www.swansurgery.co.uk*
Vets: *www.stpetersvets.co.uk*
Walking for Health: *www.walkingforhealth.org.uk/walkfinder*

Independent Traders
Duet: *01730 268100*
Fabric House: *01730 262262*
General Wine Company: *www.thegeneralwine.co.uk*
Handmade Happiness: *jenny-handmadehappiness.blogspot.com/*
Happy Cow: *www.thehappycow.biz*
John Peter: *www.johnpeterandcompany.co.uk*
Lavant Rowe: *www.lavantrowe.co.uk*
Mimosa: *sarah@mimosaretail.co.uk*
One Tree Books: *www.onetreebooks.com*
Petaprint: *www.petaprint.co.uk*
Petersfield Cobbler: *01730 266188*
Petersfield Photographic: *www.petersfieldphotographic.com*
Plumage: *www.plumageboutique.com*
Rama: *www.ramahairgroup.co.uk*
Review: *www.review-hair.com*
Rhona Russell: *www.rhonarussell.com*
Secret Garden: *www.secretgardenuk.co.uk*
Sue Johnson Interiors: *www.suejohnsoninteriors.co.uk*
Syn-Star: *www.syn-star.co.uk*
Tara Interiors: *www.tarawake.com*
Tiger Rose: *josie@tigerrose.net*
Tile Store: *www.the-tile-store.co.uk*
Vintage and Vogue: *www.vintageandvogueboutique.com*
White and Rees: *www.whiteandrees.co.uk*
Wild Damson: *www.wilddamson.co.uk*

Petersfield's Lanes
Ann's Prams: *www.annspramcentre.co.uk*
Bakery Lane Barber: *07841 697193*
Bonica: *www.bonica.co.uk*
Butterflies Lingerie: *www.suelovelingerie.co.uk*
Cute: *www.cuteshop.co.uk*
Dower's: *www.dowers-bespoke-interiors.co.uk*
Far Horizons Gallery: *farhorizonsgallery.co.uk*
Fez: *www.fezpetersfield.com*
Gypsy Kitchen: *www.gypsykitchen.co.uk*
Inside Out: *www.insideoutshop.co.uk*
Julie's Tearooms: *07874 263838*
Monoloco: *www.monoloco.co.uk*
Nutmeg: *www.nutmegretail.com*
Petersfieldtube: *www.petersfieldtube.com*
The Blacksmiths Daughter: *www.theblacksmithsdaughter.co.uk*
The Garage: *www.facebook.com/thegaragepetersfield*
The Sweet Stop: *thesweetstop@btinternet.com*

Markets
Farmers' Market: *www.hampshirefarmersmarkets.co.uk*

Music
Children's Choirs and Concerts: *www.childrensconcerts.org.uk*
Choir Company: *thechoircompany@gmail.com*
Community Choir: *www.petersfieldcommunitychoir.co.uk*
Gemini Consort: *ann.pinhey@gmail.com*
Just Sing: *www.sing petersfield@yahoo.co.uk*
Petersfield Choral Society: *www.petersfieldchoralsociety.org.uk*
Petersfield Music Festival: *www.petersfieldmusicalfestival.org.uk*
Petersfield Orchestra: *www.petersfieldorchestra.org.uk*
Southern Pro Musica: *www.southernpromusica.org*
The Petersfield Choir: *www.petersfieldchoir@gmail.com*

Nature & Environment
BioDiversity and Petersfield Nature: *01730 264182*
Community Garden: *www.goodlifecommunitygarden@wordpress.com*
Friends of Petersfield Heath: *www.foph.net*
Petersfield Physic Garden: *www.petersfieldphysicgarden.org.uk*
Rotherlands Conservation Group: *www.Rotherlands.org.uk*

Out of Town
Butser Ancient Farm: *www.butserancientfarm.co.uk*
Hangers Way: *www3.hants.gov.uk/longdistance/hangers-way*
Queen Elizabeth Country Park: *www.hants.gov.uk/qecp*
Shipwrights Way: *www3.hants.gov.uk/shipwrightsway*
South Downs National Park: *www.southdowns.gov.uk*
South Downs Way: *www.nationaltrail.co.uk/south-downs-way*

Petersfield Town Council and Festival Hall

Festival Hall: *www.thefestivalhall.co.uk*
New Savoy Cinema: *www.moviola.org/petersfield*
Petersfield Neighbourhood Plan: *www.petersfieldsplan.co.uk*
Petersfield Town Council: *www.petersfield-tc.gov.uk*

Pubs

Black Sheep: *www.theblacksheeppub.co.uk*
Cricketers Inn: *www.thecricketersinnsteep.co.uk*
Folly Ale House: *www.follydownstairs.co.uk*
George Inn: *www.thegeorgepetersfield.co.uk*
Good Intent: *www.thegoodintentpetersfield.co.uk*
Half Moon: *www.halfmoonsheet.co.uk*
Harrow Inn: *www.harrow-inn.co.uk*
Old Drum: *www.theolddrum.co.uk*
Queens Head: *www.thequeensheadsheet.com*
Red Lion: *www.jdwetherspoon.co.uk/home/pubs/the-red-lion-petersfield*
Square Brewery: *www.thesquarebrewery.com*

Restaurants & Cafes

Annie Jones: *www.anniejones.co.uk*
Café Mezzo: *www.cafemezzo.co.uk*
Cloisters Café: *www.cloisterscafe.com*
Folly Wine Bar: *www.follywinebar.co.uk*
JSW: *www.jswrestaurant.com*
Langrish House: *www.langrishhouse.co.uk*
La Piazzetta: *www.italian-restaurant-petersfield.co.uk*
Lemon Grass: *www.lmpetersfield.co.uk*
Malabon: *www.malabonrestaurant.co.uk*
Natural Apothecary: *www.thenaturalapothecary.co.uk*
Plump Duck: *quack@theplumpduck.co.uk*

Schools

Bedales School: *www.bedales.org.uk*
Churcher's College: *www.churcherscollege.com*
Ditcham Park School: *www.ditchampark.com*
Herne Junior School: *www.hernejunior.com*
Petersfield Infant School: *www.petersfieldinfantschool.co.uk*
The Petersfield School: *www.petersfieldschool.com/*

Sport

Bowling & Snooker Club: *www.petersfieldbowlingandsnookerclub.com*
Nomads Badminton Club: *www.nomadsbadminton.co.uk*
Out-fit: *www.get-outfit.co.uk*
Parkrun: *www.parkrun.org.uk/queenelizabeth/*
Petersfield Badminton Club: *www.petersfieldbadminton.co.uk*
Petersfield Cricket Club: *www.petersfield.play-cricket.com*
Petersfield Golf Club: *www.petersfieldgolfclub.co.uk*
Petersfield Hockey Club: *www.pitchero.com/clubs/petersfieldhockeyclub*
Petersfield Pilates: *www.petersfieldpilates.com*
Petersfield Mountain Bikers: *www.petersfieldmountainbikers.org.uk*
Petersfield Rugby Football Club: *www.pitchero.com/clubs/petersfield*
Petersfield Squash Club: *www.petersfieldsquashclub.org.uk*
Petersfield Town Football Club: *www.petersfieldtownfc.co.uk*
Petersfield Town Juniors: *www.petersfieldtownjuniors.co.uk*
Petersfield Triathlon Club: *www.petersfieldtriathlonclub.co.uk*
Taro Leisure Centre: *www. placesforpeopleleisure.org/centres/taro-leisure-centre*

Theatre

Bedales Theatre: *www.bedales.org.uk*
Lion & Unicorn Players: *www.lionandunicornplayers.co.uk*
Petersfield Shakespeare Festival: *www.petersfieldshakespearefestival.co.uk*
Petersfield Theatre Group: *www.petersfieldtheatregroup.org*
Petersfield Youth Theatre: *www.petersfieldyouththeatre.org.uk*
Winton Players: *www.wintonplayers.org.uk*

Young People

Air Cadets, Petersfield Squadron: *www. 1927squadron.org*
Butserfest: *www.butserfest.co.uk*
Festival for Young People: *gnwells@btinternet.com*
Guides: *01730 827264*
King's Arms: *www.thekingsarms.org.uk*
Petersfield Academy of Dance: *www.padance.biz*
Scouts: *www.petersfielddistrictscouts.org.uk*